PC Magazine®
Windows® XP Speed Solutions

PC Magazine® Windows® XP Speed Solutions

Curt Simmons

Wiley Publishing, Inc.

PC Magazine® Windows ® XP Speed Solutions

Published by
Wiley Publishing, Inc.
10475 Crosspoint Boulevard
Indianapolis, IN 46256
www.wiley.com

Published simultaneously in Canada

ISBN: 0-7645-7814-6

Manufactured in the United States of America

10 9 8 7 6 5 4 3 2 1

Library of Congress Cataloging-in-Publication Data

Simmons, Curt, 1968–
Pc Magazine Windows XP speed solutions/Curt Simmons.
p. cm.
Includes index.
ISBN 0-7645-7814-6 (paper/website)
1. Microsoft Windows (Computer file) 2. Operating systems (Computers) I. Title
QA76.76.O63S558554 2004
005.4′46—dc22 2004018573

To my niece, Katelyn Riley,
whose love of knowledge and sense of wonder
always inspire me

About the Author

Curt Simmons, MCSE, MCSA, MCP, A+, CTT, is a technology author and trainer. The author of more than 50 computing books on a wide variety of topics, Curt most enjoys writing about operating systems and other gadgets. He is the author of *Windows XP for Power Users: Power Pack*, *iPhoto For Dummies*, and *FrontPage 2003 Bible*, as well as many others. When Curt is not writing, he enjoys spending time with his wife, Dawn, and daughters, Hannah and Mattie.

Credits

EXECUTIVE EDITOR
Chris Webb

DEVELOPMENT EDITOR
Marcia Ellett

TECHNICAL EDITOR
Steve Sinchak

COPY EDITOR
Stefan Gruenwedel

INDEXER
Melanie Belkin Associates

EDITORIAL MANAGER
Mary Beth Wakefield

VICE PRESIDENT & EXECUTIVE GROUP PUBLISHER
Richard Swadley

VICE PRESIDENT AND PUBLISHER
Joseph B. Wikert

Contents at a Glance

Part V Appendixes

Contents

Part V Appendixes

Acknowledgments

Thanks to all the folks at Wiley, who are so great to work with. Thanks to Chris Webb for giving me the green light on this book and to Marcia Ellett for all her hard work and attention to detail. Thanks to Steve Sinchak for the eagle eye, and to Stefan Gruenwedel for making sure everything looked great. Thanks to my agent, Margot, and to my family for their support.

Introduction

If you are like me, you have at some point experienced the great Windows XP "slowdown." You bought Windows XP, started using it, and were probably happy with its speed. But, over time, your operating system has grown sluggish and seems about as fast as a turtle.

Regardless, Windows XP is a great operating system, the best that Microsoft has produced to date, in my humble opinion. Yet Windows XP is also the most complex operating system that Microsoft has ever produced, and with complicated operating systems, you tend to get complicated problems. Speed is no exception to that rule. The operating system that once zoomed along can certainly slow to a crawl instead.

Fortunately, you can fix the great majority of problems that cause an operating system like Windows XP to slow down. In these pages, you'll find all kinds of tips, tweaks, hacks, and configuration settings that should help you regain some speed control over Windows XP. I'll also show you how to get rid of the clutter and junk that Windows XP picks up over time as you use it and the Internet. Finally, I'll address concerns for keeping your data safe and private when you use the Internet. Armed with all of this knowledge, you should see great speed gains and end up with a cleaner and meaner Windows XP.

This book is designed for the "smart user." I assume you know a thing or two about using Windows XP, so I won't waste your time covering basic Windows skills. I don't assume that you know everything, however, so I have tried to make the steps and processes throughout this book clear and easy to follow, even if you don't have a lot of Windows XP experience.

I've organized this book into five parts:

- **Part I, "Programs, Junk, and Other Things That Get in the Way":** See how to manage programs, remove the junk and clutter from the operating system, and manage startup items and your Notification Area.

- **Part II, "Supercharging Windows":** Take a look at solutions that will help you supercharge Windows XP. Learn how to make Windows XP work more quickly, clean up the Registry, take care of hard disks, manage hardware, and perform a number of other speed tricks and tactics.

- **Part III, "Internet, E-mail, and Digital Media":** See how to manage the Internet, e-mail, and your digital data. Find out how to make things work more efficiently and how to deal with common problems, such as spam, adware, spyware, and other frustrating issues. Also, learn about cookies and Internet security options.

- **Part IV, "Keeping Your PC Healthy and Happy"**: Discover how to maintain your PC's health and automate some management tasks so you can spend your time enjoying your PC instead of taking care of it.
- **Part V, "Appendixes"**: Finally, find more helpful tips and suggestions in the appendixes.

I've written all of this in an organized, step-by-step manner, and I've included some Tips and Notes as well as sidebars along the way.

Before you get started, there are two quick issues I need to mention. First, almost everything you do in this book will require you to log on to Windows XP with an account that has administrator privileges. So, use the default administrator account or make sure your account is an administrator account. Second, a number of fixes require you to edit the Registry. I should warn you that editing the Registry is serious business, and doing it incorrectly can cause systemwide problems with Windows XP. Therefore, if you have never edited the Registry before, I suggest you start with Chapter 6, which includes a primer on Registry editing. This will make sure your skills are up to date before you start using the book.

I hope you find this book helpful and that it assists you in restoring some speed to your Windows XP computer. I'd love to hear from you, so please drop me an e-mail or visit me on the Web.

curt_simmons@hotmail.com
www.curtsimmons.com

PC Magazine®
Windows® XP Speed Solutions

Part I

Programs, Junk, and Other Things that Get in the Way

IN THIS PART

Chapter 1

Removing Programs and Unneeded Files

Microsoft Windows XP is a storehouse of programs, information, and data. After all, keeping up with digital information is the reason you have a computer in the first place. However, after a period of time you may end up with too many programs and certainly too many files lurking around your computer. All of these programs and files can slow things down because the more that Windows XP has to keep track of and manage programs and files, the slower the operating system is likely to work. So to speed up Windows XP, you should get in the habit of removing old programs you no longer use and removing old files the system no longer needs. This process is much like cleaning out your closet. The more clutter you can remove, the more quickly Windows XP can find what it needs. This chapter explores how to remove old programs and clean out unneeded files. It also discusses some utilities and automatic settings that can help Windows XP stay trim and fit.

Removing Old Programs

A program is a collection of computer codes designed to provide you with some feature or complete some task. Most everything you do in Windows XP involves running some kind of program. Programs include internal programs, such as Windows XP Media Player, as well as various programs you might install and use on the computer, such as Microsoft Office, various games and utilities, Internet programs, e-mail programs, and so on. Programs are necessary and important if you want Windows XP to meet your specific computing needs. However, too many programs have a tendency to clutter the system, and poorly written programs and older games can even conflict with each other and cause you problems. Windows XP allows you to use as many programs as your hard drive can hold, but too many programs running at the same time can consume your computer's memory and slow things down.

Removing Programs with Add or Remove Programs

If you want Windows XP to work as fast as possible, it's a good idea to remove old programs periodically that you no longer use. My basic philosophy is to keep any program installed on my computer that I find useful. We all have a tendency to "over install" programs, so from time to time it's a good idea to clean out Windows XP's closet of programs and remove old programs you no longer want or need. Windows XP makes removing programs rather easy with Add or Remove Programs in Control Panel. The following steps show you how to remove an old program you no longer want. If you are familiar with using Add or Remove Programs, you can skip this section.

Note

Many programs generate files. For example, let's suppose you are using Adobe Photoshop Elements to edit photos. You can save those photos as Photoshop Elements files. However, if you remove Photoshop Elements from your computer, Windows XP will no longer be able to read your photo files. Because Windows XP needs a program to open a file, it will search the system for a suitable program to open a specific file type. If there is no compatible program, the file cannot be opened.

The lesson is simply this: Do not remove programs that produce specific files you will later want to open. If you need to remove the program, first open those files and save them as a different file type that another program on your computer can open.

1. Click Start ➪ Control Panel.
2. Click Add or Remove Programs.
3. In the Add or Remove Programs dialog box (see Figure 1-1), see the list of programs installed on your computer. Scroll through the list and locate a program that you want to remove and select it. Notice that Windows XP tells you how much disk space the program consumes, how often you use the program, and when you last used it.
4. Click the Change/Remove button.
5. A dialog box appears asking if you are sure you want to delete the program. Click Yes.
6. The program is uninstalled from your computer and the Add or Remove Programs dialog box is updated to reflect the deletion.

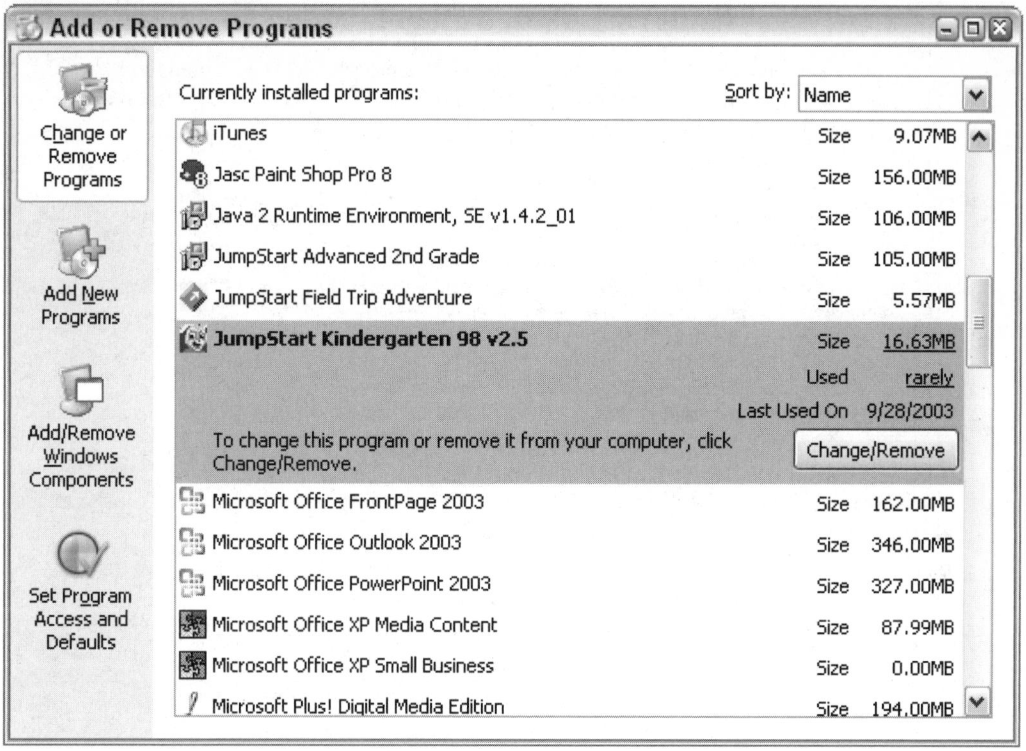

Figure 1-1: Select a program to see usage information about it.

Tip

If you start to remove a program and you get a message telling you that the program cannot be removed because it is in use, press Ctrl-Alt-Del. This opens the Windows Task Manager. On the Applications tab, select the application you are trying to delete and click End Task. Close the Task Manager. You will now be able to delete the program. If this still doesn't work, you can reboot your computer in Safe Mode (hold down the F8 key at startup). Once in Safe Mode, you should be able to remove the program.

Removing Shared Files

It is not uncommon for various applications to share internal program files among themselves. For example, the Microsoft Office suite is a collection of applications that work together. To save disk space and reduce file redundancy, the programs may share various

Removing Shared Files *(Continued)*

resource files. As such, when you choose to delete a program from your computer, you may see a dialog box, such as the one shown in Figure 1-2, telling you that a shared file exists in the program you are deleting. When this happens, what should you do?

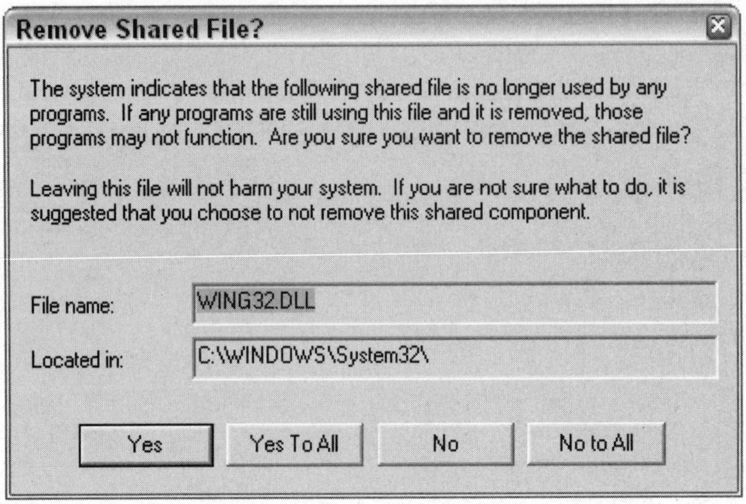
Remove Shared File?
The system indicates that the following shared file is no longer used by any programs. If any programs are still using this file and it is removed, those programs may not function. Are you sure you want to remove the shared file?
Leaving this file will not harm your system. If you are not sure what to do, it is suggested that you choose to not remove this shared component.
File name:
WING32.DLL
Located in:
C:\WINDOWS\System32\
Yes
Yes To All
No
No to All

Figure 1-2: You can safely remove shared files that are no longer in use.

The dialog box gives you a clue about the file's importance. For example, Figure 1-2 tells you that Windows XP has checked the file and determined that it is no longer in use. In this case, it is safe simply to click Yes and remove the file. However, if the dialog box tells you that other programs are using the file, you should click No and keep the file on your computer. There is nothing worse than removing a program only to find out later that the program's removal made other programs stop working correctly. So if you feel safe in removing the file, go ahead; when in doubt, leave the file on your system in case it is needed by another program.

Manually Removing Programs

Add or Remove Programs gives you an easy way to remove programs you no longer want. However, in some cases, not all programs installed in Windows XP show up in Add or Remove Programs. In fact, only programs that are written for Windows XP appear there. Other programs that may work fine in Windows XP are not necessarily written for that operating system. You frequently see this in games or utilities you download from the

Internet that still use .ini files. In this case, you can remove the program directly using the uninstall feature built into the program.

If you click Start ➪ All Programs, you can see a listing of programs installed on your computer, including those that may not appear in Add or Remove Programs. If you point to a particular program, you'll often see a context menu appear that also has an uninstall option. Click the uninstall option; the program will walk you through a series of short steps that remove the program from your computer.

In some cases, you may not have an uninstall option. This typically occurs with poorly written programs or specific utilities that you may have download from the Internet. As a last-ditch effort, you can remove the program by simply deleting the program's folder in C:\Program Files. When you delete the program's folder, you remove the core code of the program, but you do not remove any Registry settings and other file configurations, which could spawn error messages and other hiccups from time to time. However, if you can't seem to remove a program in any other way, try the manual deletion method. Click Start ➪ Run. Then type **c:\program files** and click OK. This opens the Program Files folder where you can locate the folder of the desired application. Right-click the program's folder and click Delete. Keep in mind that this action should be a last-ditch effort.

Tip

If you install a program that seems to wreak havoc on your system, remember that Windows XP has an excellent restore feature that allows you to return your computer to its previous state before you installed the program. Click Start ➪ All Programs ➪ Accessories ➪ System Tools ➪ System Restore and follow the simple wizard that appears. The restore feature will not remove any files you have created or delete any e-mail, so your personal items are safe and sound.

In some cases, once you have removed a program, Add or Remove Programs still shows the program as being installed. This occurs when the uninstall process doesn't actually remove the program listing from Windows XP, even though the actual program has been removed. You can remove these bogus entries in two different ways. First, visit `www.microsoft.com` and download the TweakUI utility for Windows XP. This utility helps you remove leftover entries. You can also edit the Registry directly and remove the offending entries. The following steps show you how.

Caution

Incorrectly editing the Registry can cause serious damage to Windows XP. It is always best to perform actions in Windows XP without editing the Registry unless absolutely necessary. If you

choose to edit the Registry (which I touch on in various places throughout this book), make sure you work carefully and follow the steps presented exactly.

1. Click Start ➪ Run. Type **regedit** in the dialog box and click OK.
2. In the Registry Editor, navigate to the following Registry key: HKEY_LOCAL_MACHINE\ Software\Microsoft\Windows\CurrentVersion\Uninstall.
3. After you click the Uninstall key, right-click the Uninstall folder and select Export.
4. In the dialog box that appears, click Desktop in the Save In box, type **delete** in the File Name box, and click Save.
5. Each key under Uninstall represents a program that appears in Add or Remove Programs. To determine which key represents which program, click the key and view the following values, which tell you the display name in Add or Remove Programs.
6. After you locate the desired key that represents the offending program listing, right-click the key and click Delete.
7. After you delete the key, open Add or Remove Programs and verify that the program has been deleted from the list.
8. If the program list is not correct in Add or Remove Programs, you can double-click the delete.reg file on your desktop to restore the original list of programs in the Registry. If the program list is correct in Add or Remove Programs, right-click the delete.reg file on your desktop and select Delete.

Removing Spyware and Adware

For all the wonderful things the Internet provides, it also offers a lot of junk that can creep into your system without your knowledge. One of those common annoyances is "spyware" or "adware." Both are programs that run in Windows XP without your knowledge. For instance, you may notice that Internet Explorer keeps popping up ads or the default home page in your browser randomly changes. All of these actions are caused by spyware and adware programs. Essentially, these types of programs contain malicious code that steals personal information about you from your computer and communicates that information to Internet servers or dumps random ads on your computer from the Internet. The end result is that companies end up getting information about you that you do not want to share and a bunch of junk shows up on your computer.

Spyware and adware programs are difficult to track down and uninstall yourself but I wholeheartedly recommend two free utilities that can decisively do the job for you. The first is Spybot, which is available for download from `www.safer-networking.org`. Spybot is a small, safe utility recommended by *PC Magazine* that periodically scans your system for personal invasion programs and deletes them from your system. Spybot provides you with a simple interface (see Figure 1-3).

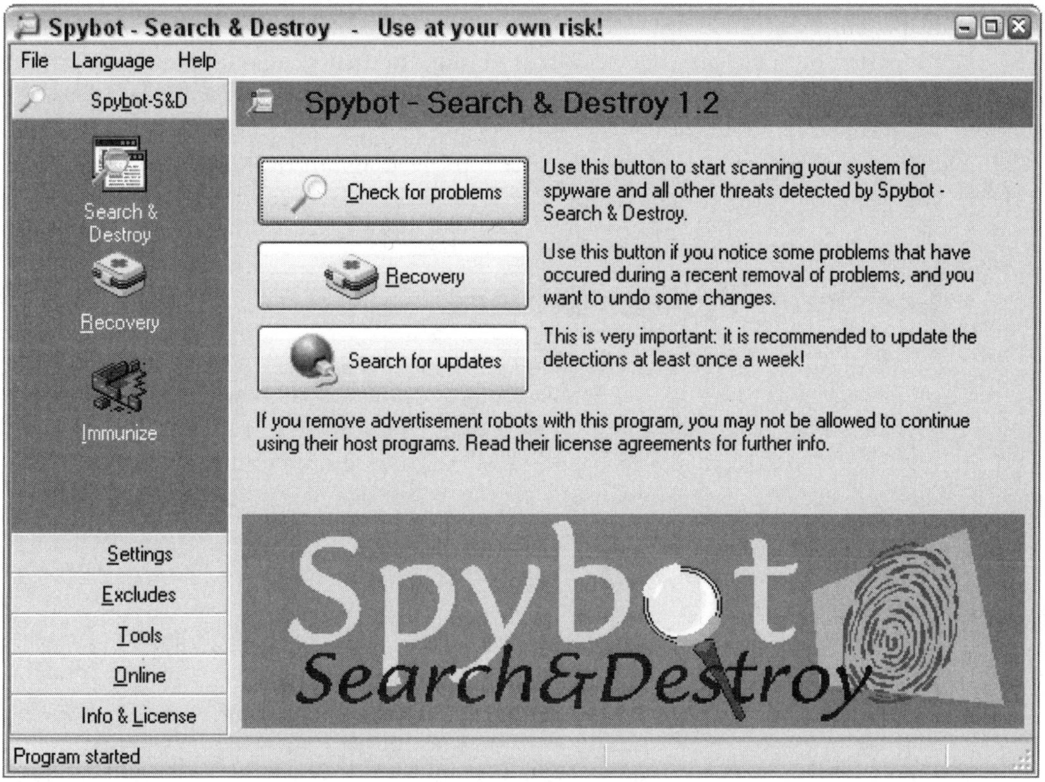
Spybot - Search & Destroy - Use at your own risk!
File Language Help
Spybot-S&D
Spybot - Search & Destroy 1.2
Search & Destroy
Recovery
Immunize
Check for problems
Use this button to start scanning your system for spyware and all other threats detected by Spybot - Search & Destroy.
Recovery
Use this button if you notice some problems that have occured during a recent removal of problems, and you want to undo some changes.
Search for updates
This is very important: it is recommended to update the detections at least once a week!
If you remove advertisement robots with this program, you may not be allowed to continue using their host programs. Read their license agreements for further info.
Settings
Excludes
Tools
Online
Info & License
Spybot
Search&Destroy
Program started

Figure 1-3: Spybot makes removing spyware and adware a cinch.

Another great utility is Ad-Aware. This utility, available for free at `www.lavasoftusa.com`, essentially performs the same functions as Spybot and features a similar simple-to-use interface. You can scan your system for problems and then choose to fix those problems once the scan completes its job.

Either of these programs will get the job done. I strongly recommend you use one of them.

Making Programs Start Faster

As humans, we have brains that can easily do several things at one time. As such, we want our computers to keep up with us. One of the frustrating things about computing is waiting for our computer to start an application that we want to use. We hate to wait. We want those applications to start quickly so we can get busy with the task at hand.

Windows XP generally does a good job of starting programs quickly. However, you can help it out, especially if you notice that program startup becomes sluggish. Keep in mind that many programs are complicated, especially advanced processing programs such as Microsoft Excel or Publisher or graphics programs such as Adobe Photoshop. Windows XP has to load a lot of information into memory and start the program's processes before you can use the program. So a little patience is warranted, but there are still some tricks that will help your programs start faster.

Configuring Prefetch Settings

Windows XP includes a unique feature called "prefetching," which means it guesses which programs you are likely to use. As you use your computer, Windows XP remembers the programs you use so that when you next boot Windows XP or access programs on it, portions of the program files are copied to the Prefetch folder on your hard drive. The next time you open the program, part of it is already available in the Prefetch folder, making it appear to open more quickly than before. In reality, the prefetching works by caching a small portion of the program paging setup and runtime information to the disk so that the program opens quickly.

In truth, if you use only two or three programs, prefetching works great and makes programs open more quickly. However, if you use a bunch of programs only once or rarely, the Prefetch folder will fill up with junk. Because Windows XP doesn't know your intentions, it keeps a portion of each program you use in the Prefetch folder at all times. Repeating this process over and over with many programs eventually causes the system to run more slowly than if you never used prefetching at all.

Fortunately, you can easily make changes to Windows XP's prefetching process. The following sections show you what to do.

Note

There is some controversy about working with the prefetch folder. Many people say it helps performance, while others say it does not. The effect you get on your system will probably vary. The least that cleaning the prefetch folder will do for you is help clear out some junk on your hard

disk. However, after you clean the prefetch folder, you may notice that some applications open more slowly the first time they run.

CLEANING THE PREFETCH FOLDER

Think of the Prefetch folder as you do the Temp folder on your computer. Naturally, the more programs you use, the bigger the Prefetch folder grows. Over time, prefetching will actually slow things down. To regain some speed, delete the contents of the Prefetch folder about once a month. Remember that prefetching is designed to make programs load more quickly, so don't delete the contents more than once a month; this may actually cause programs to load more slowly because you will be preventing prefetching from doing its job. To delete the contents of the Prefetch folder, follow these steps:

1. Click Start ➪ Run. In the dialog box that appears, type **c:\windows\prefetch**.
2. In the Prefetch folder (see Figure 1-4), click Edit ➪ Select All. Right-click the selected files and click Delete, or just press the Delete key on your keyboard.

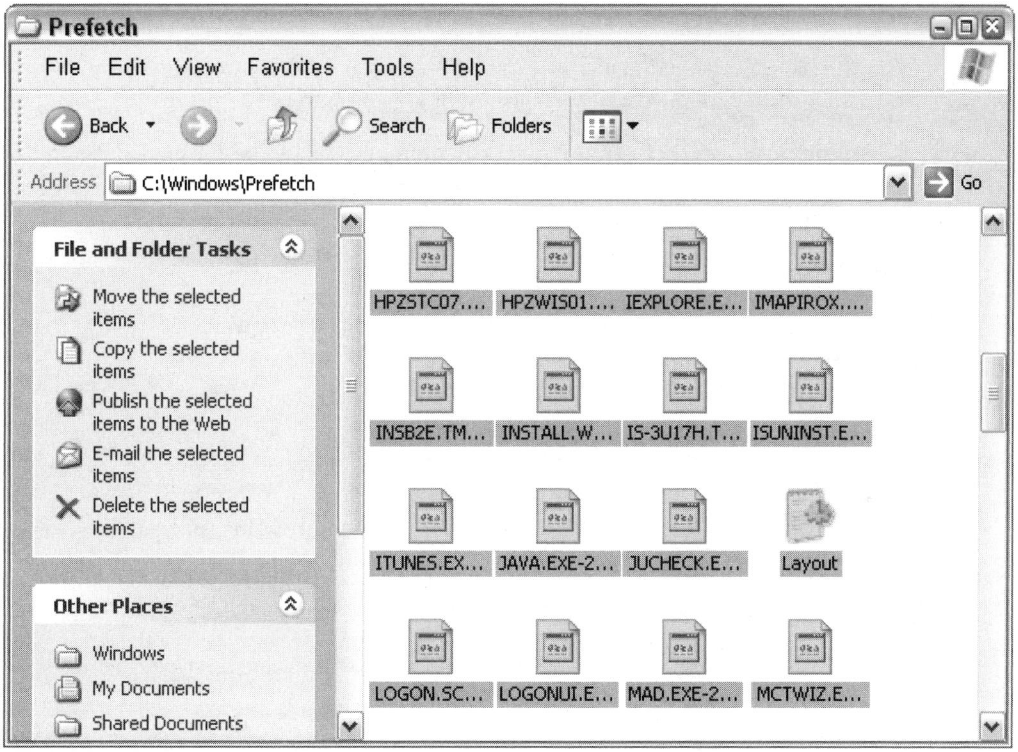

Figure 1-4: Delete all the files in the Prefetch folder.

Note

You may notice a Layout.ini file, also shown in Figure 1-4. This file is used by the Disk Defragmenter in Windows XP and contains a record of how the tool reorganized information after its most recent run. It is fine to delete this file along with the others.

ADJUSTING PREFETCH SETTINGS

By editing the Registry, you can adjust how prefetching works in Windows XP. Depending on your system, the prefetching values may already be optimized, but you should check them out anyway. When you access prefetching in the Registry, you can configure the following values for prefetching:

- 0: Disables prefetching
- 1: Enables Application Launch Prefetch
- 2: Enables Boot Prefetch
- 3: Prefetches everything

If your computer has 512 MB RAM or more, setting 3 is probably best. It gives prefetching the most power; and because you have ample RAM installed, you should take advantage of the feature. However, if your computer has 256 MB RAM or so, you may want to experiment with setting 1 or 2. These give you faster launch times for applications but prevent excessive prefetching.

To examine your system's current configuration and make desired changes, follow these steps:

1. Click Start ➪ Run. Type **regedit** and click OK in the dialog box provided.
2. In the Registry Editor, navigate to HKEY_LOCAL_MACHINE\SYSTEM\CurrentControlSet\Control\Session Manager\Memory Management\PrefetchParameters (see Figure 1-5).
3. In the right pane, locate the EnablePrefetcher key. Double-click the key to open it.
4. In the key's dialog box, enter the desired value for the Value Data (see Figure 1-6).
5. Click OK and close the Registry Editor.

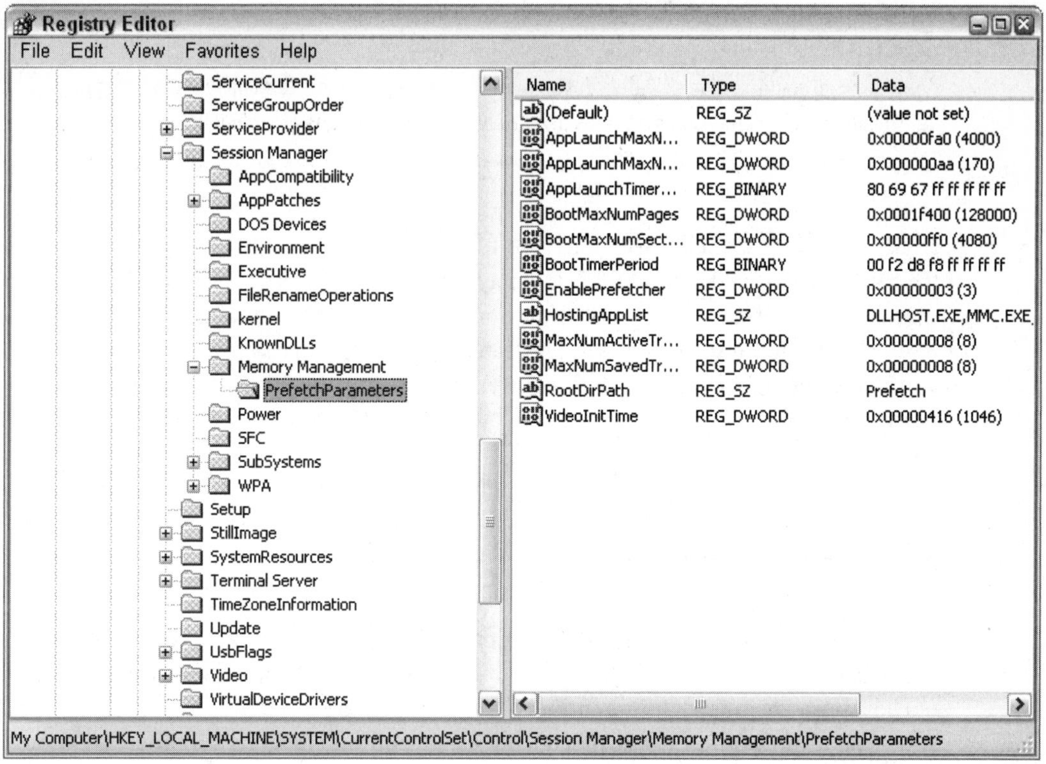

Figure 1-5: Navigate to PrefetchParameters.

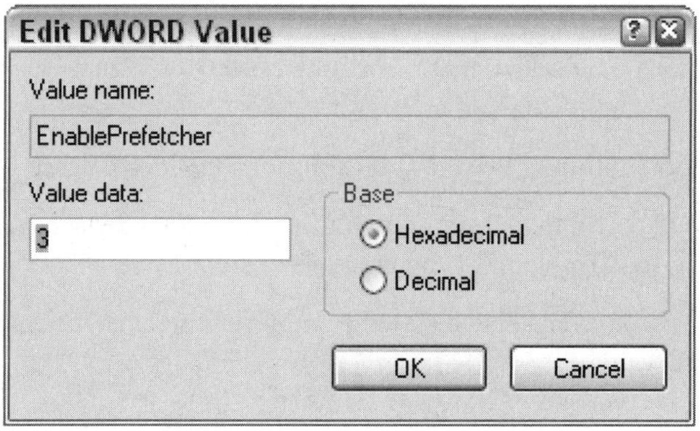

Figure 1-6: Enter a value from 0 to 3 in the Value Data field.

Caution

Keep in mind that a setting of 3 decreases overall boot time and makes applications start more quickly. Do not change this setting unless your computer does not have sufficient RAM.

DISABLING PREFETCH ON SLOW SYSTEMS

If your Windows XP computer has low memory, such as 128 MB RAM or so, your best solution is to disable prefetching. Because you are low on RAM, you want all of the memory resources directed at the task at hand instead of applications that you may not use anyway. To disable prefetching, follow the Registry editing steps shown in the previous section but enter a value of **0** as the data value. This effectively turns off prefetching on your computer.

Using the Intel Application Accelerator

The Intel Application Accelerator is performance software for Intel-powered computers. This application provides faster delivery of data from the hard drive to the processor and other system-level hardware. The end result is that applications start and run more quickly, boot time is reduced, and there is accelerated input/output for games, graphics applications, disk utilities, and media authoring applications. For all of you digital media lovers, this utility can certainly help speed up your system. The software also functions as a data prefetcher for Intel Pentium 4 processors and supports hard drives up to 137 GB.

Before you decide to use the Intel Application Accelerator, take note of the requirements:

- Windows 98 SE, Windows Me, Windows 2000, Windows NT 4.0, or Windows XP
- Motherboard with a supported chipset (see the next listing for supported chipsets)
- Intel Pentium 4, Intel Pentium III, Intel Pentium II, Intel Celeron, Intel Xeon, Intel Pentium III Xeon, or Intel Pentium II Xeon processor
- Ultra ATA/66 or Ultra ATA/100 compatible logic either on the motherboard or on an Ultra DMA PCI adapter card
- Ultra DMA BIOS
- Ultra ATA/66 or Ultra ATA/100 compatible IDE device (such as a hard drive)
- Intel Chipset Software (discussed later in this section)

You also need a supported chipset:

- Intel 810
- Intel 810E
- Intel 810E2
- Intel 815
- Intel 815E
- Intel 815EP
- Intel 815P
- Intel 820
- Intel 820E
- Intel 840
- Intel 845
- Intel 850
- Intel 860

Check your computer's hardware documentation to verify that it meets these requirements. Once you are sure that your computer meets them, you'll first need to download and install the Intel Chipset Software Installation Utility from `www.intel.com/design/software/drivers/platform/inf.htm`. Install the software and reboot your computer. After you are done installing the utility, you need to download and install the Intel Application Accelerator, available from `www.intel.com/support/chipsets/IAA`. Install the accelerator and reboot your computer. You should notice an improvement in the speed of your applications.

Setting Application Priority

Windows XP enables you to set a priority for the applications that run on your computer. In a nutshell, if you have several applications and processes at work, which you always do because Windows XP runs may internal processes, you can boost a certain application you are using by adjusting the priority of that application. When you change the priority of the application, you make that application the "top dog"; it gets preference for processor cycles over other applications and processes. This feature can be useful when you are working on applications such as photo editing and multimedia applications, which demand a great amount of system resources.

You can easily adjust the priority of an application. Make sure you have opened the application; then follow these steps:

1. Press Ctrl-Alt-Del to bring up the Windows Task Manager.
2. Click the Processes tab and locate the process for the application you want to prioritize.
3. Right-click the application process, point to Set Priority, and then choose the desired priority from the pop-up menu (see Figure 1-7). Generally, a setting of AboveNormal or High will give your application a boost. Be careful about the Realtime setting; it prevents Windows from managing multiple processes and could bring your operating system to a standstill.

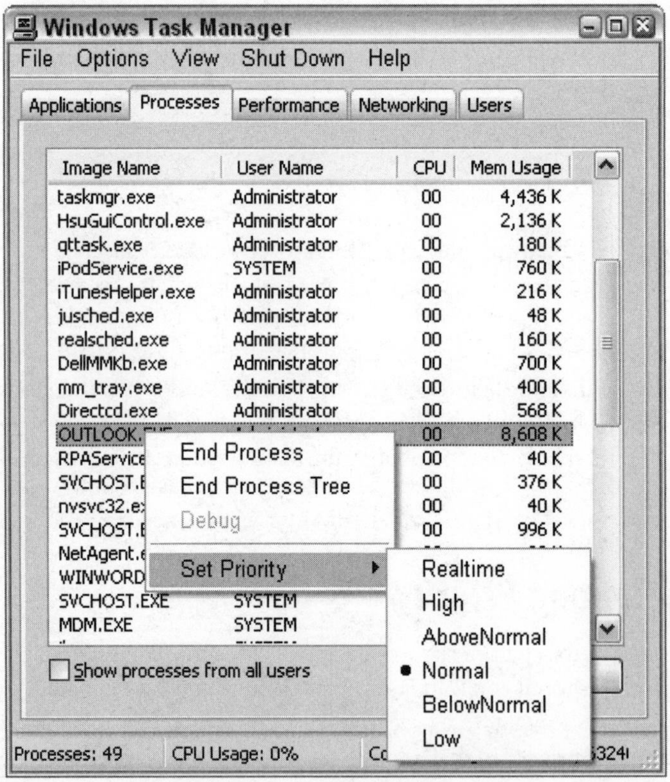

Figure 1-7: Set an application's priority to AboveNormal or High.

Antivirus Software and Speed

Antivirus software is a necessary evil in these days of computer viruses. If you have never experienced a computer virus, count yourself lucky. But don't depend on luck to keep you virus-free. Antivirus software is highly important—and a minimal investment for the service you receive. However, antivirus software performs a number of scanning processes that tend to make boot time and some applications, such as e-mail programs, slower. Unfortunately, the software is working as fast as your computer processor and RAM will allow, and there isn't much you can do to speed up the application. Because antivirus software does a lot of work, you can expect some slowdowns here and there on your system.

Typically, antivirus software slows down the opening and closing of applications and zipped files because the antivirus software scans those files when the operating system accesses them. As a general rule, you may want to study the settings for your antivirus software and make sure it's not over-scanning your system. The software should scan at regular intervals, and it should scan your incoming e-mail because this is one place where you are likely to get a virus. However, the software may not need to scan your system every single day. You'll have to strike a balance between speed and safety. In the case of computer viruses, you should err on the side of caution. It doesn't do any good for your computer to work faster if you end up with lost data or a butchered operating system due to a computer virus. In this case, safety is much better than speed.

Cleaning Up Files

Why do files slow down a computer? Think of your computer as a filing cabinet. The more stuff you cram into a filing cabinet, the longer it takes you to locate what you need. The same scenario is true in your computer. The Windows XP file system maintains a master file table that it uses to look up where each file is located on the hard disk. When the master file table gets too big, it starts to fragment, which can cause your system to slow down because Windows XP has more difficulty finding what it needs in the master file table.

Cross-Reference

The more files you store, save, and resave, the more fragmentation of those files naturally occurs. Fragmentation can make your computer run more slowly. I cover fragmentation in more detail in Chapter 7.

Organizing Your Personal Files

Windows XP provides you with a default folder structure called My Documents to organize different kinds of files you generate. You can use those default folders any way you like. The point is simply this: Organizing your personal data helps you work faster in Windows XP. Storing your personal data in those folders does not speed up Windows XP per se but it greatly speeds up your ability to find what you are looking for.

For older data files that you no longer use regularly, consider moving them to removable storage media, such as CDs or DVDs. You can store data on the removable disk and then delete it from your computer to free up disk space and reduce clutter on your computer. You can also store personal files on the Web as an easy way to create redundant copies of your data files for remote storage. Check out Xdrive (`www.xdrive.com`) or SwapDrive (`www.swapdrive.com`) to get started.

Removing Temporary Files

Windows XP uses many temporary files—often created when you use various programs as well as when you look at Web pages. Temporary files are a necessary part of the Windows operating system but, like prefetching, the system can get bogged down as temporary files pile up.

Your first step in cleaning up temporary files and giving your system an extra boost in speed is to run the Disk Cleanup utility. This utility scans your system for temporary files that can be safely removed. Get in the habit of running Disk Cleanup about once a month if you regularly use your computer. Follow these steps:

1. Click Start ➪ My Computer.
2. Right-click the desired hard drive and click Properties.
3. On the General tab, click the Disk Cleanup button.
4. The utility performs a check on your system and eventually displays a dialog box showing the different categories of temporary files that can be deleted and the amount of disk space you can gain by deleting the files in each category. Review the dialog box and select the check box next to each category you want to clean up (see Figure 1-8).
5. If you click the More Options tab, you can also clean up Windows components you no longer want installed, old programs you no longer want to use, and System Restore point files (see Figure 1-9).

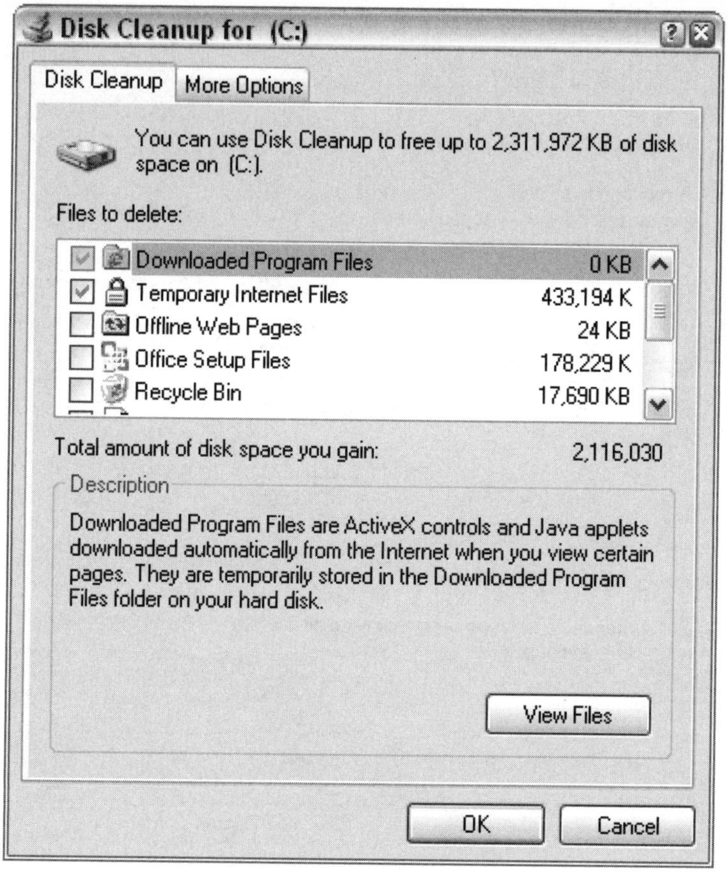

Figure 1-8: Choose the desired categories you want to clean up.

6. When you have made your selections, click OK and Yes to the confirmation message that appears. The clean-up process may take some time, depending on the number of files that must be removed.

Cleaning Up Internet Explorer Files

Microsoft Internet Explorer is designed to make your Web surfing experience the best it can be. In the process, Internet Explorer collects temporary Internet files and records a history of Web pages you visit. While these features are useful for your surfing experience, all of those files and information clutter up your system unnecessarily after a period of time. It is

Disk Cleanup for (C:)
Disk Cleanup
More Options
Windows components
You can free more disk space by removing optional Windows components that you do not use.
Clean up...
Installed programs
You can free more disk space by removing programs that you do not use.
Clean up...
System Restore
You can free more disk space by removing all but the most recent restore point.
Clean up...
OK
Cancel

Figure 1-9: Clean up additional items on the More Options tab.

always a good idea to check your Internet Explorer settings and make sure these files are not stacking up unduly. Follow these steps:

1. Click Start ➪ Control Panel ➪ Internet Options.
2. On the General tab, click the Settings button under Temporary Internet Files.
3. The best setting in the Settings dialog box is for Internet Explorer to check for new pages automatically (see Figure 1-10). Internet Explorer does a good job of checking for updated pages so it's best to use the Automatically setting. For disk space usage, around 1100 MB is a good setting, assuming you have plenty of available disk space. When you near the threshold you have configured, Internet Explorer automatically begins deleting old pages and objects from its Temp

folder. This configuration helps you keep data that is actually useful but removes data that has become old. Click OK when you're done.

Figure 1-10: Use the Automatically setting and keep a lower amount of disk space usage, typically around 1 GB.

4. On the General tab under History (see Figure 1-11) notice that the history of pages you have visited is listed and that you can clear the history if you like. History is not critical in terms of wasted space and files but a default setting of 20 days serves you well and won't cause Internet Explorer unnecessarily to store an inordinate amount of history information. Adjust this setting as desired and click OK.

Cookies and Your Privacy

Cookies are small files that contain information about you so that you can interact with various Web sites. Cookies are common and necessary, and give you the kind of Web surfing experience you expect. However, cookies can also be a source of privacy invasion.

Cookies and Your Privacy *(Continued)*

Internet Explorer attempts to reduce this possibility by enabling you to configure cookie security on the Privacy tab of Internet Options. The tab is self-explanatory. Strive for a setting that gives you a good combination of security and flexibility with your Web surfing. If you want more cookie control, there is a nice utility called Cookie Monitor that lets you see what cookies are being created and allows you to control them. You can get Cookie Monitor from Naturpic Software (`www.naturpic.com/cookie`). To learn more about Internet cookies and blocking them, see also Chapter 12.

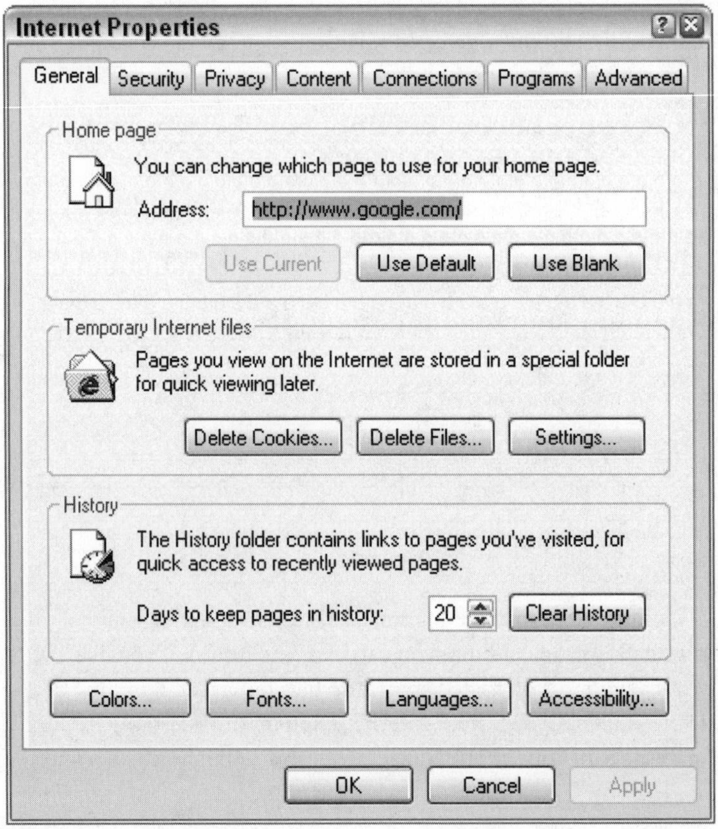

Figure 1-11: Configure the desired History setting.

Along with configuring settings for deleting temporary files, you can also have Internet Explorer automatically delete those files when you close Internet Explorer. This feature keeps Internet file junk to a minimum and prevents anyone from seeing the Internet sites you have visited, which is particularly helpful if you are viewing private sites and data, such as e-mail, online banking, credit card statements, and so on. Naturally, deleting all temporary files each time you close Internet Explorer means the browser has to download those temporary files every time you use it. However, if you have a broadband connection, you are unlikely to notice much performance difference. To configure Internet Explorer to delete temporary files automatically each time you close it, follow these steps:

1. Click Start ➪ Control Panel ➪ Internet Options.
2. Click the Advanced tab.
3. On the Advanced tab, under the Security heading, click the "Empty Temporary Internet Files folder when browser is closed" check box and then click OK (see Figure 1-12).

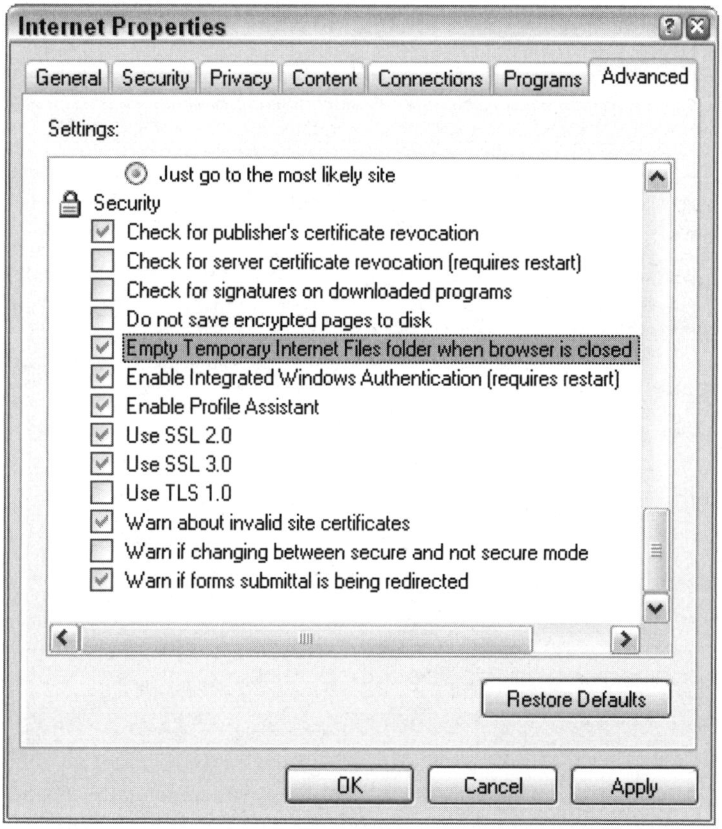

Figure 1-12: Choose this setting to have Internet Explorer delete all temporary Internet files whenever you close your browser.

Manually Cleaning Up Your Temp Folder

Disk Cleanup is a handy tool for removing items from your Temp folder but manually removing them is faster—not to mention easy and safe. Just follow these steps:

1. Click Start ➪ Run. In the dialog box that appears, type **c:\windows\temp** and click OK.
2. This opens the Temp folder (see Figure 1-13). You can delete everything in the Temp folder, including all subfolders. Click Edit ➪ Select All and then just press the Delete key on your keyboard.

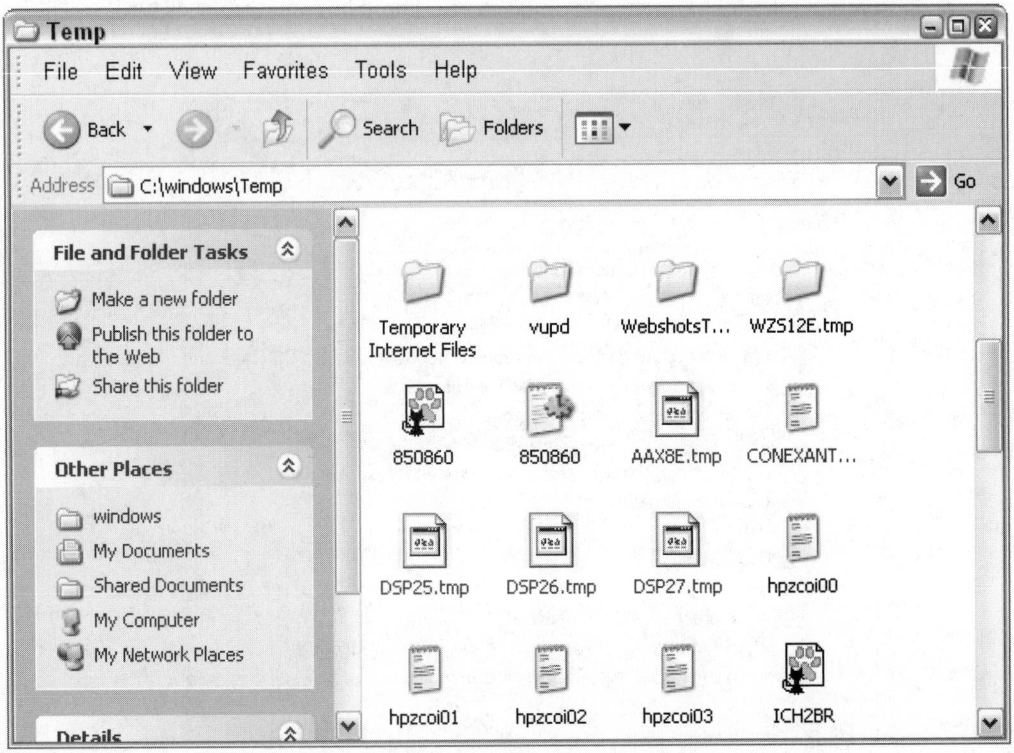

Figure 1-13: You can delete all items and subfolders in the Temp folder.

Tip

All the items in the Temp folder are moved to the Recycle Bin, so you won't really free up any disk space until you empty the Recycle Bin.

Automating Temp Folder Cleanup

If you automate the process of keeping the Temp folder cleaned out, you won't have to bother with the issue again.

First, you can use Disk Cleanup and create a Scheduled Task so that the cleanup process runs periodically without your intervention. For example, you could schedule Disk Cleanup to run each Wednesday in the middle of the night. To configure Disk Cleanup to run as a Scheduled Task, click Start ➪ Control Panel ➪ Scheduled Tasks. You can then launch the Scheduled Task wizard and follow the easy steps to select Disk Cleanup and configure when you want the utility to run.

In addition to Disk Cleanup, a number of third-party utilities handle Temp folder cleanup automatically. One good example is TempClean (`www.snapfiles.com/get/tempcleaner.html`), which allows you to determine the folder that you want to keep clean, such as the Temp folder, Internet cache, Document History, and many others. Once you configure the utility, it does the work without any intervention from you.

There is an important issue to consider when using third-party cleanup tools. Many of these tools clean the Temp folder when you start your computer. This sounds like a good idea but this action can prevent you from installing software. For example, when you install software, temporary files are kept in the Temp folder. The software makes you reboot the computer but the cleanup utility deletes all of the temporary files upon reboot. This results in a failed software installation. So keep in mind that the Temp file is important for many different processes, including software installation. For this reason, I recommend that you use Disk Cleanup and create a Scheduled Task. This action allows you to keep your hard drive free of clutter but does not interfere with software installations or other processes.

Speed Up Searching By Avoiding Compressed Files

If you have many zipped (compressed) files on your computer, the Windows XP file-searching feature can become rather sluggish as it wades through all of those compressed files. You can quickly stop the search function from looking through compressed files, which greatly speeds up search results. To enable this feature, click Start ➪ Run. In the dialog box, type the following:

regsvr32 C:\winnt\\system32\zipfldr.dll /u

If the files are installed in the Windows folder, you can substitute "windows" for "winnt" in the command line. To turn searching back on for zipped files, type the following:

regsvr32 C:\winnt\system32\zipfldr.dll

Use "windows" for "winnt" if the files are located in the Windows folder.

Chapter 2

Cleaning Up the Desktop and Start Menu

Windows XP raised people's eyebrows when Microsoft first introduced it. For one thing, the desktop looked different. Gone were all the icons, with the exception of the Recycle Bin, and the Start menu looked and behaved quite differently. These changes were designed to streamline the desktop and make it look neater. The Start menu holds more information and gives you a quick access point to the things you are most likely to use. That's all well and good but after you work with Windows XP a bit, the desktop and Start menu typically become cluttered, unless you are highly organized to begin with. Fortunately, you can clean up the desktop and Start menu without much trouble. These solutions do not actually speed up Windows XP but they make your work with Windows XP easier. At the end of this chapter, I describe some desktop configuration issues that may help Windows XP run more quickly.

Cleaning Up the Desktop

By default, only the Recycle Bin exists on the desktop. Windows XP provides you with the Taskbar and the Recycle Bin but, beyond that, your first experience with Windows XP leaves you looking at some graphic wallpaper on the desktop and nothing else. This is by design so that the desktop remains clean. Of course, Windows XP gives you the flexibility you want. You are free to put icons and files on the desktop, as you always have been. You can even drag icons, such as My Computer, from the Start menu and put them on the desktop. The choice is entirely up to you.

Cleaning up the desktop primarily requires you to drag files and icons around, as needed, and put them in other folders. Keep in mind that Windows XP intends for you to put your files in My Documents; it even gives you a number of subfolders, such as My Pictures and My Movies, to help you organize your various types of files. You can even create your own folders within My Documents if you like.

Of course, you don't have to organize your data this way. You are free to create your own folders and organize them however you want. For example, when I write a book, such as this one, I create a folder for the book on my desktop. Within that folder is a folder for each chapter. The chapter folders then contain the actual chapter and all of the screen shots in the book's figures. This method keeps everything in the right place as I work on the book. When I'm done, I compress the folder and store it in a Projects folder in My Documents. I also make a backup copy on CD, just in case anything catastrophic should happen to my computer. This method works well for me but you'll have to determine a storage system of your own. If you do not use a lot of files anyway, the process is rather easy. However, if you create many files, or if you are a digital photography enthusiast and you end up with hundreds or thousands of digital photos on your computer, you must spend a little time thinking about organization and creating a system that makes sense in your own mind. The goal, of course, is to keep information easy to locate so you can get to it whenever you want.

Tip

Speaking of digital photos, there are a number of programs that catalog your photos and manage them for you in a library. You can then work directly with the photos from the library without having to worry about manually storing them. I recommend Adobe Photoshop Album software (`www.adobe.com`) and Jasc Paint Shop Photo Album (`www.jasc.com`).

If you are manually cleaning up your desktop, there are two primary tasks to complete:

- **Organize files as necessary by dragging to desired folders.** You are free to create folders directly on the desktop (right-click the desktop and point to New). Once you are done working with those folders, you can drag them to another storage location off your desktop or even to removable storage. You can also have Windows XP arrange your icons in an orderly fashion. Right-click the desktop and point to Arrange By. You'll see a menu of arrangement options.
- **Many programs automatically create shortcuts on your desktop.** These shortcuts are small files that contain a pointer to the location of the actual program. They are designed to make program access easier. These are fine to use, but you don't have to use them, and you can safely drag any shortcuts that you do not want into the Recycle Bin. This action removes only the shortcut, not the actual program. You can still access the program from Start ➪ All Programs.

Using the Desktop Cleanup Wizard

The Desktop Cleanup Wizard is a little tool that helps you organize and manage desktop shortcuts. You can also manage shortcuts manually with about just as much ease.

The Desktop Cleanup Wizard tracks how often you use the shortcuts on your desktop. The program moves shortcuts you do not regularly use into a desktop folder called Unused Shortcuts. You can always retrieve older shortcuts from that folder.

Now you don't have to use this wizard. You can manage shortcuts yourself and organize them as desired, but if you have many shortcuts on your desktop, you may find that the wizard helps you get everything in order more quickly.

To use the Desktop Cleanup Wizard, follow these steps:

1. Right-click the desktop and point to Arrange Icons By. On the context menu that appears, click Run Desktop Cleanup Wizard.
2. Click Next on the Welcome screen.
3. In the next window, all of the shortcuts on your desktop are listed (see Figure 2-1). Notice that you can see when you last used the shortcut, or if you have everused it at all. The selected items are bound for the folder that the wizard

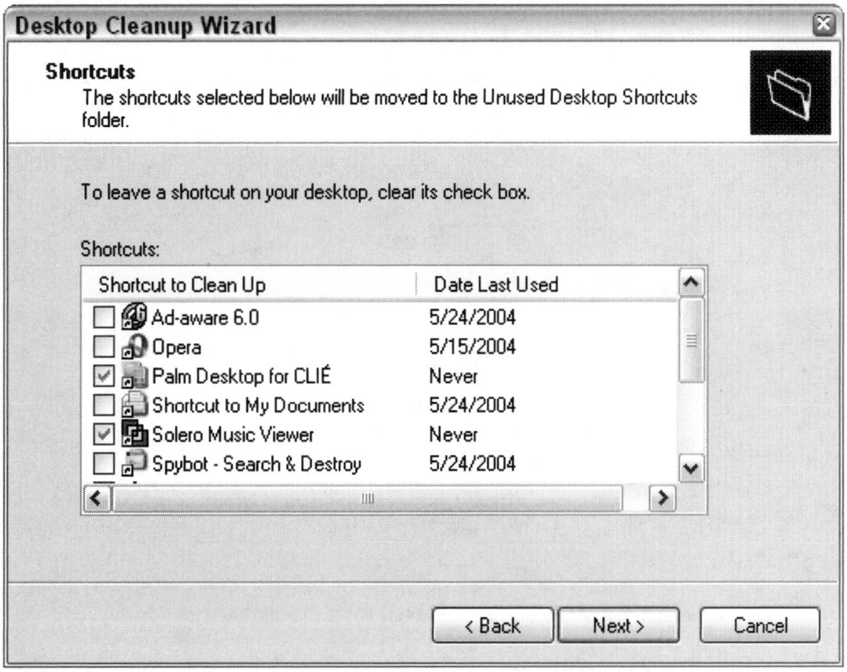

Figure 2-1: Select the shortcuts you want to move to the Unused Shortcuts folder.

will create, so uncheck any shortcuts you do not want to move and select any shortcuts you do want to move, even if the wizard has not selected them. Click Next.

4. Click Finish.

Configuring the Recycle Bin

When you delete a file from your system (anything at all—a document, picture, shortcut, or whatever), it isn't really deleted. It is sent to the Recycle Bin, where it waits to be deleted. It stays in the Recycle Bin until you choose to empty the Recycle Bin or the Recycle Bin becomes too full. Only then is the item deleted permanently. The Recycle Bin is an excellent Windows feature that prevents you from losing data that you may actually want to keep.

USING THE RECYCLE BIN

You can empty the Recycle Bin by right-clicking the Recycle Bin icon and clicking Empty Recycle Bin. Also, you can double-click the Recycle Bin and see the items there that are waiting to be deleted (see Figure 2-2).

Figure 2-2: Double-click the Recycle Bin to open it.

As you can see, the Recycle Bin is just a folder; it has the same typical options as other folders. Clicking the Empty Recycle Bin button deletes the items in the Recycle Bin. Once you choose to empty the Recycle Bin, all items in the Recycle Bin are permanently deleted from your computer. You *cannot* recover these items once they have been emptied from the Recycle Bin.

What if you accidentally delete a file and it is moved to the Recycle Bin? No problem—click the Restore All button to move the file back to its original location on your computer. If you deleted 30 files and want to restore only one of them, just select the file in the list by clicking it. The Restore All button changes to Restore This Item. Click the button to put the file back in its original location.

Tip

You can move an item out of the Recycle Bin by dragging it back to the desktop, as well. Note that you cannot open an item that is in the Recycle Bin to view it. You must drag it out of the Recycle Bin before you can open the item.

CHANGING THE RECYCLE BIN'S PROPERTIES

You can easily adjust the Recycle Bin's properties so that it manages trash more efficiently. Right-click the Recycle Bin and click Properties on the contextual menu that appears. You see a Recycle Bin Properties window that has a Global and Local Disk (C:) tab (see Figure 2-3).

The top two option buttons enable you to configure your drives independently or use the same settings for all drives. This feature applies to you only if you have more than one hard disk in your computer. In most cases, the default setting that configures all of your drives equally is all you need.

The check box that tells your computer to delete items immediately, instead of moving them to the Recycle Bin, automatically deletes items when you click Delete. This provides you absolutely no protection in the event that you accidentally delete a file you want.

Like everything else on your computer, the Recycle Bin stores items in a folder on your hard drive. The sliding bar enables you to set a limit for how big the Recycle Bin can grow before it forces you to empty the contents and permanently delete items from your system. By default, this setting is configured for 10 percent. This means that 10 percent of your hard drive's space can be used before the Recycle Bin tells you to empty it. That is, if you have a 10 GB hard drive, you can store up to 1 GB of deleted data in the Recycle Bin before it must be permanently removed from your computer. Under most circumstances, this 10 percent setting is all you need but you can change it to a higher or lower percentage if you want. Just be sure you have a good reason for doing so.

The Display Delete Confirmation Dialog check box at the bottom of the Global tab tells Windows to give you that aggravating "Are You Sure?" message every time you delete

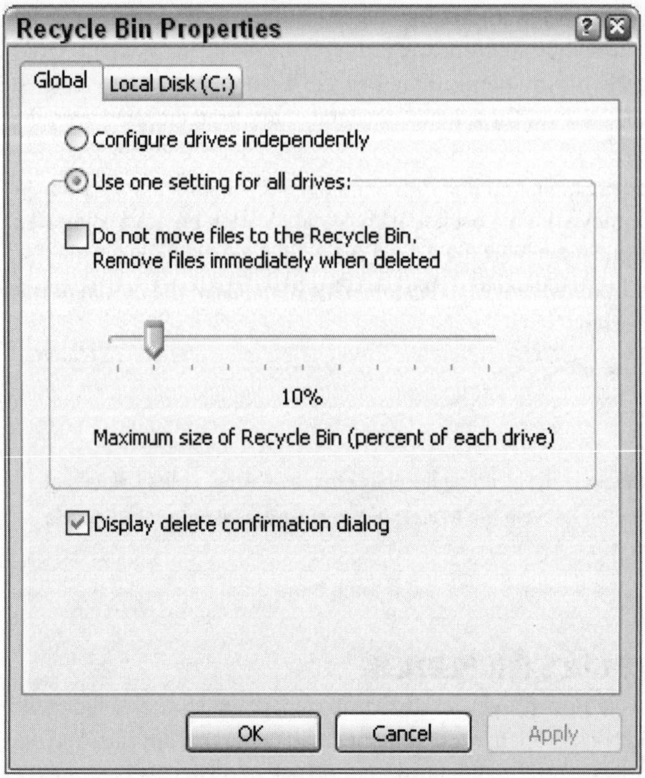

Figure 2-3: You can manage the Recycle Bin's global behavior on the Global tab.

something. This option is selected by default. Although the configuration message is sometimes a pain, it is a good safety check.

Aside from the Global tab, you have a Local Disk tab—you may have several of these tabs if your computer has more than one hard drive. You can't do anything on these tabs if you selected the Use One Setting For All Drives option button. If you want each drive to have different settings and you selected this option on the Global tab, you can configure each drive independently. The tabs have the same options, such as the slider bar for the percentage of the hard drive you want to use for the Recycle Bin. This feature is helpful if you want to configure the Recycle Bin's behavior differently on each individual hard disk.

Cleaning Up the Start Menu

The Windows XP Start menu provides you with access to documents and programs, but also operating system features and easy access to the things you use most of the time.

The Start menu appears in a two-column design (see Figure 2-4). At the top of the Start menu, you see your username and photo icon configured for use with your username. In the left column, you see access to several programs; the right column gives you access to files and other portions of the operating system.

The left side of the Start menu lists programs you commonly access. By default, Internet Explorer and your default e-mail client always appear in this list. The rest of the programs

Figure 2-4: The Start menu gives you access to commonly used items.

appear here according to your actions. For example, if you open Microsoft Word, the application icon is added to the Start menu for easy access. If you do not use Word again for a long period of time, it is dropped from the Start menu due to inactivity. So the Windows XP Start menu is rather dynamic; it tries to guess what programs you might need by keeping frequently used programs available on the Start menu for you.

I mentioned that Internet Explorer and your default e-mail client are always listed on the Start menu. What happens if you do not use these for a period of time? Internet Explorer and your default e-mail client are "pinned" to the Start menu by default, which means they are permanently placed there unless you decide to remove them. You can pin any application or even a document to the Start menu so that they are always available to you. To pin an item to the Start Menu, just right-click the item in the left column and click Pin to Start Menu. You can also remove any pinned application or document by right-clicking the icon on the Start menu and clicking Unpin from Start Menu (see Figure 2-5).

Note

The small divider bar that appears on the left side of the Start menu (see Figure 2-5) separates the pinned from the unpinned Start menu items so that you can easily keep track of them. Also, Internet Explorer and your default e-mail client display some quick access options when you right-click their icons. You can quickly browse the Internet or check e-mail this way.

On the right side of the Start menu you see common Windows items that you will need to access. Following are the included items:

- **My Documents, My Pictures, and My Music:** The My Documents folder is the default storage location for files of all kinds, including pictures, music, and movies. My Documents contains the default subfolders My Music, My Pictures, My Videos, and Remote Desktops.
- **My Computer:** My Computer is the default folder that stores information about drives connected to your computer. You can quickly access system properties by right-clicking My Computer on the Start menu and clicking Properties.
- **My Network Places:** My Network Places contains information about other computers and shared folders on your network.
- **Control Panel:** Control Panel is the default location for managing all kinds of programs and services on your XP computer.
- **Network Connections/Connect To:** Network Connections is a folder that contains your dial-up/broadband connections as well as local area network (LAN)

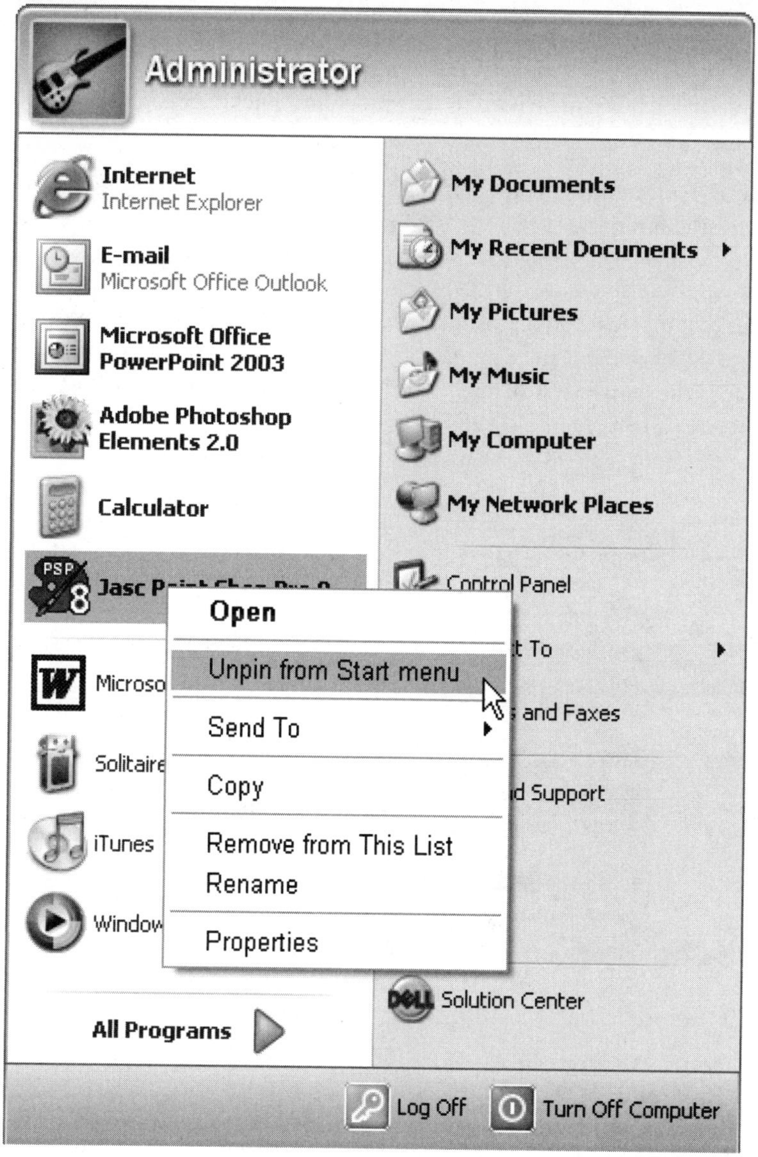

Figure 2-5: You can pin or unpin items simply by right-clicking the icons in the Start menu.

connections. If you have configured connections, you'll see a Connect To option where you can quickly access a connection and start it.

- **Help and Support:** Windows XP includes a help and support feature that can answer your questions and even locate answers on the Internet.

- **Search:** The search feature enables you to find items on your computer or items on the Internet.
- **Run:** The Run dialog box can be used to start programs quickly or connect to network shares.
- **Log Off/Turn Off Computer:** These standard icons enable you to log off or shut down/restart the computer.

Note that you can add just about anything to your Start menu simply by dragging the icon to it. Also, notice that the items on the right side of the Start menu cannot be removed by right-clicking them. Manage the Start menu icons by accessing Taskbar and Start menu properties. To configure the Start menu further, right-click an empty area of the Taskbar and click Properties; more easily, right-click the Start menu button and click Properties. The Properties dialog box appears with Taskbar and Start Menu tabs (see Figure 2-6).

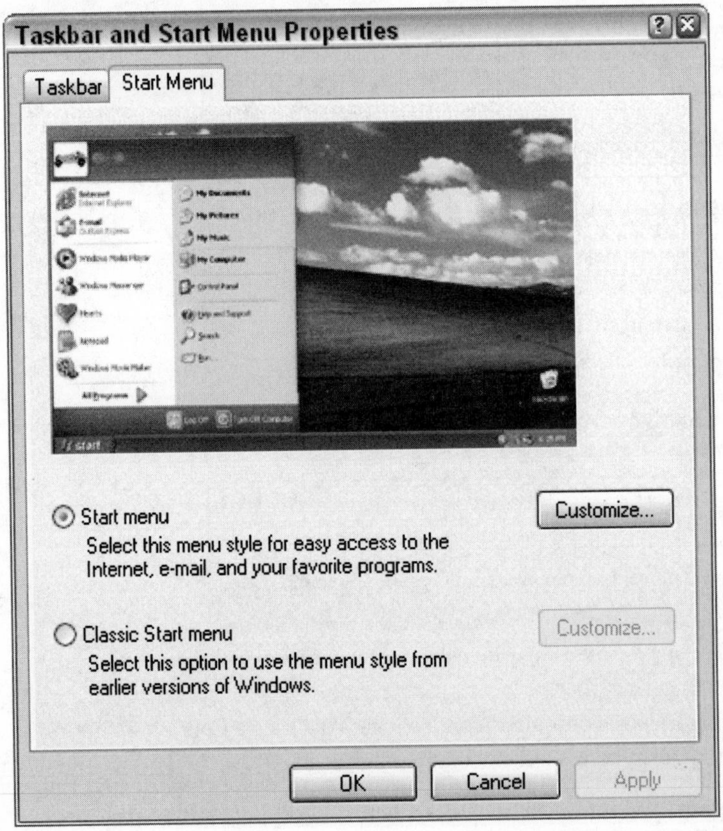
Taskbar and Start Menu Properties
Taskbar
Start Menu
Start menu
Select this menu style for easy access to the Internet, e-mail, and your favorite programs.
Customize...
Classic Start menu
Select this option to use the menu style from earlier versions of Windows.
Customize...
OK
Cancel
Apply

Figure 2-6: Taskbar and Start menu properties.

On the Start Menu properties page you have the option to use either the current Start menu or the Classic Start menu, which is simply the Start menu found in previous versions of Windows.

To continue using the Windows XP Start menu, just click the Customize button. This takes you to a Customize Start menu window, where there are General and Advanced tabs. On the General tab (see Figure 2-7) are three different customization options:

Figure 2-7: The General tab of the Customize Start Menu dialog box.

- **Select an icon size for programs:** You can choose to use large or small icons in the Start menu. Small icons may be harder to see but you can put more shortcut icons directly on the Start menu that way. Large icons are selected by default.
- **Programs:** By default, your Start menu makes five program shortcut icons appear in viewing range when you click Start. You can change this number by using the drop-down menu. The Start menu can display up to 30. Basically, this just makes your Start menu larger so it can display all 30 programs you might place on it.

- **Show on Start menu:** This option allows you to show Internet and E-mail on the Start menu, and then provides you with a drop-down menu to select the application (Internet Explorer and Outlook Express, by default). If you have other browser or e-mail clients installed on your computer, you can use the drop-down menu and select a different browser or e-mail client, or just clear the check boxes if you don't want these items displayed at all.

On the Advanced tab are some additional options that you may find very useful (see Figure 2-8).

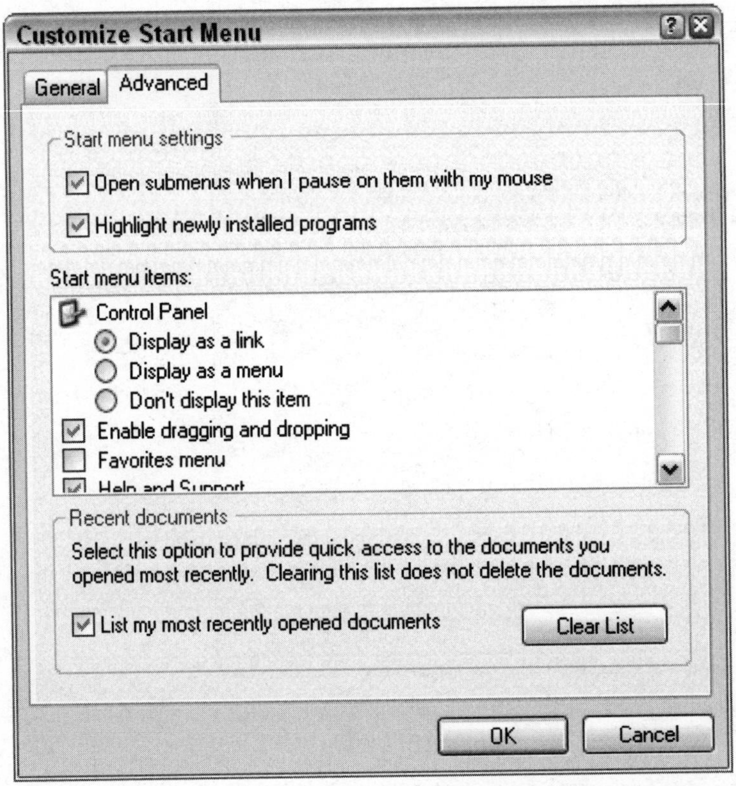

Figure 2-8: The Advanced tab of the Customize Start Menu dialog box.

The top two check boxes determine the Start menu settings:

- **Open submenus when I pause on them with my mouse:** By default, folders such as My Documents, My Computer, and so on are stored as a link on the Start menu. You can click them to open the folders in a different window. However, you can use a menu option so that a menu appears where you can choose subfolders. For example, I have a folder called Work in My Documents. Without using the menu option, I have to click My Documents and then open Work. Using the menu option, if I point to My Documents on the Start menu, a pop-out menu appears showing my other folders, including Work, which I can just click on to open. This check box simply asks if you want the pop-out menu to appear when you put your mouse over the item or if you want to have to click the item to see the contents of the folder.

- **Highlight newly installed programs:** When applications are first installed on your XP computer, they are highlighted when you click All Programs. This serves as a simple reminder that you have new stuff you haven't used. Just clear the check box if you don't want to use the feature.

The second part of the Advanced tab gives you a scroll window where you can select the folder and Windows items that appear on the Start menu and how to display those items. For example, by default, Control Panel is shown on the Start menu as a link. You can change this behavior so that it is shown as a menu, or not all. Simply scroll through the list and click the desired check boxes and option buttons to determine what Windows items you want to include and how those items are presented (link or menu). You may want to experiment with these settings until you find the combination that is right for you. Remember, you can make changes to these settings as many times you like.

The last part of this configuration dialog box allows you to show recently used documents on the Start menu. For example, say that you're writing your life story. Once you open the document and then close it, the Start menu puts it in Recent Documents, which is a folder that will now appear on the Start menu. You can easily access the document from the Start menu the next time you need it.

Using Classic Start Menu

You can use the Classic Start menu by selecting the Classic Start Menu option on the Start Menu tab of Taskbar and Start Menu Properties. This option allows you to use the Start menu you saw in previous versions of Windows. If you want to use the Classic Start menu, right-click the Start button and click Properties. Select the Classic Start Menu option button and click Apply, which gives you a single Customize Classic Start Menu interface. You'll see that you have the same basic Start menu options, just in a different format. If you want to add items to the Classic Start menu, click the Add button and let the wizard help

Using Classic Start Menu *(Continued)*

you select items on your computer to add. Use the Remove button to remove items. The Advanced button opens Windows Explorer so you can manually add and remove items you want. You can also re-sort items and clear recent documents, programs, Web sites, and so on. The Advanced window option that you see enables you to display a number of Windows items, use expandable (menu) folders, and so on. These items are self-explanatory. Feel free to experiment and try new configurations.

Reducing Graphic Effects for Slower Systems

The best way to gain speed is to make sure you have a fast processor installed on your computer and ample RAM, preferably 512 MB or more. Of course, hardware upgrades are expensive and not always practical, so you are left with trying to make Windows XP work faster in spite of any hardware deficiencies. After all, that is probably why you are reading this book in the first place.

If your computer has a processor that is a bit on the slow slide, you can change some configuration options in Windows XP to reduce the graphical effects you see on the desktop, on the Start menu, and in folders. Naturally, graphics consume processor cycles so if you reduce the graphic effects, you'll end up with a processor that has more free cycles to devote to other tasks. You don't need to make these changes if you have a fast processor and ample RAM but if you know you are limping along with slower hardware, these changes can help give you a boost in speed.

Windows XP gives you a simple interface to adjust the graphical nature of Windows XP to conserve RAM and processor cycles. If you right-click My Computer and select Properties, or just open System in Control Panel, you can click the Advanced tab and then click the Settings button under Performance.

This opens the Performance Options window (see Figure 2-9). As you can see on the Visual Effects tab, Windows XP attempts to choose its own settings by default. However, you can change this setting so that Windows XP's visual effects are adjusted for appearance or performance. You can also click the Custom option button and clear the desired visual effects check boxes to reduce RAM and processor usage on certain items. For example, you might remove the shadows features and fading features of Windows XP.

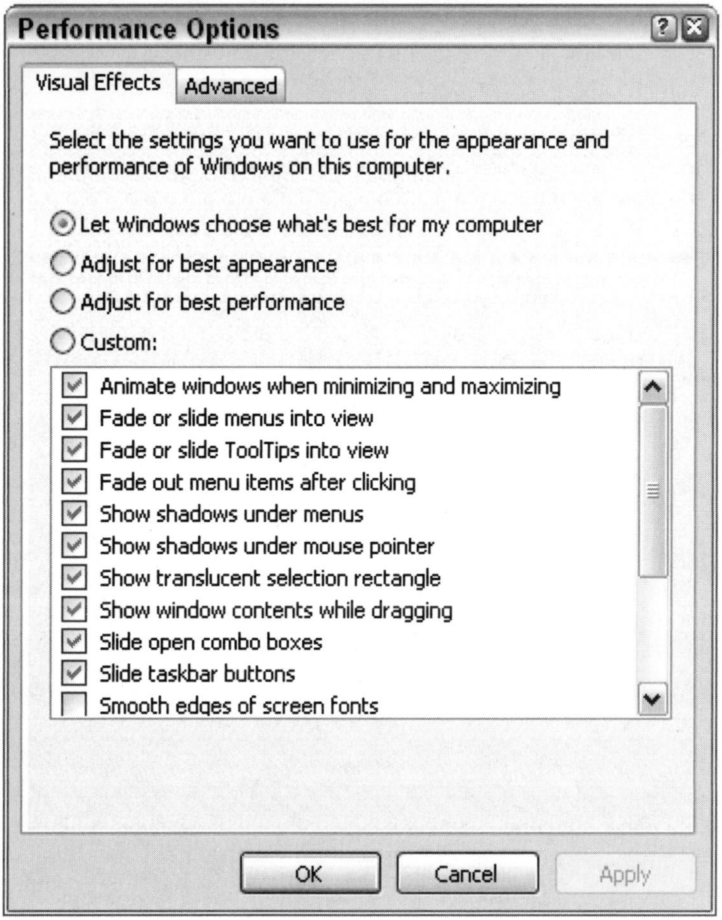

Figure 2-9: The Visual Effects tab in the Performance Option dialog box.

Chapter 3

Managing Notification Area Items and Startup Programs

Windows XP includes a Notification area that is found on the lower right side of your desktop and appears to be a part of the Taskbar. In previous versions of Windows, this area was called the System Tray but the name was changed in Windows XP to express better the purpose of the Notification area. So what is its purpose? The Notification area displays the time and also serves a quick access area for certain shortcuts. Also, when certain events occur in the system, an icon appears in the Notification area. For example, if you print a document, a printer icon appears in the Notification area; when you are sending or receiving e-mail, an icon appears. These icons give you access to management features of the particular item when you right-click them. For example, when you print a document, you can right-click the printer icon in the Notification area to open the printer queue and manage the print jobs.

What does all of this have to do with speed and performance? As you might guess, the more tasks and features that the Notification area tries to show you, the more processor cycles and system resources those features consume. Too many Notification area items can slow the system down and cause your computer to take longer to boot. This chapter takes a look at the Notification area and explores some practical tactics you can employ to control and manage it to increase speed on your computer. You'll also see how to stop programs from loading when you boot your computer.

Exploring the Notification Area

The Notification area may primarily appear as a clock in the lower-right corner of your desktop on the Taskbar. However, if you click the little arrow next to the clock and expand the Notification area, you'll be able to see all of the current programs and notices that the Notification area manages (see Figure 3-1). Keep in mind that the Notification area is dynamic: What you see in the Notification area changes according to what is currently happening on the system. For example, you only see a printer icon if you are printing something and you only see an e-mail icon if you are sending or receiving e-mail. Some programs always stay in the Notification area but you can manage those as well.

Figure 3-1: Windows XP Notification area.

Controlling the Notification Area

Like most features in Windows XP, the Notification area has some basic configuration options you can set. If you right-click the clock in the Notification area and click Customize Notifications, you'll see the Customize Notifications dialog box (see Figure 3-2). For the most part, virtually all programs are configured to hide when they are not active. In other words, you do not see items in the Notification area that are not running. However, you can prevent some previous items that have appeared in the Notification area from appearing again, or you can make some items always appear.

To change the configuration of a particular item, click the behavior of the particular item; a menu will appear. You can then use the menu to change the behavior of that particular item.

Aside from the basic configuration options, you can determine if you want to show the clock in the Notification area. By default, the clock appears and all other icons are hidden (which is why you must click the arrow to expand the Notification area). However, you can easily change this behavior so that the clock does not appear, or so all Notification area items are always visible.

Right-click the Start menu and click Properties; then click the Taskbar tab (see Figure 3-3). In the Notification Area section, clear the check boxes if you want to turn off these features.

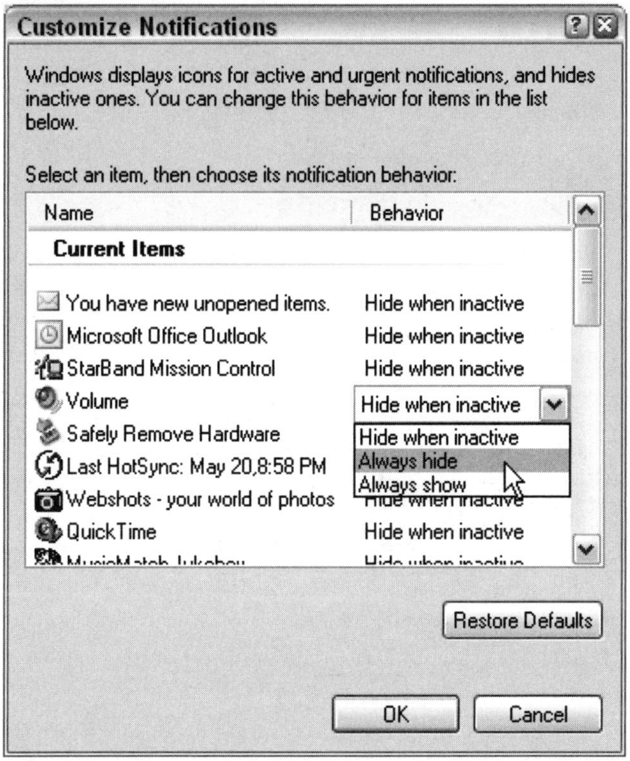

Figure 3-2: You can customize the behavior of Notification area items.

Stopping Programs in the Notification Area

Since the Notification area shows you open programs and events that are occurring in Windows XP, can you use the Notification area to control those programs? The answer is a resounding yes—and this is one commonly overlooked feature that can help you reduce the program load placed on Windows XP. The Notification area shows programs that you have opened, but also shows some of the programs that automatically start when you run Windows XP. You may want to reduce the number of those programs to decrease boot time, but you may also want to exit some of those programs from time to time to increase system performance.

All computers have a threshold of available resources. You might have a supercharged computer but, let's face it, your computer has a finite amount of RAM and processor cycles. The more programs you have running at the same time, the more those system resources are consumed. That's fine, but you do not want to waste RAM and processor cycles on

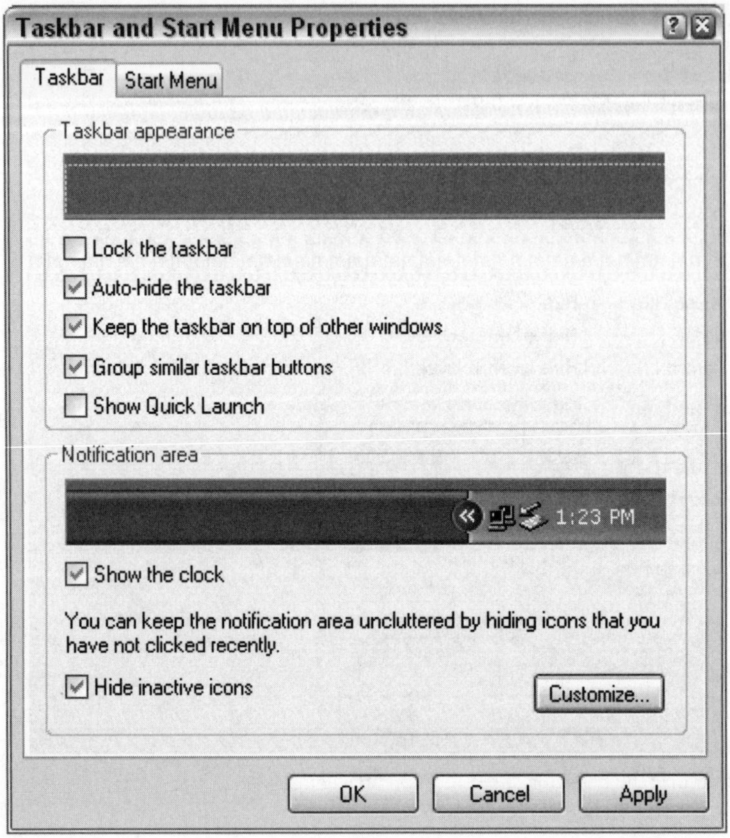

Figure 3-3: You can easily turn off the clock and make all inactive icons appear.

programs you never use. To increase system performance, you can easily and quickly exit programs that are active in the Notification area if you do not need those programs.

Simply expand the Notification area (if necessary) to see all of the program icons. You can right-click any Notification area icon to see a contextual menu of options; for each program, you should see an Exit or Close option. Just click Exit or Close to close the program. This closes the actual program, not just the Notification area icon. If you later want to use the program, you can locate it in Start ➪ All Programs.

Using the Notification Area to Boost Program Power

Users tend to see the Notification area as a passive tool in Windows XP. While its main purpose is to notify you about what programs and processes are running in Windows XP, you can also use the Notification area as a control center of sorts for your programs.

Because you can use the Notification area to exit programs easily, get in the habit of knowing what is running on your computer and use the area to exit programs that you are not using at the moment.

Here's an example. Multimedia applications have become very popular over the past few years, and rightly so. Many of us use our computers to edit and manage photos as well as video clips. Windows XP gives you the tools you need to manage multimedia, but most multimedia applications are resource hogs. It takes a lot of processor cycles and RAM to work with digital photos and movies. So when you need to work with a program that consumes a lot of system resources, it's a good idea to close other programs that you do not need. For example, when I work on a movie or photo editing, I often close my e-mail application and my antivirus application. Because I am not doing anything that could cause a virus to enter my computer, I don't need those applications to run or consume power. Using the Notification area, I can quickly exit those programs free up more power for the task at hand—and then simply restart those applications when I'm done. Use some common sense about your programs and always be aware of the programs that are running on your computer. This simple tactic can help you gain power and speed by reducing the load placed on the computer's memory and processor.

Clearing Past Icons from the Notification Area

If you took a look at the Customize Notifications dialog box, you may have noticed that Windows XP keeps track of all the prior icons that have appeared in the Notification area. This isn't a big problem but it is one of those less useful items that Windows XP spends time keeping track of. You can easily stop Windows XP from remembering these old "icon streams," as they are called in the Registry, by following these steps:

1. Click Start ➪ Run. Type **regedit** and click OK.
2. In the Registry Editor, navigate to HKEY_CURRENT_USER \Software\Microsoft\Windows\CurrentVersion\Explorer\TrayNotify.
3. Right-click IconStreams and click Delete (see Figure 3-4).
4. Right-click PastIconStreams and click Delete.
5. Close the Registry Editor and restart your computer.

Disabling Notification Area Balloon Tips

Balloon tips are a little feature in Windows XP that pops up a balloon to give you some information. At first, the balloon tips can be helpful if you are a new Windows XP user but they quickly become an annoyance because every time you point to something in the

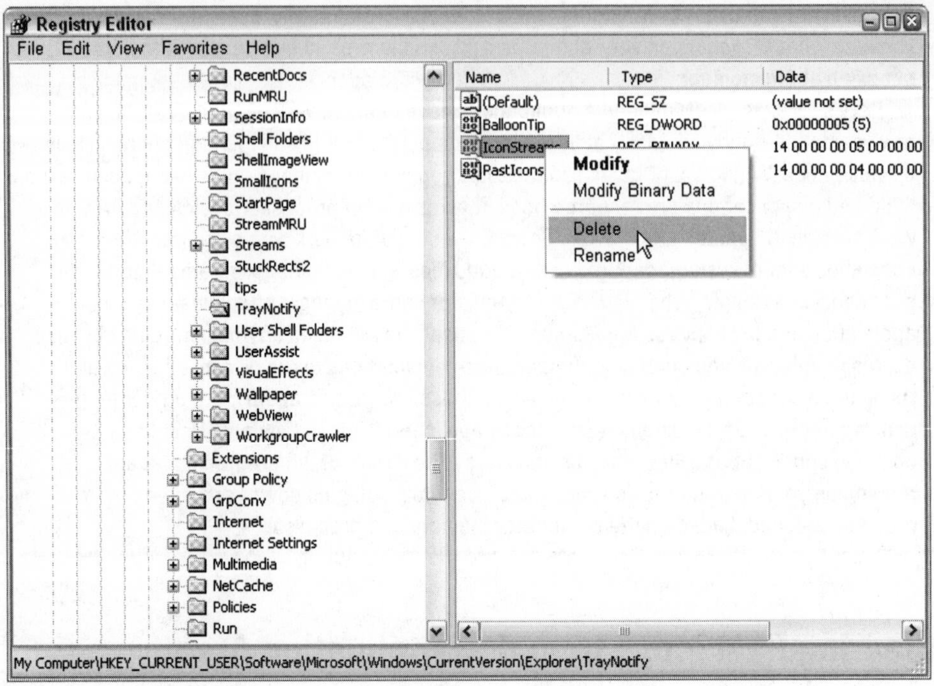

Figure 3-4: Right-click the IconStreams value and click Delete.

Notification area, a balloon tip appears telling you information you already know. Fortunately, you can quickly disable the balloon tip feature. Follow these steps:

1. Click Start ➪ Run. Type **regedit** and click OK.
2. In the Registry Editor, navigate to HKEY_CURRENT_USER\Software\Microsoft\Windows\CurrentVersion\Explorer\TrayNotify.
3. Right-click the BalloonTip value and click Modify.
4. In the modification dialog box that appears, enter a value of **0**.
5. Close the Registry Editor and then log off Windows and log back on again.

Making Windows XP Icons Appear More Quickly

While I am on the subject of icons in general, there is a quick little fix you can perform that makes icons in a folder appear more quickly. Have you noticed that sometimes when you open a folder, Windows XP takes a little time to search for the items to display? This is caused by a default configuration that makes Windows XP automatically search for network files and printers that might belong in that folder. This wastes time and makes Windows XP appear to run more slowly. No problem, though; you can easily stop this network browsing behavior:

1. Select Control Panel ⇨ Folder Options.
2. In the Folder Options dialog box, select the View tab.
3. Clear the check box that says "Automatically search for network folders and printers" (see Figure 3-5).
4. Click OK.

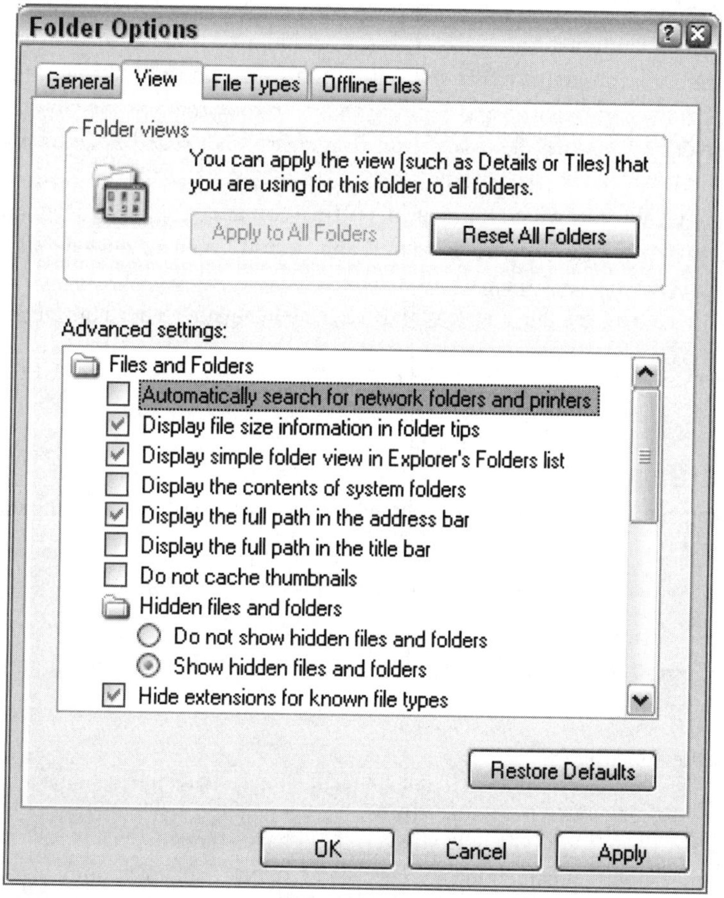

Figure 3-5: Clear the check box shown to speed up the display of folder icons.

Controlling Startup Programs

A number of programs that you might install on your Windows XP computer are designed to load when the computer starts. Naturally, Windows XP has a number of its own programs that start when the computer boots, but some programs you install may do the same thing. Antivirus software is a good example. To keep your computer protected at all times, virtually all antivirus software automatically loads when your computer boots. This allows the software to work without your intervention and prevents the possibility of you forgetting to start it. So startup programs are not bad per se; they can serve a very important function on your computer.

However, a number of unnecessary programs may also start. For example, I have a screen-capture utility that always starts when my computer boots. I also have a weather monitoring utility that automatically starts. These programs are good—I use them from time to time—but the more programs that must start when I turn on the computer, the more time it takes to get the computer up and running and the more programs that automatically end up in the Notification area. So if you want to increase boot speed as far as programs are concerned and reduce the amount of program clutter in the Notification area, examine all of the programs that start when your computer turns on and stop those programs from loading upon startup if you don't really need them. After all, you can always start those programs yourself, as you need them.

You can easily control which programs start when you turn on your computer by following these steps:

Cross-Reference

There are many other tricks and tactics that help Windows XP start faster. I explore all the startup issues in Chapter 4.

1. Click Start ➪ Run. Type **msconfig** and click OK. The System Configuration Utility appears.
2. Click the Startup tab.
3. The Startup tab (see Figure 3-6) shows you every service and program that starts when your computer boots. As you can see, I have some internal items and program helper Dynamic Link Libraries (DLLs), but I also have some programs that are designed to start up automatically. You can prevent a program from starting by simply clearing the check box next to it and clicking OK.

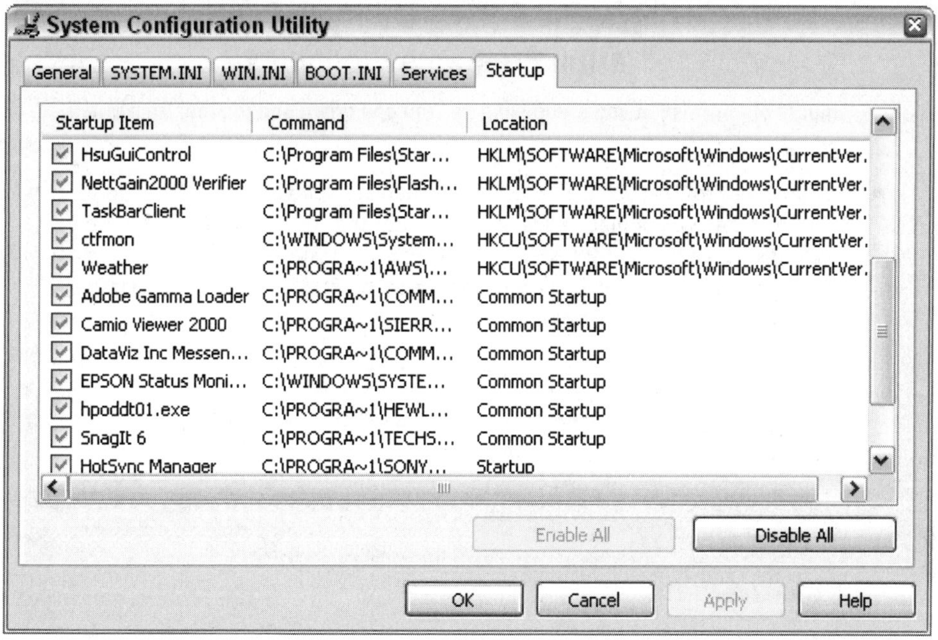

Figure 3-6: Clear the check box next to programs that you do not want to run when the computer boots up.

Caution

Make sure you do not clear any unfamiliar check boxes. Many of the features you see here give you the functionality you love in Windows XP and the programs you use, so do not randomly stop programs from loading. However, if you know there are some programs that you do not regularly use, you can safely stop those from loading.

Using a Third-Party Utility to Control Startup Programs

You can use the System Configuration Utility to control startup programs but there are also third-party tools that you may find helpful and more useful. Here are two of them you may want to check out:

- **Windows XP Startup Programs Tracker:** This program simply gives you information about all the programs that are designed to start up in Windows XP and the location of their programs (see Figure 3-7). It's a free utility that can give you that extra

Using a Third-Party Utility to Control Startup Programs *(Continued)*

amount of information you are looking for. You can download the tool from `www.dougknox.com/xp/utils/xp_starttrack.htm`.

- **Startup Cop Pro:** This utility gives you information about what programs start up on your computer, where they reside, what they do, and you can control the startup programs with this utility. It's a nice program and one you might want to add to your collection. Download requires a subscription to the PC Magazine Utility Library, where you can get a myriad of other helpful programs. Find out more at `www.pcmag.com/utilities`.

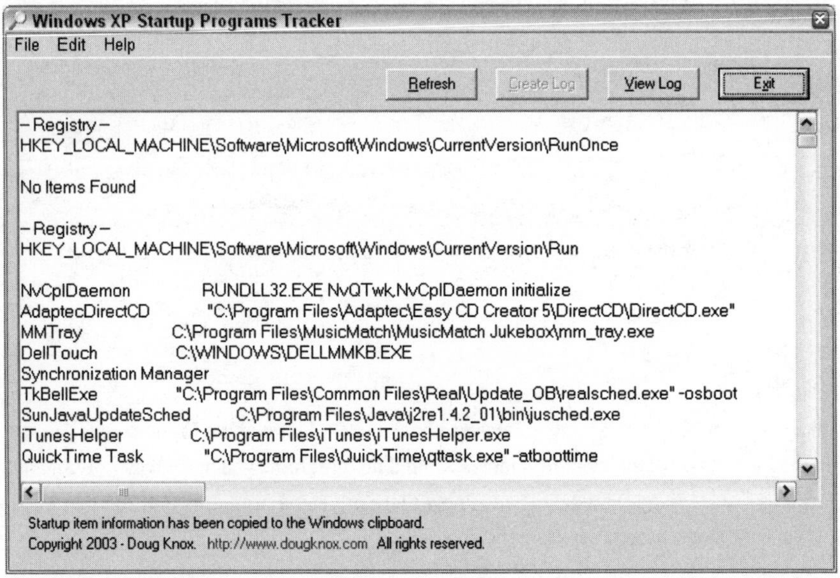

Figure 3-7: Use Windows XP Startup Programs Tracker to see what programs start when Windows XP loads, and where they are located.

Part II

Supercharging Windows

IN THIS PART

Chapter 4

Making Windows XP Start Faster

Whenever you start your computer, you are faced with a few moments of thumb twiddling while Windows XP boots and prompts you to log on. Although you should expect to wait for a few moments, sometimes Windows XP seems to boot rather slowly. In fact, you may notice that over a period of time the PC that used to roar to life seems a bit sluggish instead. Fortunately, you can perform several techniques that help Windows XP get the bootup speed you want. This chapter explores how to put these techniques to work.

Stopping Unneeded Startup Services

Along with the core operating system and programs that Windows XP runs when it starts, there is also a host of services involved. Many of these services are necessary for Windows XP to operate correctly. However, many of them are for features in Windows XP that you may not use at all. You can peruse the services and disable any service that you do not want to run. The fewer services that run, the more quickly Windows XP will boot.

Caution

Exercise caution when stopping services. If you do not know what a service does or are unsure of the ramifications of stopping the service, leave it alone. Some services are critical to Windows XP's operations, so make sure you understand what the service is before you disable it.

To reduce the number of services that start on bootup, you can access two different areas of Windows XP. The first is the System Configuration Utility. The Services tab shows you the services that start when the computer boots (see Figure 4-1).

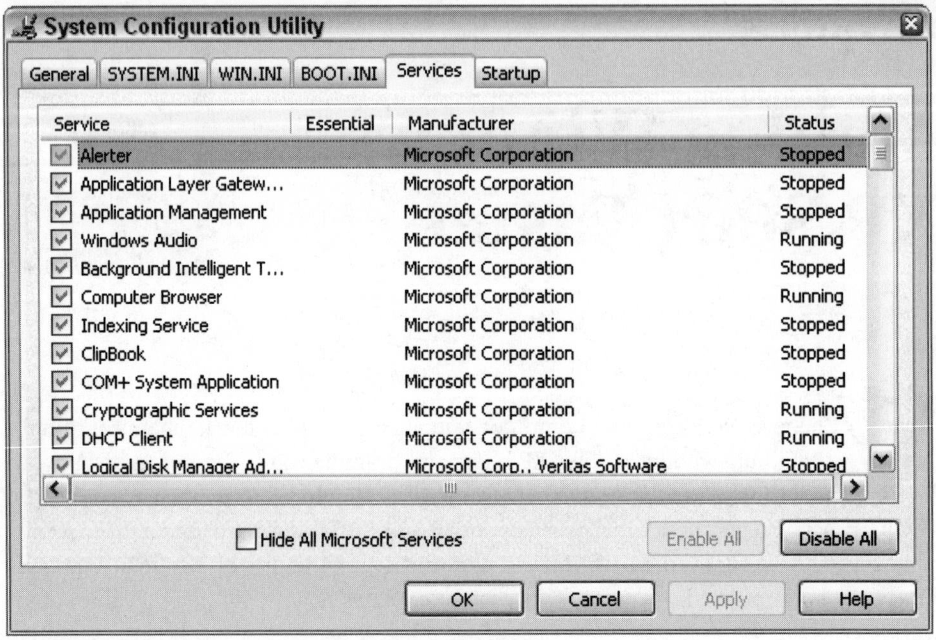

Figure 4-1: Services tab of the System Configuration Utility.

You can stop a service from starting by simply clearing the check box next to the service and clicking OK. However, before you do so, there is another way to disable services that you may prefer because the interface gives you more information about the service in question.

Open Control Panel ➪ Administrative Tools ➪ Services or else select Start ➪ Run, type **services.msc**, and click OK. Either way, you see the Services console (see Figure 4-2).

I prefer to use the Services console instead of the System Configuration Utility because it describes what the service does. Additionally, you can double-click a service and examine its properties.

Notice the Startup Type column in Figure 4-2. This information lists whether the service is automatic or manual. Manual services are only started in Windows XP when you start a process that requires the service. Some other process may require the service that has a "dependency" relationship with it; in this case, the dependency service will start, as well. Because these services do not start automatically when you boot Windows XP, you do not need to do anything with manual services.

However, all services listed as automatic start when Windows XP boots. These are the services that increase boot time. As I have mentioned, many of them are necessary and important, so you should not stop automatic services from booting unless you are sure of the ramifications. You can get this information by looking at the Description column. Here's a quick look at common services you may want to live without:

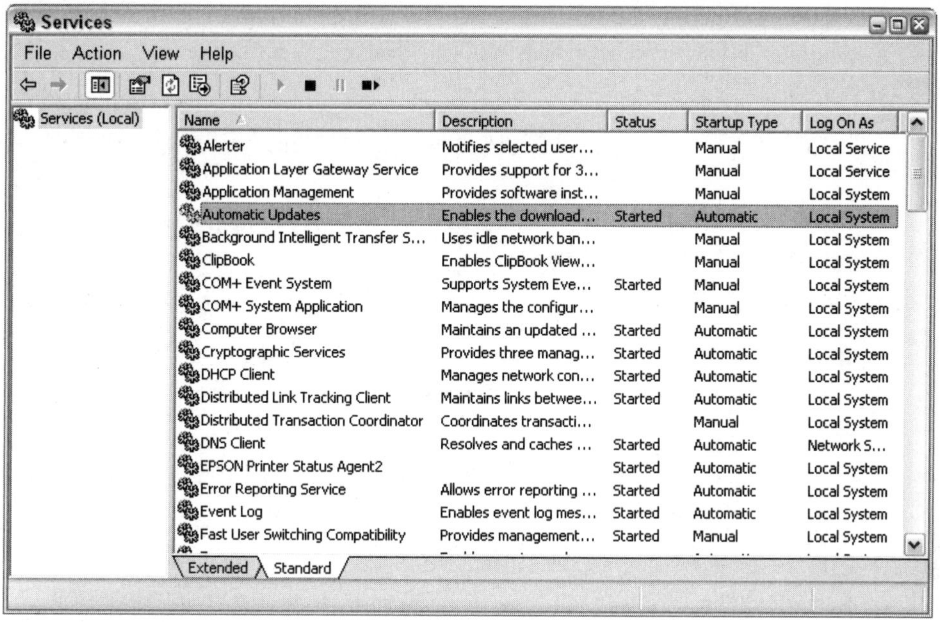

Figure 4-2: The Services console gives you additional information about services that run in Windows XP.

- **Automatic Updates:** This service enables Windows XP to check the Web automatically for updates. If you don't want to use Automatic Updates, you can disable the service. You can always check for updates manually at the Windows Update Web site.

- **Computer Browser:** If your computer is not on a network, you don't need this service. If you are on a network, leave it alone.

- **DHCP Client:** If you are not on a network, you do not need this service. If you are on a small workgroup, you can still increase boot time by configuring manual IP addresses (which I explore later in this chapter).

- **DNS Client:** If you are not on a network, you do not need this service. If you are, leave it alone.

- **Error Reporting and Event Log:** You don't have to use these services but they can be very helpful, so I would leave them configured as automatic.

- **Fax:** If you don't use your computer for fax services, you can disable this one.

- **Help and Support:** If you never use the Windows XP Help and Support Center (found on the Start menu), you can disable this service.

- **IMAPI CD-Burning COM:** This service enables you to burn CDs on your computer. If you never burn CDs, you can disable the service.
- **Indexing Service:** Your computer keeps an index of files but if you rarely search for files, the service is just a resource hog. You can stop it and turn the service to manual.
- **Windows Firewall/Internet Connection Sharing:** If you do not use these features, you can disable them.
- **Infrared Monitor:** If you do not use infrared devices, you can disable this service.
- **Messenger:** This service sends alert messages on a local area network (it is not the same as Windows Messenger). If you are not on a network, you can disable this service.
- **Print Spooler:** If you do not do any printing from the computer, you can disable this service. If you print, make sure you leave it as automatic.
- **Remote Registry:** This service allows remote users to modify the Registry on your computer. If you are not on a network, you can disable this service.
- **System Restore Service:** This service allows you to use System Restore. If you have turned off System Restore anyway, you do not need to turn off the service. If you do, you turn off System Restore.
- **Themes:** If you do not use themes, you can disable this service.
- **Windows Image Acquisition:** If you do not use scanners or digital cameras, you can disable this service.
- **Wireless Zero Configuration:** If do not use wireless networking devices, you can disable this service.

You may have a number of other automatic services, depending on software and other configurations on your computer. So it's a good idea to look through the services and learn more about them. If you double-click a service, a Properties dialog box appears (see Figure 4-3).

Notice that on the General tab, you see a Startup Type drop-down menu. If you want to change an automatic service to manual, select Manual here and click OK. As a general rule, don't disable a service unless you are sure you will never use it. However, manual configuration allows the service to be started when you find it necessary, thus speeding up your boot time.

However, before you change a service to manual, look at the Dependencies tab (see Figure 4-4). This tab shows you which other services depend upon the service you are considering changing.

Upload Manager Properties (Local Computer) [?] [X]

| General | Log On | Recovery | Dependencies |

Service name: uploadmgr

Display name: Upload Manager

Description: Manages synchronous and asynchronous file transfers between clients and servers on the

Path to executable:
C:\WINDOWS\System32\svchost.exe -k netsvcs

Startup type: Automatic

Service status: Started

[Start] [Stop] [Pause] [Resume]

You can specify the start parameters that apply when you start the service from here.

Start parameters:

[OK] [Cancel] [Apply]

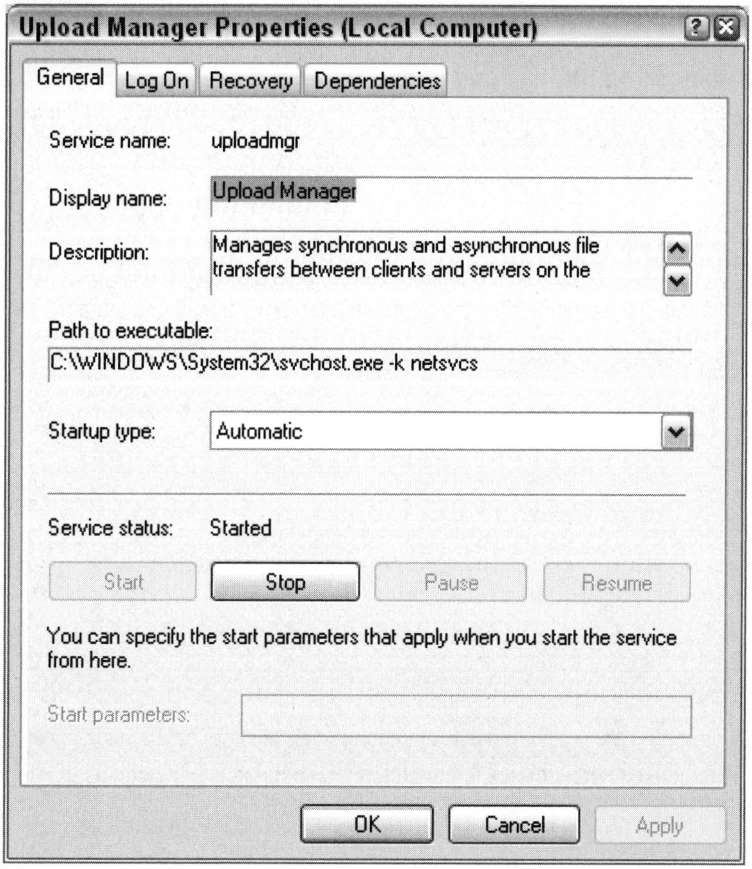

Figure 4-3: General tab of the Upload Manager Properties dialog box.

Keep in mind that services are necessary for the vast functionality you get with Windows XP. Change only those services that you understand and do not use. How you use your Windows XP computer should be the best guide in terms of optional startup services.

Tip

The Indexing service and the System Restore service take up a lot of disk space and system resources across the board. You can live without the Indexing service but I suggest that you keep using System Restore. It works great when you are in a bind and this is one case where the loss of speed may not be worth the ramifications of not using System Restore.

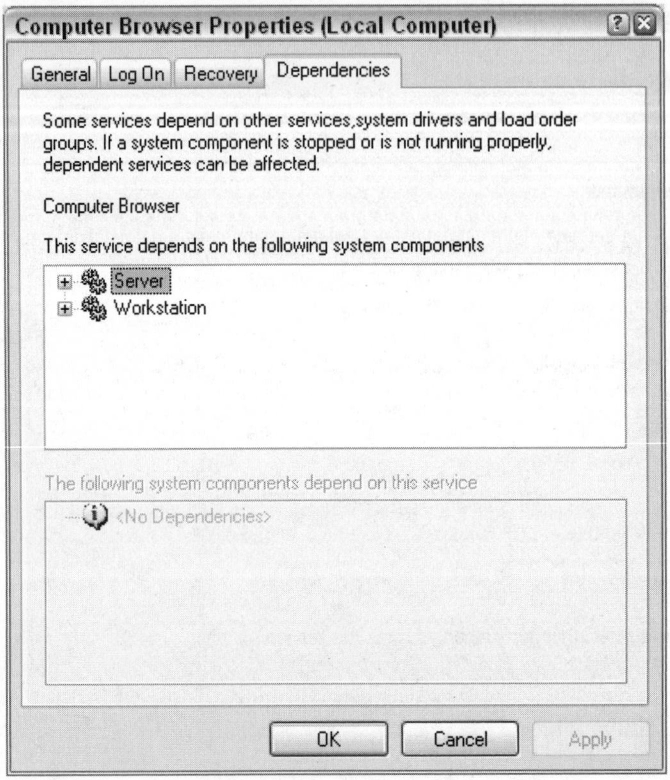
Computer Browser Properties (Local Computer)
General
Log On
Recovery
Dependencies
Some services depend on other services,system drivers and load order groups. If a system component is stopped or is not running properly, dependent services can be affected.
Computer Browser
This service depends on the following system components
Server
Workstation
The following system components depend on this service
<No Dependencies>
OK
Cancel
Apply

Figure 4-4: Check the Dependencies tab for other services that are dependant on the service in question.

Speed Tips and Tricks for Windows XP Startup

Aside from startup programs, services, and the Prefetch folder, there are a number of other startup procedures and issues you can modify to help Windows XP start faster. The following sections explore those tips and tricks.

Manual IP Addressing on Small Office/Home Networks

Windows XP is configured to help you take care of networking. It uses the TCP/IP protocol for networking in workgroups, or what you might call small office or home networks that do not use a dedicated server.

The problem is that automatic IP addressing can be slow. When your computer boots, it has to query the network to see what IP addresses are already in use and then assign itself one. If you want to speed up the boot time a bit, consider manually assigning IP addresses to all computers on the network. This way, the network computers do not have to worry about locating an automatic IP address. Because one is manually configured, the operating system doesn't have to spend time solving this problem.

This isn't a networking book, however, so I won't delve into the implications of using a manual IP address, but if you are using a computer that functions as a host computer to the Internet (using Internet Connection Sharing [ICS]), you can get into connectivity problems if you change the configuration of the IP address. However, you can still work around this problem by starting with the ICS host computer.

Select Start ➪ Connect To ➪ Show All Connections. Right-click your network adapter card and click Properties. On the General tab, select TCP/IP in the list of services and click the Properties button.

In the TCP/IP properties, you can see if you use an automatic or manual IP address. In the example in Figure 4-5, I have configured a manual IP address of 90.0.0.1 and a default

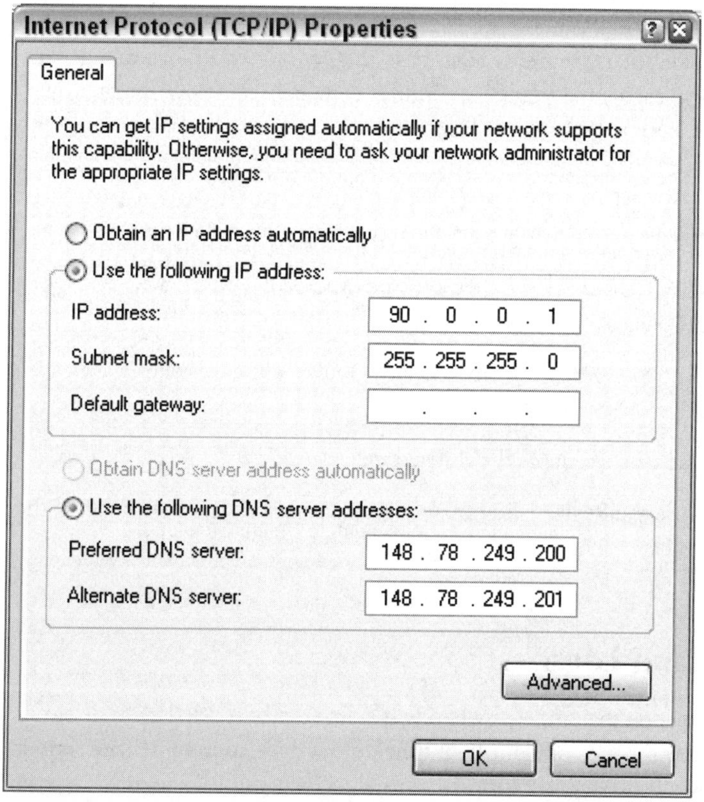

Figure 4-5: Manually assigned IP addresses can help increase startup time.

subnet mask. The other computers on my office network each use a different IP address in the same class, such as 90.0.0.2, 90.0.0.3, 90.0.0.4, and so on. This way, each computer has a permanent IP address, which helps increase boot time. Note that if you change the IP addresses of your computers, they must all use the same subnet mask. A default subject mask of 255.255.255.0 will keep you in good shape.

Make sure you understand the implications of changing IP addresses on your network. If you have no networking experience at all, you may be wiser to leave the automatic IP addressing as is and try to gain some speed using the additional suggestions in this chapter.

Disabling Recent Documents History

Windows XP includes a feature that keeps track of all recent documents you have opened or used. The idea is that you can select Start ➪ Recent Documents History and quickly reopen any document you have recently used. I use many documents each day and never use the feature myself. In my opinion, I can keep up with what I want to use without Windows XP doing it for me.

The bad thing about Recent Documents History is that Windows XP has to calculate what should be put there each time you boot Windows, which can slow things down. So, if you never use the Recent Documents History, it's a good idea to disable it. Here's how:

1. Open the Registry Editor (select Start ➪ Run, type **regedit**, and click OK).
2. Navigate to HKEY_CURRENT_USER\Software\Microsoft\Windows\CurrentVersion\Policies\Explorer.
3. Create a NoRecentDocsHistory D_WORD key. Double-click the value to open it once it is created.
4. Set the Data Value to **1** to enable the restriction.
5. Click OK and close the Registry Editor. You'll need to restart the computer for the change to take effect.

Disabling the Boot Logo

You can remove the boot logo that appears when you start Windows XP. This little tweak probably shaves only a few seconds off your boot time but seconds count if you are serious about trying to get Windows XP up and running as quickly as possible. The only negative is that if you remove the boot logo, you will also not see any boot messages, such as check disk. (But if you are not having problems with your computer, this isn't such a big deal.)

To remove the boot logo, follow these steps:

1. Select Start ➪ Run, type **msconfig**, and click OK.
2. In the System Configuration Utility, click the BOOT.INI tab.
3. On the BOOT.INI tab, click the NOGUIBOOT check box option (see Figure 4-6). Click OK.

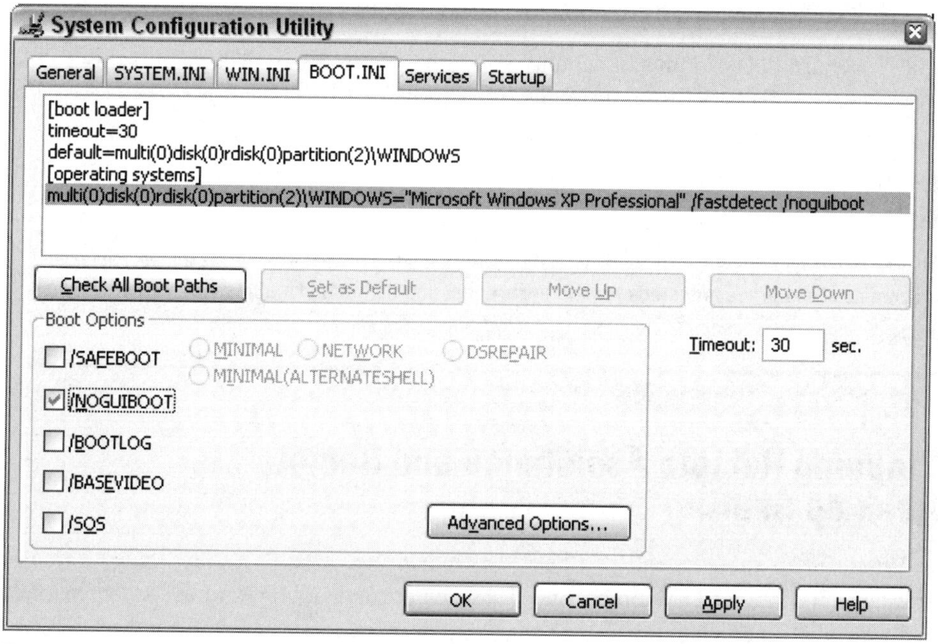

Figure 4-6: You can turn off the boot logo by selecting the NOGUIBOOT option.

Removing Unwanted Fonts

One trick that increases your boot time a bit is to lose any fonts in the Fonts folder in Control Panel that you never use. The more fonts you have, the more processing Windows XP has to do to prep all of those fonts for use. You must be a bit careful here to not remove fonts that you might want, but there is a good chance that you can live without many of them. For instance, you may have foreign language fonts and other symbol fonts (such as Wingdings) that you never use.

To delete unneeded fonts, follow these steps:

1. Open the Fonts folder in Control Panel.
2. Select Edit ➪ Select All and then Edit ➪ Copy.
3. Create a new folder on your desktop, open it, and select Edit ➪ Paste.
4. In this new folder, delete any of the fonts you do not want.
5. Return to the Fonts folder in Control Panel. Right-click the selected fonts and click Delete.
6. Go back to your new desktop folder and click Edit ➪ Select All.
7. Return to your Fonts folder and click Edit ➪ Paste. You now have only the desired fonts in the Fonts folder.

Tip

You can directly delete fonts from the Fonts folder without creating the secondary folder. However, I recommend the preceding steps to help ensure that you do not make a mistake in the deletion process.

Stopping Remote Assistance and Remote Desktop Sharing

In Windows XP Professional, you have two remote networking features called Remote Assistance and Remote Desktop Sharing. These remote networking features are very helpful in a variety of situations but if you don't use them, it is good idea to disable them to save boot time. You can always enable them later if you want to use them.

Note

If you are interested in using Remote Desktop or Remote Assistance, see my book *Windows XP for Power Users: Power Pack* published by John Wiley & Sons.

1. Open the Start menu, right-click My Computer, and choose Properties.
2. Click the Remote Tab.

3. Clear both check boxes to disable Remote Assistance and Remote Desktop (see Figure 4-7).

Figure 4-7: Stop using Remote Desktop and Remote Assistance to help reduce startup time.

Updating Device Drivers

One thing that can slow down your boot time is old device drivers. If you are using a newer computer that came preconfigured with Windows XP, you can skip this section. But if you are using older hardware that you have manually installed with the manufacturer's device drivers, it is a good idea to locate the manufacturer's Web site and see if there are any updated drivers for the hardware.

Windows XP tries very hard to be backwards-compatible with older hardware so older drivers will often work. However, older drivers tend to slow things down across the board, including the time required to boot the system. The only way you can update older drivers is to download newer drivers that the manufacturer of the device may make available on the Web. You'll have to do a bit of detective work and see if you can locate any newer drivers that can be installed. It's worth the time, though, because drivers written for Windows XP simply perform better than drivers for older versions of Windows.

Cross-Reference

Learn more about updating device drivers in Chapter 8.

Stopping Windows Messenger in Outlook Express 6

If you are using Outlook Express 6, Windows Messenger is configured to start when Windows XP starts and run in the background. That's fine if you use it, but if you don't you waste boot time and background resources because Windows Messenger is always around. You can stop this behavior, however, and save your self a little startup time by following these steps:

1. Open Outlook Express 6.
2. Select Tools ➪ Windows Messenger ➪ Options.
3. Click the Preferences tab.
4. On the Preferences tab, clear the "Allow this program to run in the background" check box (see Figure 4-8) and click OK.

Speeding Up Logons to Windows Domains

Although not technically a part of the boot process, one thing that can slow down your startup time is logging onto a Windows domain. If you do not connect to a Windows domain, you can skip this section. If you do and you notice that logging on seems to take forever, there is a simple explanation. Windows XP attempts to load up networking components asynchronously during startup. Although you can log on using cached credentials instead of waiting for a domain controller to log you on, this feature may greatly slow down your logon process to the network. You'll see your desktop more quickly but you'll have to wait

Figure 4-8: Stop Windows Messenger from running in the background.

longer to use the network. If you change this setting, your boot time will take longer. But at least once you log on you won't have to wait for the networking services to load. You can stop this behavior by changing a Group Policy setting on your computer.

Follow these steps:

1. Log on as the local computer administrator and select Start ➪ Run. Type **gpedit.msc** and click OK.
2. In the Group Policy editor, navigate to Computer Configuration ➪ Administrative Templates ➪ System ➪ Logon (see Figure 4-9).
3. Double-click "Always wait for the network at computer startup and logon."
4. Change the setting to Enabled (see Figure 4-10). Click OK and close the Group Policy console.

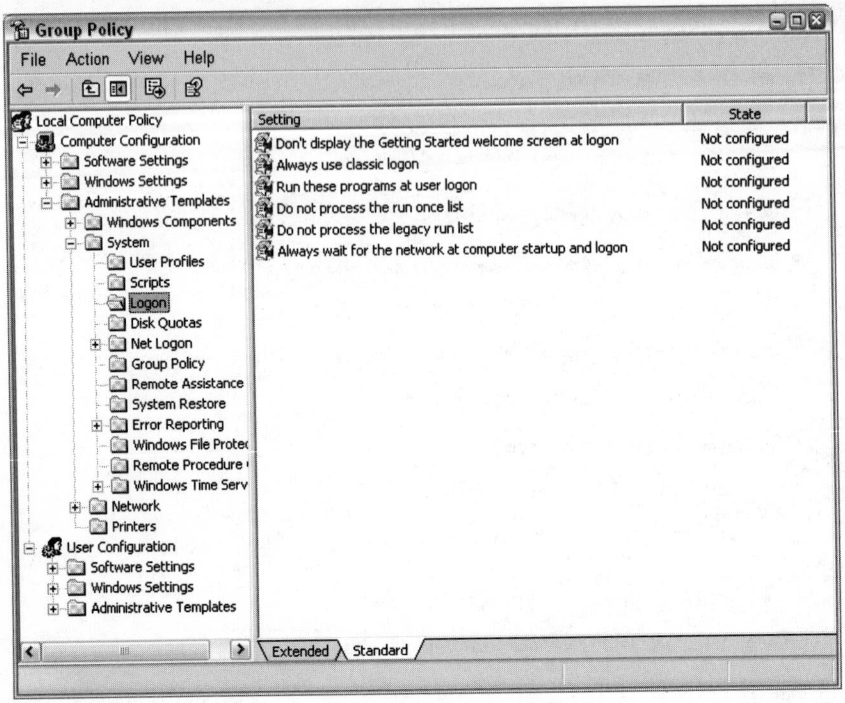

Figure 4-9: Navigate to Logon.

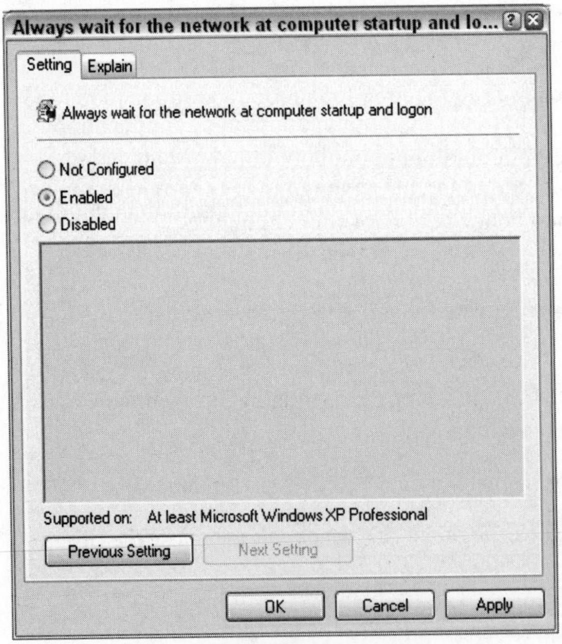

Figure 4-10: Change the setting to Enabled.

Speeding Up the Dual-Boot Timeout

If you dual-boot your computer with Windows XP and another operating system, you see an operating system selection menu on startup. If you typically boot into Windows XP and not the other operating system, you can speed up the dual-boot timeout value so that you do not wait so long for the boot process to select your default operating system and continue with the boot process. The default timeout value is 30 seconds but you can change this setting to 10. This gives you enough time to select the alternate operating system if you want but also speeds up the boot process. You can skip this section if you do not use a dual-boot configuration.

Follow these steps:

1. Locate the boot.ini file on your computer. It is a hidden file by default; mine is located in C:\boot.ini.
2. Open the file with Notepad (which is what opens it by default).
3. Change the Timeout value to **10** (see Figure 4-11).
4. Select File ➪ Save and close Notepad.

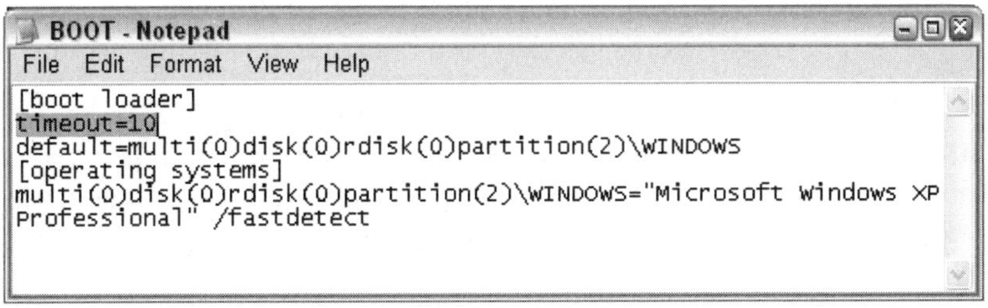

Figure 4-11: Change the timeout value to 10.

Speeding Up Your PPPoE Connection

If you use a Point-to-Point Protocol connection over Ethernet (PPPoE), you may notice a delay in using the PPPoE connection after startup. By default, there is a 120 second delay but you can stop this behavior by manually configuring an IP address for the network adapter card. If you do not use a PPPoE connection, you can skip this section.

1. Select Start ➪ Connect to ➪ Show All Connections.
2. Open the TCP/IP properties for your LAN network interface card.
3. Manually set the IP address on the TCP/IP properties to an appropriate IP address and subnet mask for your network.

Editing the PC Setup Program

Each PC has a setup program that tells the computer how to start the operating system. We often think that speeding up the boot time means speeding up Windows XP. While that's true, the PC setup program also governs some of the items that occur when the computer starts—which you can speed up as well.

Typically, you can enter the PC setup program by starting the computer and holding down the Delete key. A different key may be used for your computer's setup program, so check your computer's documentation for additional details.

Once you are in the setup program, you may have to look around a bit. Each manufacturer uses different categories and names, but essentially you can wade through the menu options and find these three common features to change to decrease your startup time:

- **Quick Power on Self-Test:** Set this option to Fast or Enabled, depending on your setup program. This change will result in skipped memory and hardware startup tests. Be aware that this setting might cause you to lose notice of a problem with RAM or the motherboard but, in most cases, you don't need this test anyway if your PC is operating without problems.
- **Floppy Search/Test:** If your floppy disk drive is working fine, there is no reason to test it every time you start your computer. Change this setting to Disable.
- **IDE Drives:** The setup program seeks to test and identify each IDE device as it boots. This is necessary but if you have IDE channels that are not in use, set this to None. If you do not understand this option, just leave it configured as it is.

Note

Cleaning up the Registry and defragmenting the hard drive can also increase your boot time. Learn more about cleaning the Registry in Chapter 6 and defragmenting the hard drive in Chapter 7.

Disabling Unused Devices

If you have devices attached to your computer or installed that you do not use, you can reduce the startup time by disabling those devices. The rule to follow is to keep enabled any device that you use or might use, but if you have devices that you do not use on a regular basis, you can disable those devices without uninstalling. When you start the computer, those devices' drivers won't have to load, which will help decrease boot time.

To disable a device, follow these steps:

1. Open the Start menu, right-click My Computer, and select Properties.
2. Click the Hardware tab and click the Device Manager button.
3. Expand the category that contains the device that you want to disable.
4. Right-click the device and click Disable (see Figure 4-12). The device is now disabled and remains disabled until you re-enable it in the same manner.

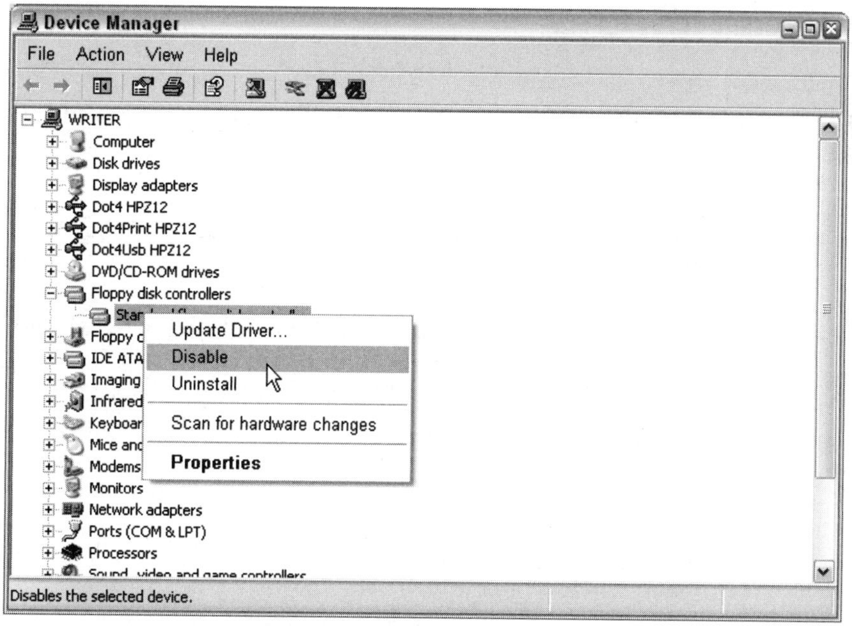

Figure 4-12: You can disable any hardware device that you do not use.

About BOOTVis

If you poke around on the Internet a bit and search for ways to reduce your computer's boot time, you may find information about a BOOTVis utility. BOOTVis is a Microsoft-developed utility for system architects who design systems for faster boot times. According to Microsoft, many published reports on the Internet state that you can download the

About BOOTVis *(Continued)*

BOOTVis utility and run it on your PC to improve your boot time. However, Microsoft also states that the utility was not developed for this purpose and it will not increase the boot time in Windows XP because Windows XP already performs the routines that BOOTVis performs. In short, it is an Internet myth that BOOTVis can help you. Do not waste your time running this utility. Visit `www.microsoft.com/whdc/system/sysperf/fastboot/bootvis.mspx` to learn more about this.

Making Your Computer Shut Down More Quickly

The flip side of the boot-faster coin is a faster shutdown. There are a couple of quick issues you can check or change that will make Windows XP shut down more quickly.

Reducing the Wait Time

When you start to shut down Windows XP, it has to quit, or "kill," any live applications or processes that are currently running. So close all applications first. However, some applications and processes are always running in the background. You can reduce the amount of time that Windows XP waits for those applications and processes to close before Windows XP kills them. Edit three different Registry settings to change this:

1. Open the Registry Editor.
2. Navigate to HKEY_CURRENT_USER\Control Panel\Desktop. Select WaitToKillAppTimeout and set the value to **1000**.
3. Select the HungAppTimeout value and set it to **1000** as well.
4. Navigate to HKEY_USERS\.DEFAULT\Control Panel\Desktop. Set the WaitToKillAppTimeout and set the value to **1000**. Select the HungAppTimeout value and set it to **1000** as well.
5. Navigate to HKEY_LOCAL_MACHINE\System\CurrentControlSet\Control. Select the WaitToKillServiceTimeout value and set it to **1000**.
6. Close the Registry Editor.

Stopping the NVIDIA Driver

If you use an NVIDIA video card, there is a service that runs that seems to slow down boot time and, especially, shutdown time. The general consensus in the hardware community is that the service doesn't actually do anything, so you should disable it. Disabling the service should not affect the NVIDIA video card but it will help your computer shut down more quickly.

Follow these steps:

1. Open the Click Start menu, right-click My Computer, and select Manage.
2. In the Computer Management console that appears, expand Services and Applications and select Services to open the services window.
3. Locate and highlight the Nvidia Driver Helper service. Right-click it and select Properties.
4. Set the Startup Type drop-down box to Disabled.
5. Click OK and close the Computer Management console.

Automatically Killing Tasks on Shutdown

You know the drill. You start to shut down the computer, you wait a few moments, and then you see a dialog box asking if you want to kill an application or service that is running. Instead of prompting you, you can make Windows XP take care of the kill task automatically. Here's how:

1. Open the Registry Editor.
2. Navigate to HKEY_CURRENT_USER\Control Panel\Desktop.
3. Highlight the value AutoEndTasks and change the value to **1**.
4. Close the Registry Editor.

Chapter 5

Working with Memory and System Settings

Without question, the two most common components that impact overall performance are Random Access Memory (RAM) and processor power. Without adequate RAM and an adequate processor, all other techniques you perform to boost speed will most likely not give you the performance you are looking for. After all, RAM and the processor are the computer system's workhorses.

Fortunately, you can check some settings that will help boost your computer's RAM and processor performance. Although no setting is going to replace RAM or processor speed, you can certainly help them along. This chapter explores some tactics to do just that.

The Hard Truth About RAM and Processors

As much as I would like to tell you that I have the perfect solution for low-RAM or slow-processor PCs, I'm afraid there is no real solution that will solve serious RAM or processor problems. After all, RAM and the computer's process are both pieces of hardware. You can boost RAM and processor performance but, in the end, your PC is only going to perform as well as the hardware allows. For example, if you have 256 MB RAM on your PC and you want to do a lot of work with multimedia applications and video production, you can try to boost the RAM all you want but you'll still need more RAM to handle these memory-hungry tasks.

The same idea is true with the processor. You can try to help your processor out but the PC's processing power is limited by the speed of the processor. The more applications you try to run, the slower the processor is going to perform as those applications make their demands on the system.

Naturally, you can help the RAM and processor by adhering to the ideas already discussed in this book. Shut down or remove unwanted applications and services, and generally try to keep things cleaned up on your system. These actions will help the RAM and processor by removing items that take up memory and processor cycles. Yet if you need more memory and speed, you probably need to upgrade the RAM and the processor. This is especially true if you have upgraded to Windows XP from a previous version of Windows. Windows XP is a power horse that needs plenty of RAM and a fast processor. In many cases, computers that have been upgraded from previous versions of Windows simply do not have the memory or processor power that Windows XP needs to run efficiently. Add a few memory and processor-hungry applications and you end up with a very slow system indeed.

I say all of this simply to tell you that there is no real replacement for upgraded RAM and a faster processor. If you know that your computer has minimal RAM and an older processor, you can try the techniques throughout this book, but the real jump in power is only going to come through upgrades. Of course, upgrading RAM and processors tends to be a bit expensive—and in many cases you might be better off simply buying a new computer that comes with all new parts and a warranty—so be sure to think through the big picture of your computing needs before you consider hardware upgrades.

Working with Memory

Windows XP, like previous versions of Windows, uses a page file process where the system's RAM manages items you are working on. As the system begins to run low on RAM, items in memory that are not currently in use are written to a portion of the hard disk called a page file. As those items are needed, the data is read from the disk and back into memory. As a general rule, the page file is a normal and necessary part of efficient memory operations in Windows XP. You should also understand that Windows XP does an excellent job of managing the page file; manual settings often hurt, rather than help performance. However, it is a good idea to take a look at your current page file configuration and make sure that it is optimized for your system.

Changing Virtual Memory Settings

As a part of desktop performance and configuration, Windows XP gives you a simple interface that allows you to adjust the graphical nature of Windows XP to conserve RAM. If a system seems sluggish, this may be your first line of defense. If you right-click My

Computer and click Properties, or just open System in Control Panel, you can click the Advanced tab and then click the Settings button under Performance.

This opens the Performance Options dialog box (see Figure 5-1). As you can see on the Visual Effects tab, Windows XP attempts to choose its own settings by default. However, you can change this setting so that Windows XP's visual effects are adjusted for appearance or performance (see Chapter 2). You can also click the Custom option and clear the desired visual effects check boxes to reduce RAM and processor usage on certain items. For example, you might remove the shadows features and fading features of Windows XP.

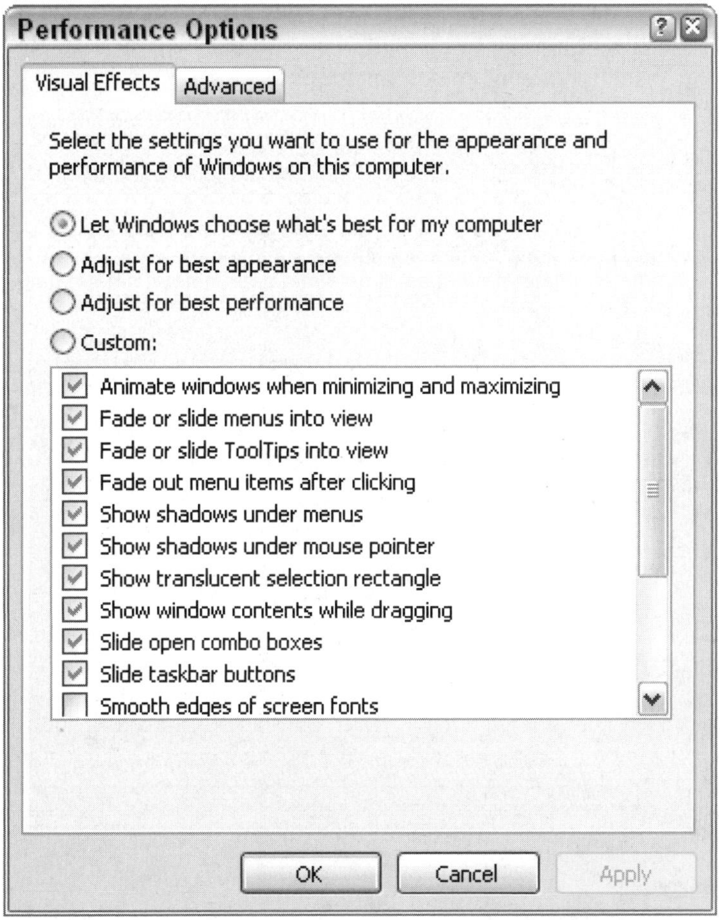

Figure 5-1: Visual Effects tab of the Performance Options dialog box.

If you click the Advanced tab, you can also access settings for virtual memory. On the Advanced tab is a Page File (Virtual Memory) Change button. If you click the Change button, you see the Virtual Memory dialog box (see Figure 5-2). By default, Windows XP is set to manage its own virtual memory settings. However, you can manually input a minimum and maximum size for the page file. The commonly recommended amount is 1.5 times the amount of physical RAM installed on the computer. So if you have 128 MB RAM, the recommended initial paging file size is 192 MB. It is important to note here, however, that Windows XP does a good job of managing its own memory settings. As a general guideline, you should allow Windows XP to handle those settings on its own. Incorrectly setting the virtual memory settings or choosing the No Paging File option is likely to have adverse affects on system performance. Also, providing more paging file room is not a replacement for physical RAM. If the computer is running too slowly because there is not enough physical RAM installed on the system, the paging file will not provide a cheap solution. In short, the paging file is used to help Windows XP physical memory, not replace it.

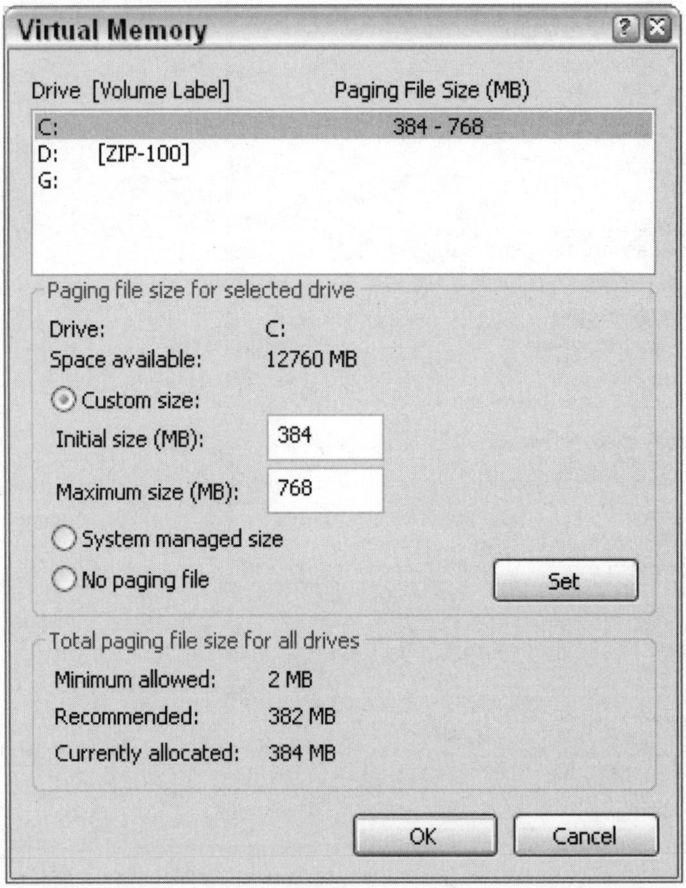

Figure 5-2: Virtual memory settings.

Boosting Virtual Memory

Aside from configuring virtual memory settings, if needed, there are a few other settings you can adjust that can help boost virtual memory performance on your system. Again, these settings are not a replacement for physical RAM but they do help optimize the way Windows XP handles virtual memory.

STOPPING THE MEMORY CACHING OF DLLS

Dynamic Link Libraries (DLLs) are files that Windows XP uses when you run programs. DLLs are loaded into memory but they often do not leave memory right away, even after you close the application. You can free up a bit of memory space by making sure DLLs close when you exit their related applications. You'll need to edit the Registry to invoke this setting.

Follow these steps:

1. Select Start ➪ Run, type **regedit**, and click OK.
2. In the Registry Editor, navigate to HKEY_LOCAL_MACHINE\Software\Microsoft\Windows\CurrentVersion\Explorer.
3. Right-click the Explorer folder and select New ➪ Key.
4. Name the new key **UnloadDLL**.
5. Set the default value for the new key to **1**. This stops Windows XP from caching DLLs in memory (see Figure 5-3).
6. Close the Registry Editor and restart your computer.

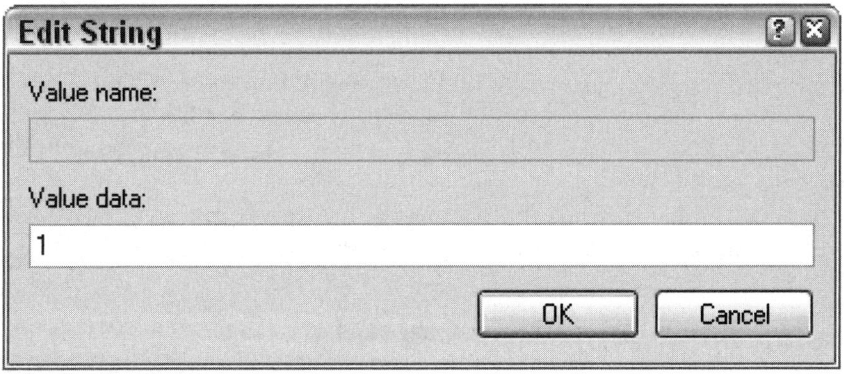

Figure 5-3: Enter a value of 1.

DISABLING VIRTUAL MEMORY FEATURES ON SYSTEMS WITH AT LEAST 512 MB RAM

Allow me to contradict myself for a moment. If you have a system that has plenty of physical RAM, such as 512 MB or more, you may see some performance gains by disabling the paging executive in the Registry as well as the large system cache. Both of the changes force Windows XP to use more physical RAM instead of the page file and the cache. I should warn you, however, that Windows XP is designed to use a page file and cache system, so unless you are certain that you have plenty of RAM, you should not try this fix. Also, I can't guarantee that this will help you, so proceed cautiously. If you do make the Registry edits and do not see performance gains, reset the changes to their default values.

Follow these steps:

1. Select Start ➪ Run, type **regedit**, and click OK.
2. In the Registry Editor, navigate to HKEY_LOCAL_MACHINE\System\CurrentControlSet\Control\Session Manager\Memory Management.
3. Double-click the DisablePagingExecutive value and change the value to **1**. Click OK.
4. Double-click the LargeSystemCache value and change the value to **1**. Click OK.
5. Close the Registry Editor.

CREATING A STRIPED VOLUME FOR THE PAGE FILE

A striped volume stores data across two different disks. If your computer is outfitted with separate hard drives on separate integrated development environment (IDE) channels, you can stripe the page file across the two drives and will likely see some performance gains. This way, Windows XP accesses both drives at the same time to write and read information from the striped page file.

To create this configuration, return to the Virtual Memory dialog box explored earlier in this chapter and assign the page file size on both drives. For example, you could place a swap file of the same size on each drive, depending on the partition size found on each disk. Ideally, you should try to duplicate a swap file size on the second drive that is the same size as the first drive.

Obviously, this fix will not work if you only have one hard disk on your computer. However, if you do have two, the reports I have seen show great improvements in performance.

Using Other Tools That Can Help

If you can't add physical RAM to your computer, there are a few inexpensive third-party utilities that may be able to give your computer's memory a boost.

RAMDISK

RamDisk is a utility that you can purchase for around $50. RamDisk essentially is software that acts like a portion of your hard drive. Because reading and writing to the hard disk is one of the slowest processes your computer performs, RamDisk acts like the hard disk for virtual memory purposes. The end result, as the software describes, is that you may see as much as 5 to 10 times the application speed you would see otherwise. RamDisk is recommended by *PC Magazine*. Find out more about it at `www.superspeed.com/ramdisk.html`.

MEMOKIT

MemoKit for Windows is a bundled program that can help optimize your system. Specifically, it helps manage various portions of the system and should cut down on crashes, memory management, and cache optimization. The software costs around $30, but it has a 30-day money-back guarantee if you are not happy with the results. (A lot of these programs do not have such a guarantee, so I thought it was worth mentioning.) Find out more about MemoKit at `www.greatware.net/computer_speed/memo_kit/`.

O&O CLEVERCACHE

CleverCache V4 Professional is similar to MemoKit in that it uses a software cache system to prevent excessive paging writes to your computer's hard disk. Because reading and writing from the hard disk takes more time than most other operations, CleverCache keeps the data stored and more accessible. The end result should be much faster responses from your system because you are bypassing the virtual memory needs of the disk subsystem. CleverCache costs around $50, but you can download a trial version first. Find out more at `www.oo-software.com/en/products/ooccpro/`.

Speeding Up the Processor

Like RAM, your computer's processor is a hardware device. As such, it has a performance limit that is determined by its speed. Various applications and processes on your computer use it to process information. The more applications and tools that need the processor, the slower the system will work because they have to wait for the processor to take care of the request. Most processors today are rather fast and you may never experience any problems. Yet that all depends on what applications you are trying to run. Multimedia applications can certainly give your computer's processor a thrashing; if you are using a slow processor, your best performance tip is to upgrade—there is no replacement technique for a new processor.

However, you can try to get as much power as possible from your existing processor. The following sections show you some quick and helpful techniques for squeezing the most power out of your processor. It is important to realize that the processor services other applications and processes on your PC. As such, half the battle for good processor performance is won by making sure other components are working as they should.

Checking the Processor Settings

The first thing you should do is make sure your computer is optimized for applications. This default setting, which is probably already set as it should be on your computer, makes certain that applications get the most priority concerning processor power. This is what you want because you will most likely experience speed problems due to applications.

Open the Start menu, right-click My Computer, and select Properties. On the Advanced tab, under Performance, click the Settings button. Click the Advanced tab. Make sure that both processor and memory settings are set to Programs. The alternative settings work well if your Windows XP computer is primarily a server to other computers on a network. Because this is probably not the case, however, you want to make sure that settings are configured for programs (see Figure 5-4).

Tip

You may see some advice on the Internet instructing you to change these settings to Background services and System cache. However, keep in mind that this shares processor priority with other services and features of Windows XP. While this is helpful is some cases, most of us need more processor power to go to the applications and programs we are trying to use at the moment. For this reason, the best setting here if you are a typical computer user is Programs.

Removing Unneeded Programs and Services

I explored the issue of unneeded programs and services in several previous chapters, but the issue warrants restatement here. The more application and services you have running, the more demand those items are likely to place on your processor. You can help reduce the load on your processor by removing programs and disabling startup services that you do not actually use. After all, the more programs and services that demand processor time, the fewer processor cycles you have available to do what you really want to do. So get rid of those unneeded programs and services.

Cleaning Up the Registry

If the Registry has a lot of junk stored in it, it can take the processor longer to run Windows XP. Because this isn't what you want, you should clean up the Registry on a regular basis.

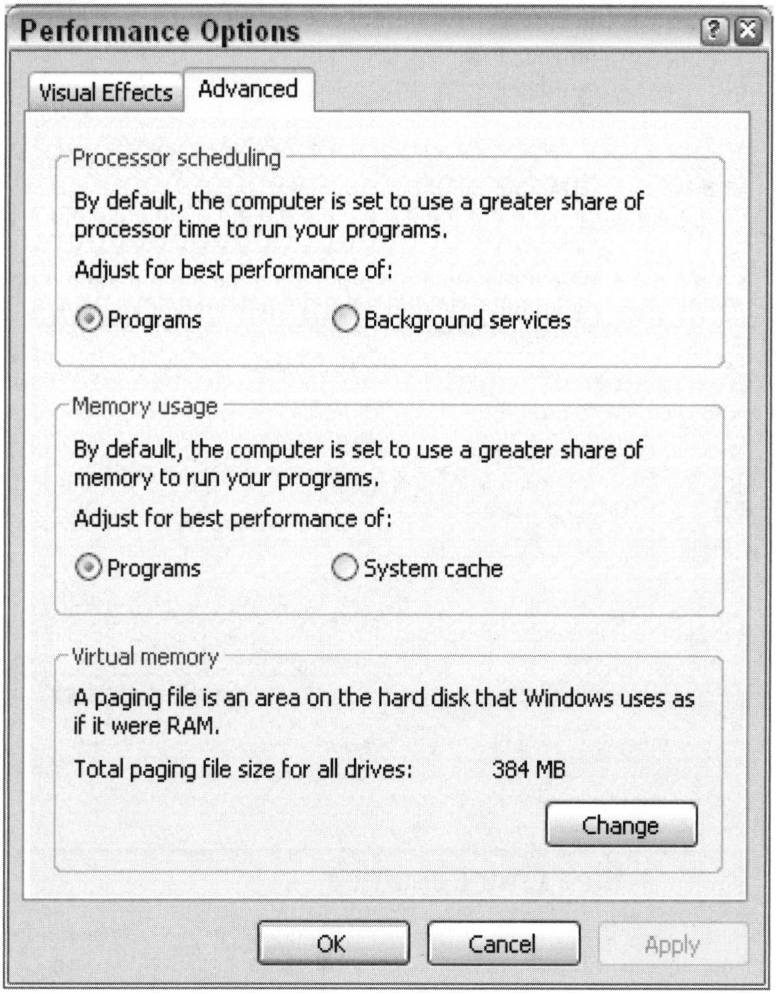
Performance Options
Visual Effects
Advanced
Processor scheduling
By default, the computer is set to use a greater share of processor time to run your programs.
Adjust for best performance of:
Programs
Background services
Memory usage
By default, the computer is set to use a greater share of memory to run your programs.
Adjust for best performance of:
Programs
System cache
Virtual memory
A paging file is an area on the hard disk that Windows uses as if it were RAM.
Total paging file size for all drives: 384 MB
Change
OK
Cancel
Apply

Figure 5-4: Make sure your computer is set for "Programs."

There are several good tools that can do this for you. See Chapter 6 to learn more about this.

Running PC PowerScan

One neat utility you may wish to use is called PC PowerScan. This tool specifically examines your Registry, files, and other system settings and looks for issues and problems that need to be fixed. Just by keeping these items fixed, you can help speed up your system. PC PowerScan checks these items and fixes them for you (see Figure 5-5). You can download and run the utility for free but you must purchase it to fix problems it finds. Learn more about PC PowerScan at www.pcpowerscan.com.

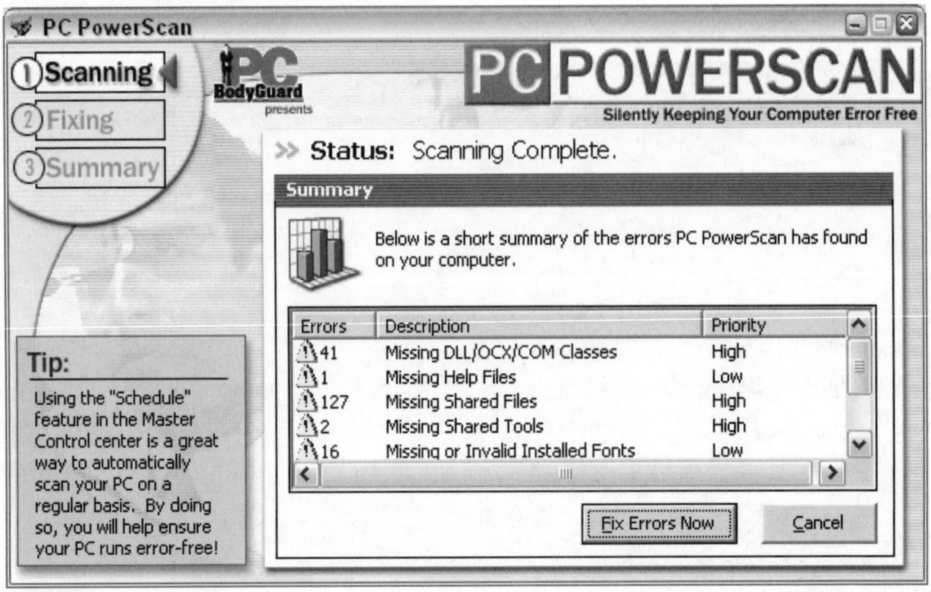
PC PowerScan
Scanning
Fixing
Summary
PC BodyGuard presents
PC POWERSCAN
Silently Keeping Your Computer Error Free
Status: Scanning Complete.
Summary
Below is a short summary of the errors PC PowerScan has found on your computer.
Errors Description Priority
41 Missing DLL/OCX/COM Classes High
1 Missing Help Files Low
127 Missing Shared Files High
2 Missing Shared Tools High
16 Missing or Invalid Installed Fonts Low
Fix Errors Now
Cancel
Tip:
Using the "Schedule" feature in the Master Control center is a great way to automatically scan your PC on a regular basis. By doing so, you will help ensure your PC runs error-free!

Figure 5-5: PC PowerScan can find and fix problems on your computer.

Stop Error Reporting

Error reporting is a good feature of Windows XP because it records errors and warnings that occur on your system and creates a log file. You can then use Event Viewer to take a look at those errors and warnings (see Chapter 16 to learn more). However, even though error reporting is a good feature, it does have a tendency to eat up processor cycles. So if you want to squeeze more power from Windows XP, you can stop error reporting so that Windows XP does not have to generate the data for you. Even if you stop error reporting, you can still be notified of critical errors. Naturally, error reporting is a good feature, so you have to decide if stopping it is really worth the bit of extra speed you might get.

If you choose to stop error reporting, follow these steps:

1. Open the Start menu, right-click My Computer, and select Properties.
2. Click the Advanced tab and click the Error Reporting button.

3. In the Error Reporting dialog box (see Figure 5-6), choose the Disable Error Reporting option but choose to keep the check box enabled that reports critical errors.

4. Click OK, and then OK again to close out of the dialog boxes.

Figure 5-6: You can disable error reporting to free up memory resources.

Chapter 6

Cleaning Up the Registry

The Registry is essentially a big database of information about Windows XP. The Registry holds all your system settings, hardware settings, user settings, and just about anything else that governs the way Windows XP behaves. As you might imagine, any storehouse of data can get filled up with junk from time to time. If you want Windows XP to have the kind of speed that makes you smile, you need to make sure you clean up the Registry on a systematic and periodic basis. Many users never clean up the Registry or even know it exists but a squeaky-clean Registry can certainly give you a speed boost. This chapter first presents an overview of the Registry and then shows you how to clean it up.

Getting to Know the Registry

In previous chapters I have shown you some Registry edits that can help speed up certain processes and functions in Windows XP. This section gives you an overview of the Registry and how to edit it. If you already know how to use the Registry Editor, you can skip this section.

Although Microsoft does not recommend that you edit the Registry, Windows XP provides a Registry Editor that enables you to do just that. Editing the Registry directly is a good way to fix problems and invoke some speed solutions that I'll explore throughout this book. However, editing the Registry is a bit dangerous. The changes you make are invoked immediately; if you make a critical mistake, you could potentially render your operating system unbootable. In other words, Registry editing is a skill that can help you in several ways but it also deserves respect because it doesn't give you an easy out like so many interface configurations in Windows XP.

The Registry is nothing new in Windows XP. In fact, it has been around since the early days of Windows. So the Registry is really just an old feature of Microsoft operating systems that has been revamped for today. The Registry is all about storing data. Essentially, it is a database of settings and configurations that determines how Windows XP operates. Every time you make a change in Windows XP, the setting is recorded to the Registry, which enables Windows XP to keep those changes each time you boot. The Registry is the place where everything that Windows does and how it behaves is recorded, so you can imagine the necessity and importance of it.

For the most part, the Registry does away with those old WIN.INI and SYSTEM.INI files that required too much manual editing work. The Registry brings all of the INI data into one central location and under a central organization so that it is easier for Windows to take care of. Every time you use the Windows XP Setup program, install additional hardware, or install 32-bit Windows software, the Registry stores data about it. Every time you make a configuration change to Windows XP, the data is stored in the Registry. The Registry is Windows XP's storehouse.

Note

Some programs still use INI files to save their settings. Windows XP supports them to maintain backwards-compatibility with older applications.

The Registry's Structure

The Registry looks like a collection of folders and subfolders when you view it with the Registry Editor. You start out with top-level folders and drill down to the folder that contains the data you want. This hierarchical structure makes it easy to find and organize data. The Registry consists of five subtrees, and each subtree is designed to hold specific kinds of information and settings Software developers use the subtrees as an organizational method to write programs that are installed and function under Windows XP. Table 6-1 describes each subtree briefly.

Table 6-1 Windows XP Registry Subtrees

Root Key Name	***Description***
HKEY_CLASSES_ROOT	This root contains class identification and associations between applications and different file types. It also holds OLE Registry information and file-class associations.
HKEY_CURRENT_USER	This root contains information about the user who is currently logged on to the computer. That information includes user profiles, environment variables, desktop settings, application preferences, network connections, and printer information.

Root Key Name	*Description*
HKEY_LOCAL_MACHINE	This root contains information about the local computer system. Here you find settings for hardware and operating system options, such as bus type, system, memory, device drivers, and startup control data.
HKEY_USERS	This root contains every user profile that is currently loaded. Here you find data about the current user and the Administrator accounts and profiles.
HKEY_CURRENT_CONFIG	This root contains information for the current hardware configuration and profile.

Understanding the Registry Keys

Each subtree within the Registry holds individual keys. A key is like a folder; it may actually hold data but it can hold other subkeys as well. If the subkey holds data, it can have one data value or it might hold several data values. Just as a folder can hold one item, many items, or additional folders, a subkey works in the same way. Each subkey has three basic parts:

- Name of the subkey
- Data type
- Actual value of the subkey

A subkey can hold five data types, as shown in Table 6-2.

Table 6-2 Windows XP Registry Data Types

Data Types	*Description*
REG_BINARY	Raw binary data that is typically displayed in hexadecimal notation. You generally cannot read this data because of its binary nature.
REG_DWORD	A four-byte number that is displayed in binary, hexadecimal, or decimal format. This data type is often used for device drivers and services. Throughout the book, I show you several Registry edits where you create a new DWORD.
REG_EXPAND_SZ	An expandable data string that holds a variable that is replaced when it is called by an application. It often looks something like *%systemroot%*, which is replaced by the actual folder name containing your WindowsXP files.

Continued

Table 6-2 Windows XP Registry Data Types *(Continued)*

Data Types	***Description***
REG_MUTLI_SZ	A multiple string that usually holds a list of values. You can generally read these because they are not stored in a binary format.
REG_SZ	A simple text string that you can read.

HIVES

If you used a PC back in the days of Windows 95 and 98 (or NT 3.x), you are familiar with System.dat and User.dat. Essentially, these two files stored Registry settings. Beginning in Windows NT 4.0 and forward, the Registry replaced these files, but the data is still split into different parts now called hives. A hive is a discrete body of keys, subkeys, and values rooted at the top of the Registry hierarchy. In other words, hives store permanent components of the Registry that do not change, not the parts you edit. In actuality, most hives are stored in the C:\Windows\System32\Config folder, as shown in Figure 6-1 and listed in Table 6-3.

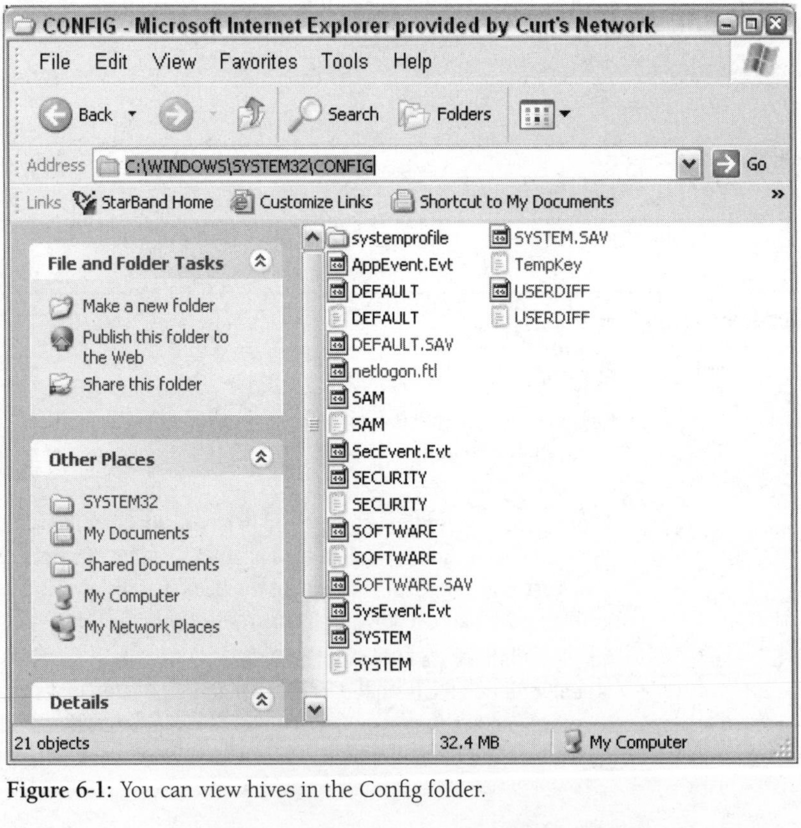

Figure 6-1: You can view hives in the Config folder.

Table 6-3 Registry Hives in \System32\Config

Registry Segment	Related Files
HKEY_CURRENT_CONFIG	system, system.alt, system.log, system.sav
HKEY_LOCAL_MACHINE\SAM	sam, sam.log, sam.sav
HKEY_LOCAL_MACHINE\Security	security, security.log, security.sav
HKEY_LOCAL_MACHINE\Software	software, software.log, software.sav
HKEY_LOCAL_MACHINE\System	system, system.alt, system.log, system.sav
HKEY_USERS\.Default	default, default.log, default.sav
HKEY_CURRENT_USER	ntuser.dat, ntuser.log

Note

If you look closely, you may see user.diff and userdiff.log files in System32\Config. You'll only see these here if you upgraded Windows XP from an earlier version of Windows.

HIVE COPIES

As you can see from Table 6-3, each hive has several files associated with it. Each of those files has different extensions; if you do not see an extension with the file, you are actually looking at a copy of the hive. Other files you see may have the .log extension, which is a transaction log showing changes to keys and value entries in the hive. The Software, SAM, Security, System, and Default hives use a .sav extension; these are actually copies of the hive that were created during Windows XP's installation.

Note

HKEY_LOCAL_MACHINE\System has an extra backup created for it named System.alt. This extra backup is just for safety because the System hive is so critical to the operation of Windows XP.

Restoring the Registry

The Registry is so important that Windows XP backs it up every time you shut down your computer. This way, should something change on your PC that corrupts the Registry, you can easily restore it from the backup copy. You need to know how to do this if you are going to consider Registry editing at all because you never know when something will go wrong. Should the day come that you try to boot Windows XP and receive an error message that the Registry is corrupted and Windows XP cannot boot, you'll know what to do. In this case, you invoke a Safe Menu option called Last Known Good Configuration, which is essentially the last saved version of the Registry that was good. When you choose this option, Windows XP can then boot using the Last Known Good Configuration, but you'll lose any changes you made to your system since that last successful Registry save.

The following steps show you how to restore the Registry using the last known good version:

1. If your computer does not boot because an error message says the Registry is corrupted, shut down your computer.
2. Wait about 10 seconds and then turn on the power again.
3. When the computer starts, hold down the F8 key.
4. The Safe Mode menu appears. Use your arrow keys to move the cursor down and select the Last Known Good Configuration option.
5. Press the Enter key and follow the remaining instructions on your screen.

Using the Registry Editor

The Registry Editor included in Windows XP is called RegEdit, and you can access it from the Run dialog box. RegEdit provides you with a graphical, folder view of the Registry where you can navigate through its different parts and locate the value that you want to change or the place where you want to create the value that is needed. RegEdit allows you to view the Registry, make changes, delete items, and create new values. The tool itself is rather easy and straightforward but it gives you no warnings of any kind. Again, remember that editing the Registry requires care. Microsoft recommends that you only make changes to Windows through Control Panel settings; however, Control Panel does not give you the option to change many things you might want to adjust for speed solutions. So editing the Registry is sometimes necessary.

To keep RegEdit out of the hands of less experienced users, there is no icon for it and it does not appear as a program. Yet you can open RegEdit quickly and easily by typing the name in the Run dialog box on the Start menu and clicking OK. As you can see in Figure 6-2, the Registry Editor looks like any other MMC console. You see the Registry keys in the left pane and whatever you select appears in the right pane. The selected key shows you what it holds in the right pane, including the name of the data value, its type, and the data itself.

Tip

You can quickly expand a key by selecting it in the left pane, then hold down the Alt key on your keyboard and press the asterisk (*) key on the numeric keypad. This action expands the entire key.

To collapse it, just double-click the key. To make a key return to the default action of only expanding one subcategory at a time, collapse the key and press F5 on your keyboard.

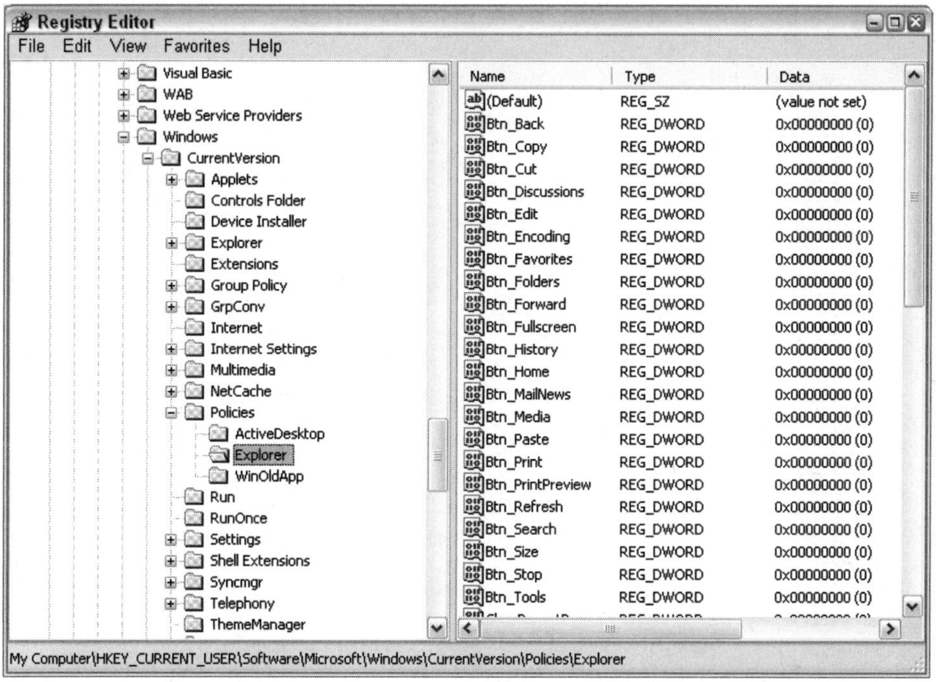

Figure 6-2: The Registry Editor.

Exploring the Subtrees

As you learned earlier in this chapter, the Registry is made up of distinct subtrees, all of which classify and hold information about different system components, applications, and so forth. Using RegEdit, you can take a look at each subtree and explore the content found in that subtree. The following sections give you a brief overview of each subtree.

HKEY_CLASSES_ROOT

The HKEY_CLASSES_ROOT tree holds the information that relates file types to applications, as well as data types and COM objects (see Figure 6-3). The key is rather large when you expand it because there are many of these file associations and COM objects on your computer. The more software you install on your computer, the bigger this key grows. The value data here is often difficult to decipher and this is not a root where you do much (if any) Registry editing.

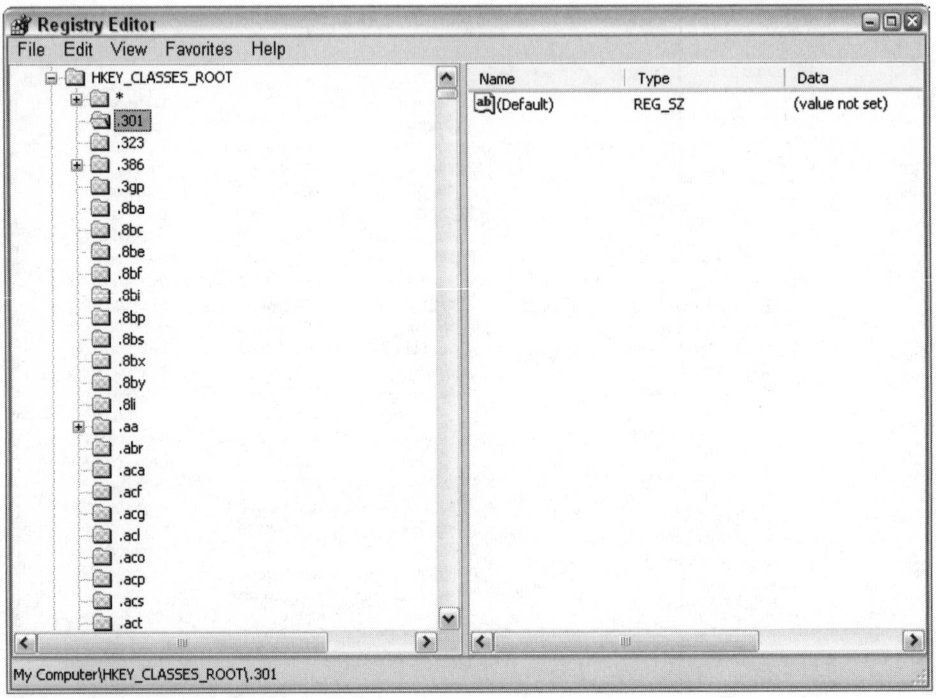

Figure 6-3: The HKEY_CLASSES_ROOT tree.

HKEY_CURRENT_USER

The HKEY_CURRENT_USER subtree contains information about the current user who is logged on. This information includes the user's profile; any settings that the user invokes, such as wallpaper and themes, are stored here. This feature enables different users to have different system settings within Windows XP (see Figure 6-4). You may note that some settings you find in HKEY_CURRENT_USER are also found in HKEY_LOCAL_MACHINE. However, HKEY_CURRENT_USER settings are always given priority over HKEY_LOCAL_MACHINE settings. When users log on to a Windows XP computer, their user profile is taken from the HKEY_USERS key and copied into the CURRENT_USER key. If no user profile exists for the user who is logging on to the computer (for example, a guest or a new user), Windows XP uses the Default User profile. Table 6-4 explains the subkeys in HKEY_CURRENT_USER.

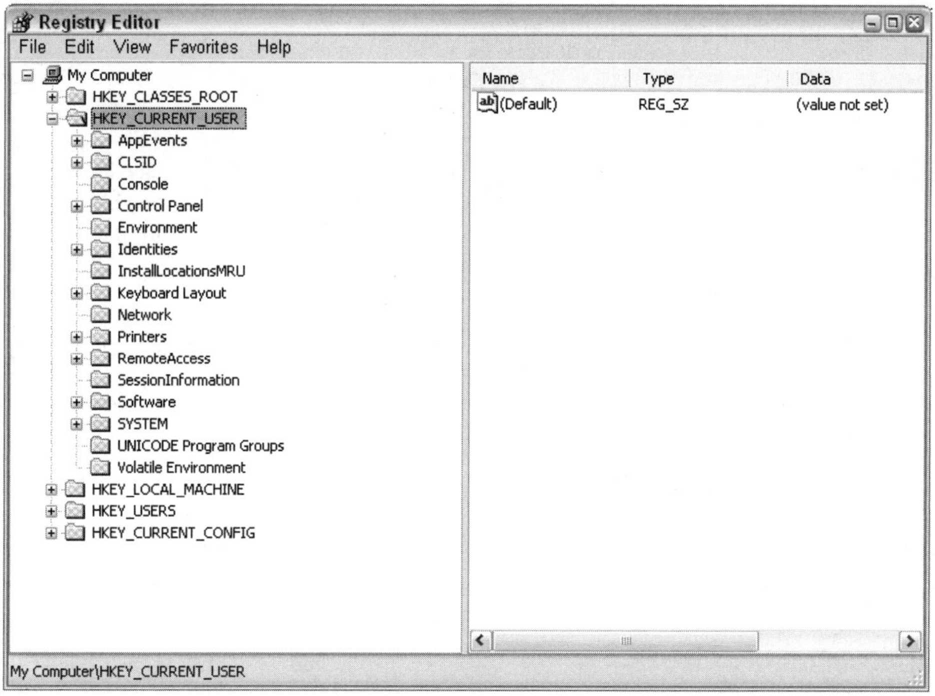

Figure 6-4: The HKEY_CURRENT_USER subtree.

Table 6-4 HKEY_CURRENT_USER Subkeys

Subkey	***What the Key Contains***
AppEvents	Sound and Multimedia applet settings in the Control Panel.
Console	Window size, along with options for any console tools.
Control Panel	Mouse, Keyboard, and Display Options applets in the Control Panel.
Environment	Environment settings that are determined using the System applet in the Control Panel.
Identities	Multiple identities in Outlook Express 5. Under each subkey, you can find the actual user name belonging to the identity.
Keyboard Layout	Keyboard language information relating to the Input Locales you choose in the Regional Options applet in the Control Panel.
SessionInformation	Data relating to the current user's Windows session.

Continued

Table 6-4 HKEY_CURRENT_USER Subkeys *(Continued)*

Subkey	***What the Key Contains***
Printers	Information about each physically installed printer.
Software	Application-specific settings. These entries are usually created when you install software. Much of the data here has a similar structure to the data in the HKEY_LOCAL_MACHINE\Software subkey.
System	Information about system settings.
Unicode Program Group	Starting with Windows NT 4.0, this key is no longer used. It is left in place for compatibility reasons.

HKEY_LOCAL_MACHINE

The HKEY_LOCAL_MACHINE subtree contains all of the configuration information about your computer. The data in this key cannot be edited directly, even using the Registry Editor. There are five subkeys in HKEY_LOCAL_MACHINE (see Figure 6-5).

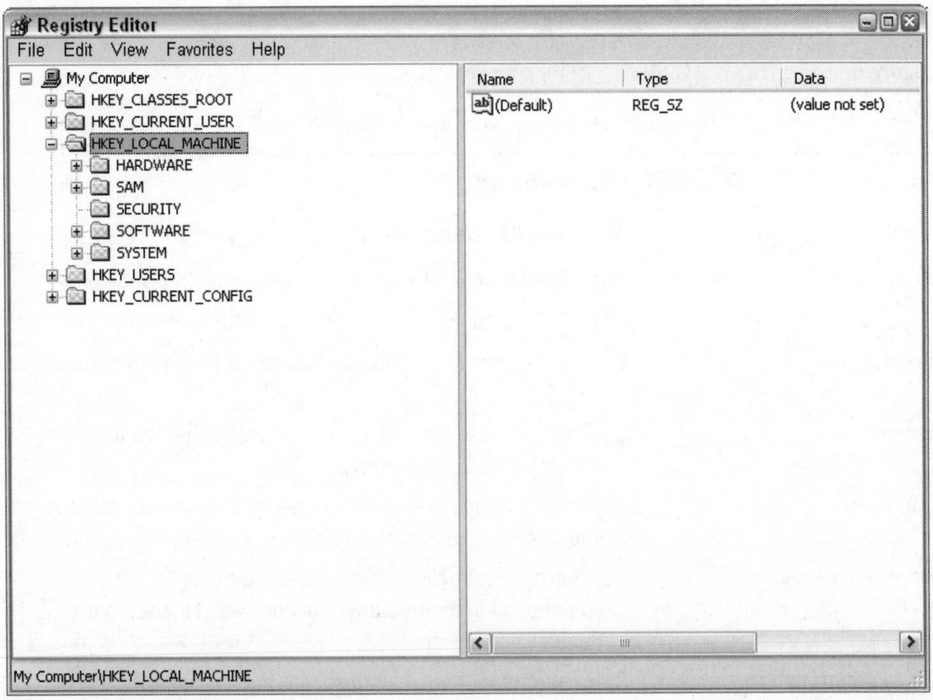

Figure 6-5: The HKEY_LOCAL_MACHINE subtree.

Hardware

The HKEY_LOCAL_MACHINE\HARDWARE subkey contains the dynamic hardware configuration data for the computer. Every time your computer boots, this key is refreshed with updated information, as needed. This updated information is then discarded when the system shuts down.

SAM and Security Keys

SAM is the Windows XP Security Account Manager. These two keys handle security information. They manage the way a Windows XP computer is connected to a Windows network server using the Active Directory.

Software

The HKEY_LOCAL_MACHINE\SOFTWARE subkey contains configuration information about the software installed on the computer. The subkeys under this key differ depending on what applications have been installed, but there will always be common subkeys among computers. You can access the CurrentVersion container here to see information about Windows XP (see Figure 6-6).

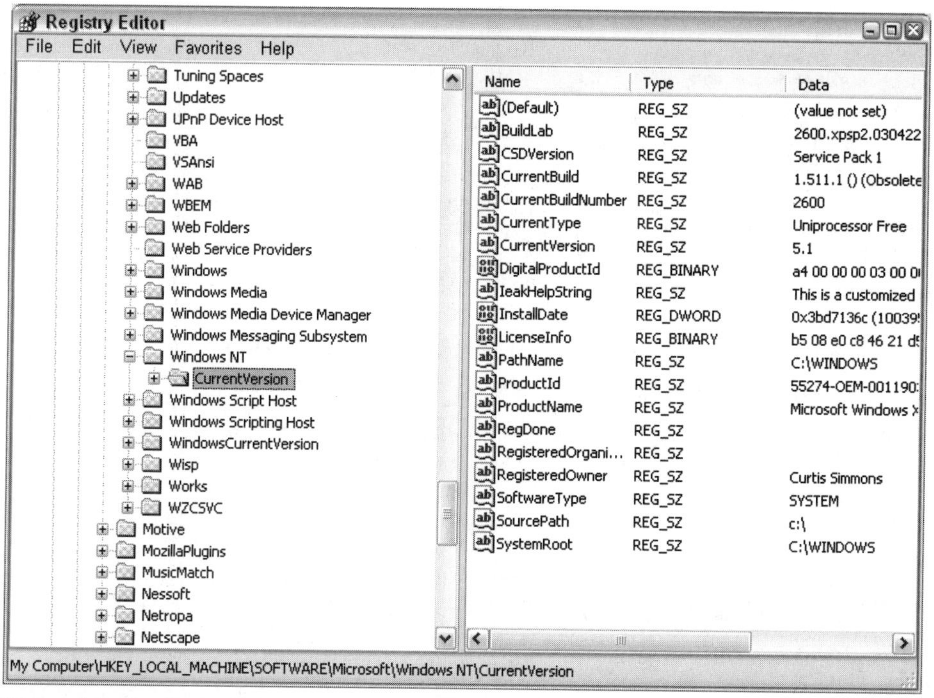

Figure 6-6: The CurrentVersion container gives you information about your computer's configuration.

System

The HKEY_LOCAL_MACHINE\SYSTEM subkey holds all the data that Windows uses that cannot be initialized during the startup process. Instead, the information is stored here in the System subkey.

You'll see subkeys called *Control Sets,* which contain startup data. While there can be up to four control sets—labeled ControlSet001, ControlSet002, and so on—there are usually only two, the current control set plus one backup. Information on the various control sets is tracked in the HKEY_LOCAL_MACHINE\SYSTEM\Select subkey (see Figure 6-7). Four value entries in this subkey track the following:

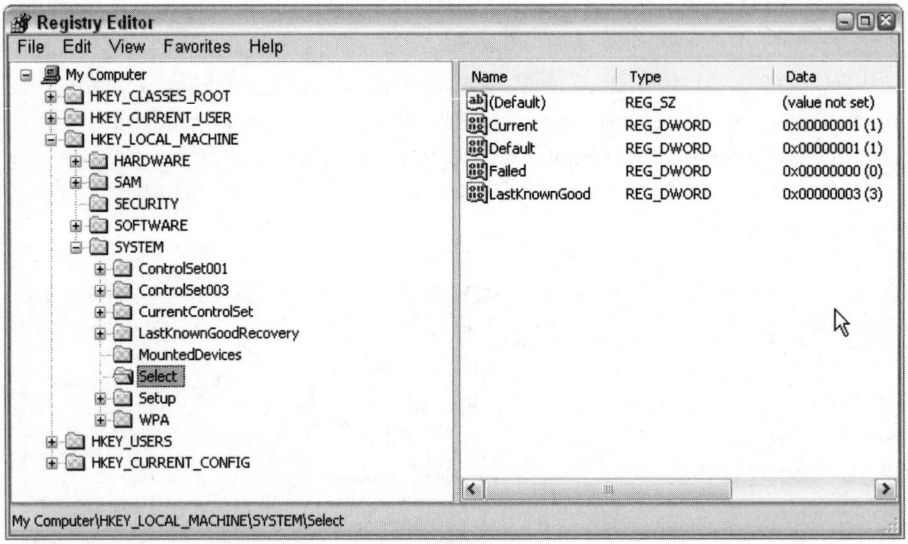

Figure 6-7: The HKEY_LOCAL_MACHINE\SYSTEM\Select subkey keeps track of the control set.

- **Default:** This is the number of the control set that will be used at the next system startup, unless the LastKnownGood configuration is selected.
- **Current:** This is the control set that started the system for the current session.
- **Failed:** This control set was replaced when the LastKnownGood control set was used to start the system.
- **LastKnownGood:** This set is an unmodified copy of the last set that was used to successfully start the system.

HKEY_USERS

HKEY_USERS is a subtree that holds user profiles; it generally contains two of them. The first profile is for the user who is logged on to the computer. The second profile is the default user profile, located in the subkey HKEY_USERS\.DEFAULT, which is in use when no one is logged on to the computer.

HKEY_CURRENT_CONFIG

HKEY_CURRENT_CONFIG is a key that is added to achieve compatibility with the Windows 95 Registry. Although this may seem unimportant to you, many users still use Windows 95 programs; without this key, those programs cannot function in Windows XP.

Using the Registry Editor

Editing the Registry consists of adding or deleting keys, adding new constants and their values to be associated with the keys, and modifying those constants and their values. For the most part, editing is easy work but it is knowing what keys, constants, and values to add, rename, or delete that is important. The good news is I tell you where to navigate and what to do for each Registry change I describe in this book.

Cleaning Up the Registry

All your work editing the Registry may be in vain if you do not clean the Registry itself from time to time. After all, the Registry is essentially a database of information and databases tend to collect junk over time. The larger the Registry, the more information Windows XP has to keep up and the slower it tends to work.

Registry cleaning is one of those tasks that is best left to tools that can examine the Registry. In other words, cleanup is not a manual action you should attempt to take in any way. Several great Registry cleaning tools are free, and you should grab one of them. Here's a quick look at my favorites.

Regclean

RegClean V 4.1a (the latest at the time of this writing) is a great tool that scans your Registry and deletes values have been left behind by old programs that you have installed or uninstalled on your computer. Because programs are a main source of Registry junk that gets left behind, the tool can really help clean things up. Also, the tool creates an undo.reg file so you can undo RegClean's work if something goes wrong. Find RegClean at `www.pcworld.com`.

Note

This tool has been tested and approved by Microsoft, although it is not directly supported.

Regseeker

RegSeeker is another great tool that scans the Registry, deleting old, left-behind items and duplicates. This software has been tested with Windows XP and appears completely safe. It allows you to interact with the process and remove the stuff you want, creating backup files as it works in case something goes wrong. Find RegSeeker at `www.hoverdesk.net/freeware.htm`.

Registry Mechanic

This general-purpose tool does a good job of cleaning Windows XP's Registry and generally keeping the registry in tiptop shape. This tool costs you $30 to download for a single computer but the interface and tools found in the Registry Mechanic are easy to use and understand. Find out more about Registry Mechanic at `www.winguides.com/regmech`.

Registry Tuneup

This tool does a good job of searching through the Registry and removing all the junk it has accumulated over time. It shows you what entries are invalid and creates backups in case something goes wrong. Download a 30-day trial of this tool and check it out at `www.acelogix.com`.

Chapter 7

Optimizing Disk Performance

Hard disks can be a problem for performance on any computer—no matter what the operating system. Windows XP is no exception. Each time your computer has to read and write to the hard disk, you lose some performance because the disk subsystem, by its nature, tends to be the slowest component of your computer system. There's not much you can do about that fact, but you can take a number of actions to make certain the computer's hard disk(s) always run in tiptop shape. Fortunately, Windows XP helps you with at least part of this task; there are additional configurations you make on your own, and many third-party utilities can help you, as well. This chapter explores these issues to help you make sure your computer's hard disk is working as it should.

Fundamentals of Hard Disk Configuration

Before I get into the performance of the hard disk, let's take a few moments to make sure you are up to speed on the hard disk configuration available in Windows XP. This is especially true if your computer has more than one hard disk. Beginning in Windows 2000, Microsoft introduced the strategy of dynamic disks, which allowed for more flexibility in how hard disks are configured and how data is managed across the disks. If you are an old pro at managing and configuring hard disks in Windows XP, you can skip this section, but if disk management is relatively new to you, this primer will set your feet on solid ground.

Windows XP gives you the Disk Management console found in Computer Management. You can find this by opening the Start menu and choosing Control Panel ➪ Administrative Tools ➪ Computer Management. Select Disk Management in the left console pane and see the disks and their configuration in the right console pane (see Figure 7-1).

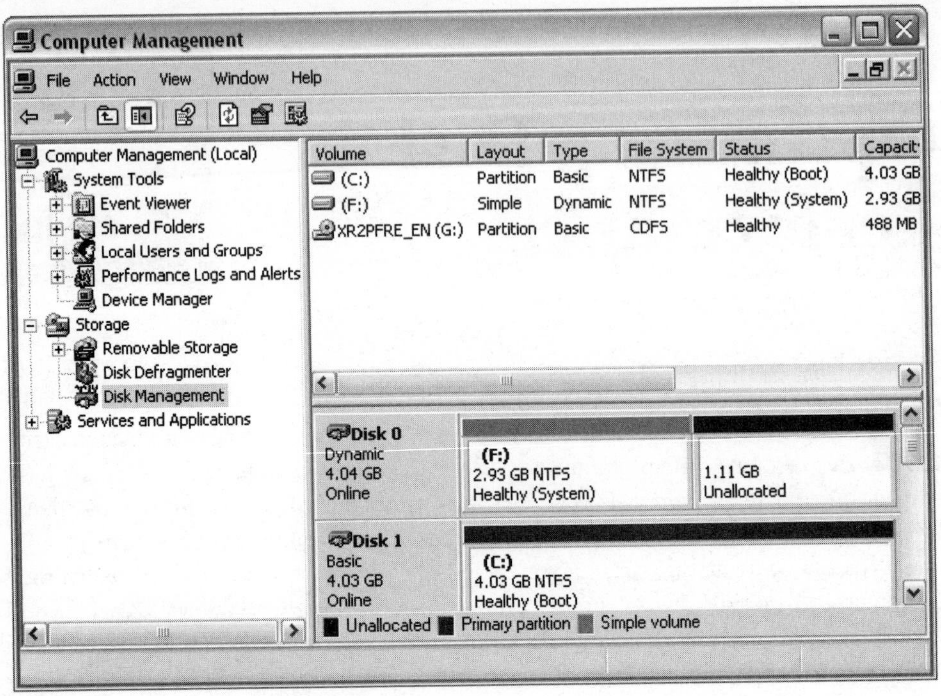

Figure 7-1: Disk Management console.

Comparing Basic and Dynamic Disks

Windows XP supports two kinds of disks: basic and dynamic. A basic disk is the same kind of disk that you have always worked with in the past. It is a standard hard disk that supports standard configurations. A basic disk can have a primary partition and extended partitions that make up logical disk drives. For example, you can configure the basic disk so that it has a C drive (primary) and a D drive (extended). You can use the D drive for storage or other purposes (or to set up a dual-boot configuration). On a basic disk, you can have up to four primary *partitions,* or alternative configurations, such as three primary partitions and one extended partition, and so on. One of the primary partitions is considered active and is used to start the computer. In other words, this active partition contains your boot files and the master boot record.

Basic disks behave like disks have in the past and do not provide the advanced management features supported under Windows XP Professional. Disks are always basic when first installed but you can convert them to dynamic to take advantage of all that Windows XP Professional has to offer.

Generally, you should convert any basic disk to a dynamic disk on your Windows XP computer. The only exception to this rule is when you have a dual-boot configuration, where you are dual-booting with an earlier version of Windows. Windows versions earlier than Windows 2000 cannot read dynamic disks so if you are dual-booting, you should keep the disk configured as a basic disk so that the earlier operating system can read from it.

A dynamic disk is a drive configured by the Disk Management console so that it can support volume management. This refers to the logical organization of a disk for storage purposes. Volume management does not limit you to a primary partition and a few extended partitions. Volumes are much more flexible and much easier to work with. The Disk Management console's utilities configure the drive so that it can make use of Windows XP Professional's disk management features. In essence, if you want to take advantage of volume management and lose the partition restrictions placed on basic disks, you need to convert the disk to a dynamic disk. Note that there are no performance features associated with dynamic disks, so if you have no intention of using volume management, there is no reason to convert a basic disk to dynamic. However, if you want to take advantage of volume management, you can easily convert your existing drives to dynamic disks.

The following steps show you how to convert a basic disk to a dynamic disk:

1. In the Disk Management console, right-click the disk number in the graphical portion of the Disk Management display and select Convert to Dynamic Disk. You can also select Action ➪ All Tasks ➪ Convert to Dynamic Disk. This option only appears if the disks are not currently dynamic disks.

2. In the Convert to Dynamic Disk dialog box (see Figure 7-2), select the disk you want to convert and click OK.

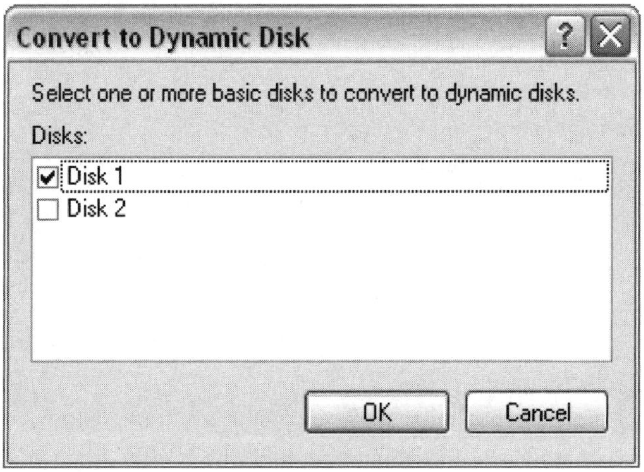

Figure 7-2: Convert to Dynamic Disk dialog box.

3. In the Disks to Convert dialog box, review the settings (see Figure 7-3). Click Convert to continue.

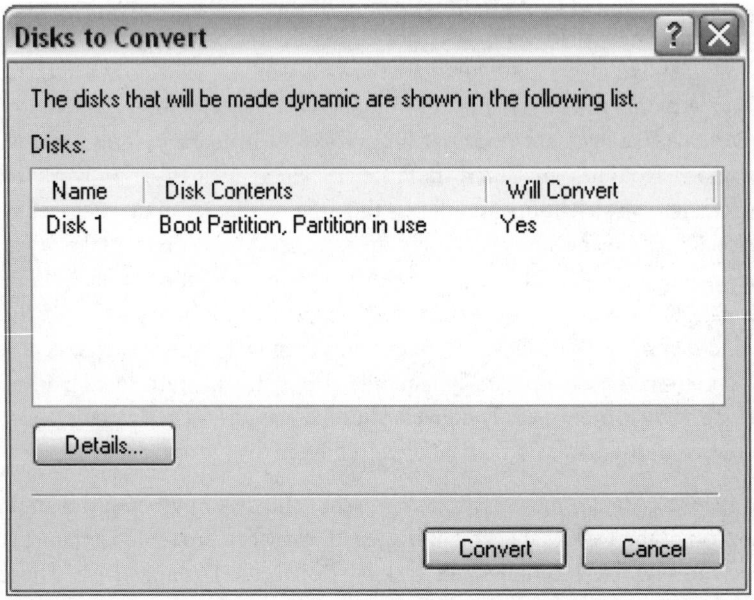

Figure 7-3: Conversion summary in the Disks to Convert dialog box.

4. A message will tell you that other operating systems will not be able to start from the disk once the conversion has taken place (this means all other operating systems, such as Windows NT, Windows 9x, and Windows Me). Click OK to continue.
5. You may see a message telling you that any mounted disks will need to be dismounted. Click OK to continue.
6. After the conversion process is completed, it prompts you to reboot the computer. After you reboot, you can see that the disk's status has changed from basic to dynamic in the Disk Management console.

Getting to Know Dynamic Disks

When you use a dynamic disk, you have more options and flexibility with disk management. Also, dynamic disks give you information about the status of the disk, and you can create various types of volumes, as needed. The following sections explore these features.

DYNAMIC DISK STATES

Dynamic disks are capable of displaying several different states. This information tells you the current status of the disk and helps you understand problems that may exist. The following list explains the states that a dynamic disk may display:

- **Online:** The disk is online and functioning with no errors.
- **Online (Errors):** The disk is online but there have been some errors. These are usually minor and can be fixed by running the Error Checking tool found on the Tools menu of the disk's properties.
- **Offline:** The disk is not accessible. This problem can occur due to corruption or an I/O problem. Try right-clicking the disk and selecting Reactivate Disk to bring the disk back online.
- **Missing:** The disk is not accessible, is disconnected, or corruption has caused the disk to be unreadable. Try right-clicking the disk and selecting Reactivate Disk to bring the disk back online.
- **Initializing:** This message occurs when the disk is temporarily unavailable due to a conversion to dynamic state.
- **Not Initialized:** This message occurs when the disk does not have a valid signature—for example, when you install a new disk. When the Disk Management console appears, the disk appears as Not Initialized. To write a valid signature so that you can format and begin using the disk, simply right-click the disk and select Initialize.
- **Foreign:** This status appears when a physical, dynamic disk is moved from one Windows 2000/XP Professional computer to another Windows 2000/XP Professional computer. When this message appears, right-click the disk and select Import Foreign Disk.
- **Unreadable:** This status appears when I/O errors keep the disk from being readable. Select Action ➪ Rescan Disks to fix the problem.
- **No Media:** This status appears on removable drives when no media is inserted into the drive.

CONFIGURING DRIVE LETTERS AND PATHS

Windows XP makes it easy to configure drive letters and paths. You can assign a drive any alphabet letter, and you can also assign a drive to any empty NT File System (NTFS) folder. First of all, if you want to make a change to a dynamic disk volume, simply right-click the volume in the Disk Management console and select Change Drive Letter and Paths. A simple Change Drive Letter and Paths dialog box appears (see Figure 7-4).

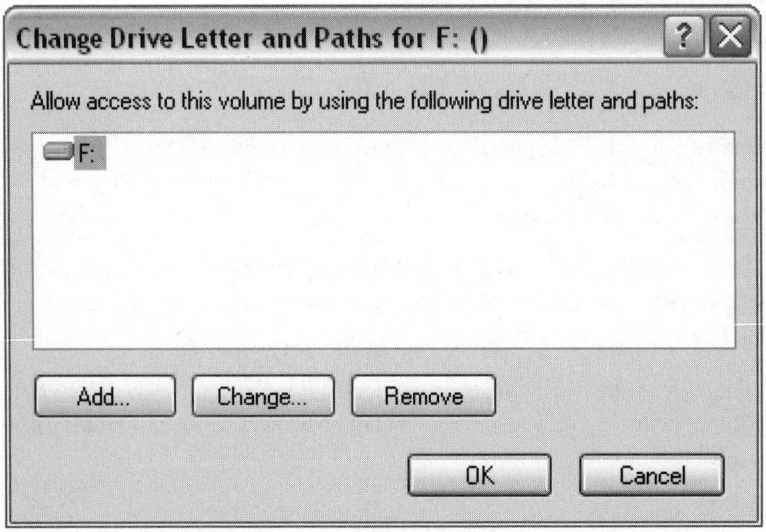

Figure 7-4: Change Drive Letter and Paths dialog box.

You can perform the following actions:

- **Add:** When you click the Add button, a second window appears where you can mount the drive to an empty NTFS folder (discussed later in this section). Because a drive can only have one drive letter, you cannot assign multiple drive letters for the same drive.
- **Change:** When you click the Change button, the Change Drive Letter or Path dialog box appears (see Figure 7-5). You can choose a different drive letter from the drop-down menu.
- **Remove:** You can also remove the drive letter. Dynamic disks do not require that a drive be identified by a drive letter or path. However, some programs may not function if you remove the drive letter, nor will you be able to access the drive.

Aside from assigning a different drive letter, you can also mount a volume to a local, empty NTFS folder. The purpose of doing this is to give you freedom and flexibility beyond the 26-letter alphabet limitation. When you mount a volume to an empty NTFS folder, a

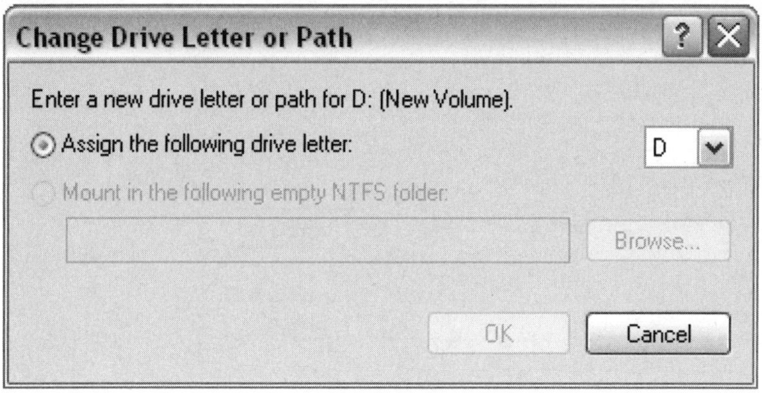

Figure 7-5: Changing drive letters.

drive path is used instead of a drive number. For example, suppose you have a local volume that is only used for storage. You could create an NTFS folder called "Volume." Then you could mount the drive to the empty storage volume. You could then access the drive by simply accessing C:\Volume, just as you would a folder. The result is that you can have an unlimited number of drives and use them like folders rather than standard drive letters that you must keep track of.

You can use both a drive letter and a mounted volume on the same drive, if you like. Keep in mind that the drive must be mounted to an empty folder. After the mount takes place, you can move data to that folder to store it on the volume. This feature works only on NTFS folders; you cannot mount to a folder on a FAT drive.

To mount a drive to an empty NTFS folder, just follow these steps:

1. In the Disk Management console, right-click the volume that you want to mount to an empty NTFS folder and select Change Drive Letter and Paths.

2. In the Change Drive Letter and Paths dialog box, click the Add button.

3. In the Add Drive Letter or Path dialog box (see Figure 7-6), select the "Mount in the following empty NTFS folder" option button and then enter the path to the folder you want to mount, or click the Browse button to select the folder directly.

4. If you browse for the folder, a browse window appears (see Figure 7-7). Locate the folder or create a new one by clicking the New Folder button. Make your selection and click OK.

5. Click OK again in the Add Drive Letter or Path dialog box.

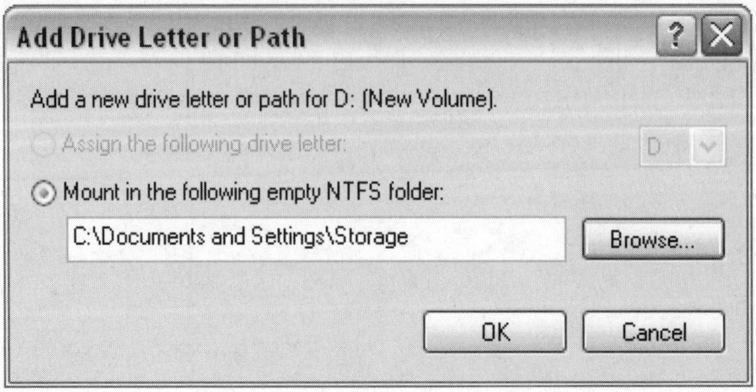

Figure 7-6: Folder mount option.

Figure 7-7: Browsing for, or creating, a new NTFS folder.

Working with Disk Volumes

Using dynamic disks opens a new world of management possibilities for you. You lose the restrictions often faced with basic disks. When a disk is first converted to a dynamic disk, it appears in the disk console as unallocated space. This means that the disk has no volumes and has not been formatted. In other words, the disk is not usable by the operating system in its current state. Figure 7-8 shows you an unallocated disk in the Disk Management console. This disk has been converted to dynamic but has no volumes and no file system; it therefore cannot be used by the operating system. To use a dynamic disk, you must create and format disk volumes. The following sections explain the different kinds of volumes that are available to you and how to create them.

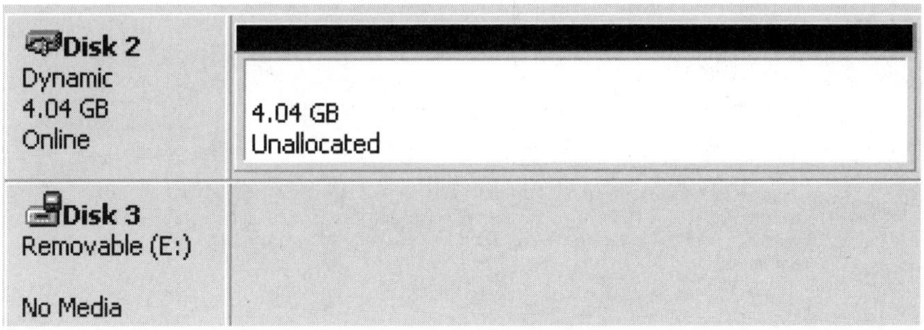

Figure 7-8: Unallocated disk space in a newly converted dynamic disk.

Creating Simple Volumes

A simple volume is a standard disk volume. It is a unit of disk space that has been configured and formatted so that it can store data. A hard disk can be formatted as one volume, or you can format a portion of it to use multiple disk volumes. The following steps show you how to create a simple disk volume:

1. In the Disk Management console, right-click the dynamic disk's unallocated space and select New Volume.
2. The New Volume Wizard appears. Click Next to continue.
3. In the Select Volume Type screen (see Figure 7-9), select the Simple option button and click Next.
4. In the Select Disks screen (see Figure 7-10), select the disk you want to configure (already chosen for you in this wizard) then enter the size of the volume (in megabytes) that you want to create. The maximum amount of available space is listed here for you as well. Click Next.
5. In the Assign Drive Letter or Path screen, choose a drive, assign an empty NTFS folder, or do not assign either. Click Next.
6. In the Format Volume screen (see Figure 7-11), you can decide whether to format the volume or not, and you can choose to use the quick format feature and

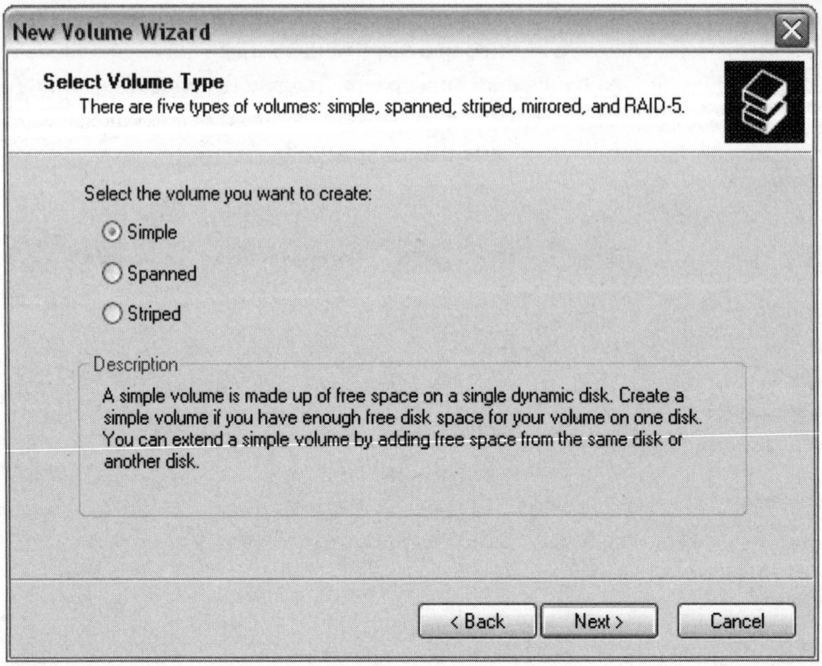
New Volume Wizard
Select Volume Type
There are five types of volumes: simple, spanned, striped, mirrored, and RAID-5.
Select the volume you want to create:
Simple
Spanned
Striped
Description
A simple volume is made up of free space on a single dynamic disk. Create a simple volume if you have enough free disk space for your volume on one disk. You can extend a simple volume by adding free space from the same disk or another disk.
< Back
Next >
Cancel

Figure 7-9: Choosing the simple volume option.

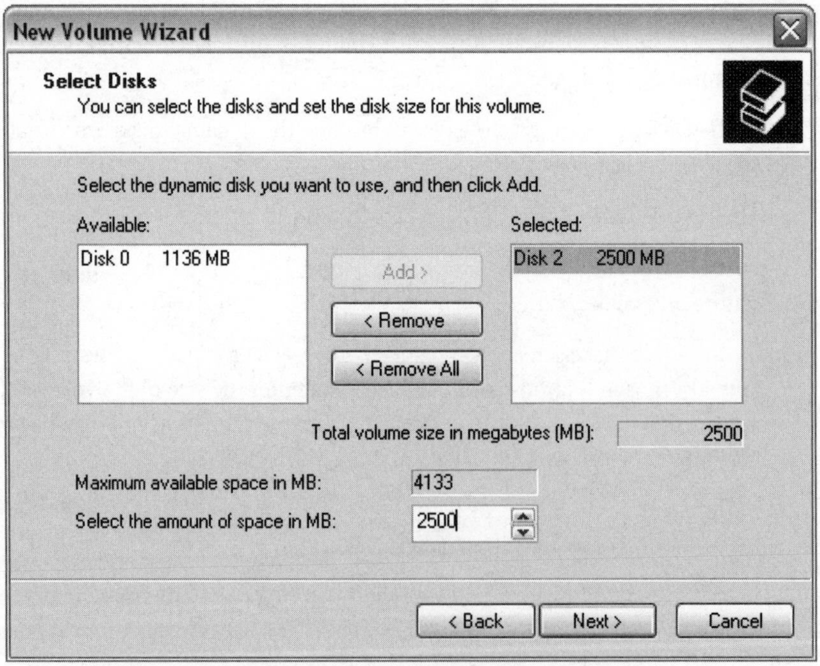
New Volume Wizard
Select Disks
You can select the disks and set the disk size for this volume.
Select the dynamic disk you want to use, and then click Add.
Available:
Disk 0 1136 MB
Add >
< Remove
< Remove All
Selected:
Disk 2 2500 MB
Total volume size in megabytes (MB):
2500
Maximum available space in MB:
4133
Select the amount of space in MB:
2500
< Back
Next >
Cancel

Figure 7-10: Selecting the disk and the desired megabyte space for the volume.

New Volume Wizard ☒

Format Volume
To store data on this volume, you must format it first.

Choose whether you want to format this volume, and if so, what settings you want to use.

○ Do not format this volume

⊙ Format this volume with the following settings:

File system: NTFS ▾

Allocation unit size: Default ▾

Volume label: New Volume

☑ Perform a quick format
☑ Enable file and folder compression

< Back | Next > | Cancel

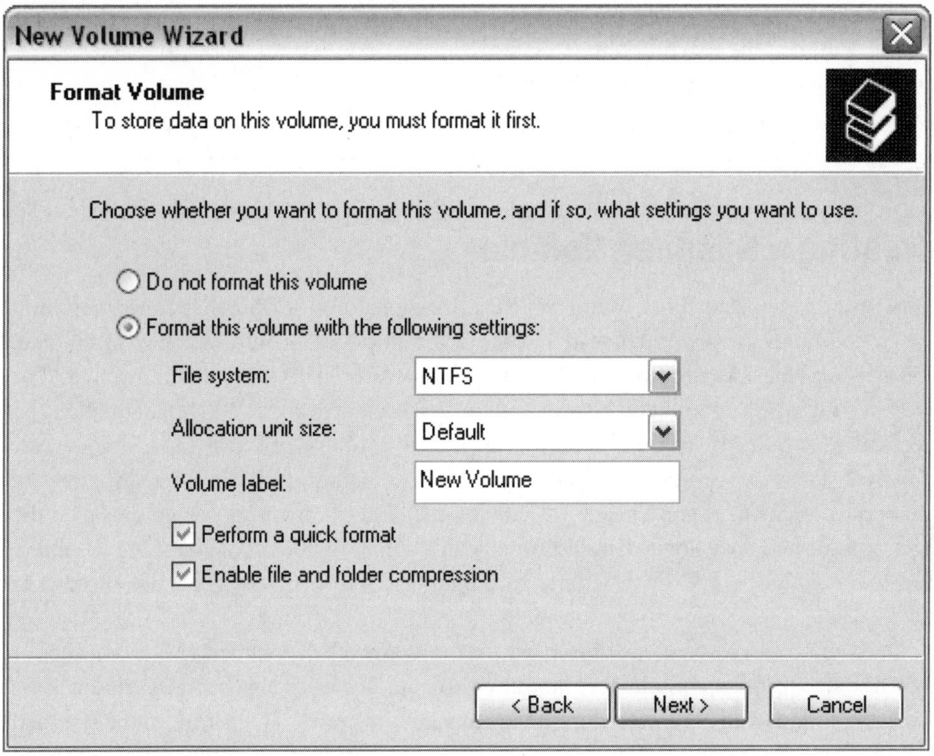

Figure 7-11: Formatting the volume.

enable file and folder compression for the volume. Make your selections and click Next.

7. Click Finish. The new volume is created and appears in the Disk Management console.

Extending a Simple Volume

Suppose you create a simple volume with a certain amount of space and then see you still have extra free space on the same disk. At a later time, you decide that the volume should have been larger. Fortunately, you do not have to remove your data from the volume and create a new one; you simply extend the existing volume by grabbing some of the additional unallocated space on the disk. This feature allows you to gain additional space quickly without any harm to your data currently stored on the existing volume. For example, suppose you have a 10 GB volume and 2 GB of free space available on the same disk. You can extend the 10 GB volume so it includes the 2 GB of free space—effectively creating a 12 GB volume.

To extend a volume, right-click the volume in the Disk Management console and select Extend Volume. The Extend Volume Wizard appears. This wizard works the same way as the New Volume Wizard. Simply walk through the steps and determine the amount of space you want to add to the existing volume. The extended volume appears as a new volume in the Disk Management console but it is actually an extension of the existing volume.

Creating a Spanned Volume

Aside from a simple volume, Windows XP Professional also supports spanned volumes, which combines areas of unallocated space on multiple disks into one logical volume. You can combine between two and 32 areas of unallocated space from different drives. For example, suppose a computer has three hard drives, each with about 500 MB of unallocated free space. A 500 MB volume is rather small and not very practical for everyday use. However, using the spanned volume option, you can combine all three 500 MB areas of unallocated space to create a single 1.5 GB volume. You can then use the volume as if the storage is located on a single disk. Essentially, this configuration gives you more flexibility and fewer volumes (and drive letters) to remember; it also makes good use of leftover space.

Once you create a spanned volume, you see it as any other volume in My Computer or the Disk Management console. It is important to note, however, that spanned volumes are storage solutions only—they do not provide any fault tolerance. If one disk in the spanned volume fails, all data on the spanned volume is lost. However, you can back up a spanned volume just as you would any other volume.

Like a simple volume, you can easily extend a spanned volume at any time by adding existing free space. However, you cannot remove a volume from a spanned volume without losing the entire volume, so do keep this in mind as you plan your disk configuration.

To create a spanned volume, follow these steps:

1. In the Disk Management console, right-click one of the areas of unallocated disk space on one of the disks and select New Volume.
2. The New Volume Wizard appears. Click Next to continue.
3. In the Select Volume Type screen (see Figure 7-12), choose the Spanned option and then click Next.
4. In the Select Disks screen, the current disk appears. Choose the free space on the desired disk(s) that appears in the Available section and click the Add button. Repeat the process until all unallocated areas you want to use appear in the Selected box. Click Next.

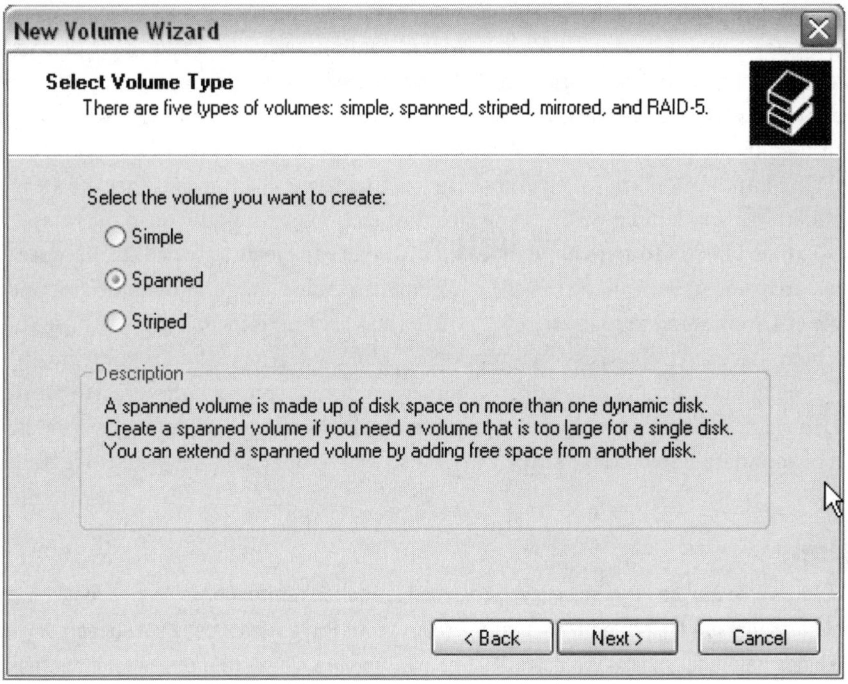
New Volume Wizard
Select Volume Type
There are five types of volumes: simple, spanned, striped, mirrored, and RAID-5.
Select the volume you want to create:
Simple
Spanned
Striped
Description
A spanned volume is made up of disk space on more than one dynamic disk.
Create a spanned volume if you need a volume that is too large for a single disk.
You can extend a spanned volume by adding free space from another disk.
< Back
Next >
Cancel

Figure 7-12: Creating a spanned volume.

5. In the Assign Drive Letter or Path screen, choose a drive letter or mount the drive to an empty NTFS folder. You can also choose not to assign a drive letter or path at this time. Click Next.

6. In the Format Volume screen, choose whether or not to format the volume at the time and whether or not to perform a quick format and enable file and folder compression. Click Next.

7. Click Finish. The volume is created and now appears in the Disk Management console.

Creating Striped Volumes

Striped volumes are similar to spanned volumes. They combine areas of free disk space (between two and 32 areas of unallocated space on different drives) to create one logical volume. However, the big difference is that striped volumes write data across the disks instead of filling one portion of free space first, followed by the next portion, and so on.

You are likely to get faster read and write performance with a striped volume than with a simple spanned volume. Like a spanned volume, you can create a striped volume by right-clicking one of the areas of unallocated space and selecting Create Volume. In the Create New Volume Wizard, choose to create a striped volume and follow the same steps I outlined in the previous section.

One important point to remember concerning striped volumes is that the areas of unallocated free space must be the same size. For example, suppose you want to use 500 MB, 800 MB, and 900 MB areas of unallocated disk space to create a striped set. Because the areas have to be the same size, the Disk Management console configures only the amount of available space common to each area (500 MB in this case). This means you still have some unallocated space left over. This configuration enables data to be written evenly across the disks.

Finally, keep in mind that striped volumes are storage solutions designed to provide better performance. They do not, however, provide any fault tolerance. If one disk in the stripe fails, all of your data stored on the stripe will be lost. Make sure you have an effective backup plan.

Note

As you work with the New Volume Wizard, you may notice references to some additional volume solutions that are fault-tolerant. In reality, Windows XP Professional does not support any kind of disk fault tolerance, unlike Windows 2000 or .NET servers. These references refer to Microsoft's overall disk management solutions, even though the fault-tolerant options are not available in Windows XP Professional, or even Windows 2000 Professional for that matter.

Speeding Up Hard Disk Performance

Now that you have a handle on disk configuration in Windows XP, there are some speed solutions available that help your hard disks work better and enable them to retrieve information more quickly. After all, the quicker that hard disks can locate and write information, the better performance you'll see from them. The following sections point out issues and tactics you can follow to speed up disk performance.

Converting to NTFS

NTFS is the file system of choice in Windows XP. While NTFS does have some overhead associated with it (which I show you how to reduce in the next section), it is overwhelmingly better than FAT and enables you to use some management features of Windows XP that FAT does not support. So you should certainly convert any FAT drives to NTFS. The only exception to this rule is if you use a dual-boot system which boots earlier versions of Windows that do not support NTFS, such as Windows 98 or Windows Me.

Keep the following two issues in mind when converting to NTFS:

- **You can convert a FAT or FAT32 drive to NTFS while preserving your data.** Conversion is a one-way process, however. Once you convert to NTFS, you cannot revert back to FAT without reformatting the disk.
- **You cannot convert an NTFS drive to FAT or FAT32 without reformatting the drive.** All your data on the hard disk will be destroyed during the formatting process. You will have to restore all data from backups.

Although the conversion process is safe and effective, volumes that are converted lack some of the performance benefits of drives that were initially formatted with NTFS. Also, the Master File Table is different on converted volumes, which also affects performance to a degree. Still, conversion is the easiest way to change a FAT drive to NTFS without reformatting and having to restore data currently held in the FAT volume.

Converting to NTFS is easy; the following steps show you how:

1. Select Start ➪ Run, type **command**, and click OK.
2. At the command prompt, you will use the CONVERT command to convert the FAT drive to NTFS. Keep in mind that the conversion process is completely safe and all of your data will remain as it is. The command and syntax is as follows:

   ```
   convert driveletter: /FS:NTFS
   ```
3. Conversion may take several minutes, depending on the size of the drive. When the process is completed, type **exit** to leave the command interface. If you converted the boot partition, you will be prompted to reboot the computer.

Reducing NTFS Overhead

As I previously mentioned, NTFS is a powerful file system that provides many of the features you enjoy with Windows XP (such as compression and encryption). However, there is some overhead that can get in the way. The following sections show you some tactics for reducing that overhead.

DISABLING 8.3 FILENAMES

For compatibility with MS-DOS and older Windows 3.x systems, NTFS supports 8.3 filenames. This means that files are named with eight characters, followed by a dot and a three-character extension. There's nothing wrong with this but the overhead is unnecessary if you are not supporting older programs and systems (which you are probably not at this point). However, one word of warning: Some older programs depend on 8.3 filenames so it is possible that if you turn off the 8.3 filename feature, some programs may not work correctly. Although this is unlikely at this point, it is still an issue you should keep in mind. Otherwise, lose the 8.3 filename feature to reduce NTFS overhead by following these steps:

1. Select Start ➪ Run, type **regedit**, and click OK.
2. In the Registry Editor, navigate to HKEY_LOCAL_MACHINE\SYSTEM\CurrentControlSet\Control\Filesystem.
3. Locate the NtfsDisable8dot3NameCreation entry and change the value to **1**. This disables the creation of 8.3 filenames.
4. Close the Registry Editor.

CREATING MORE SPACE FOR THE MASTER FILE TABLE

NTFS uses a master file table to record data about files. You can add a Registry entry to ensure that the table is large enough and has the space it needs. This takes up more space on the hard disk but reduces overall NTFS overhead, which can help general performance. Follow these steps:

1. Select Start ➪ Run, type **regedit**, and click OK.
2. In the Registry Editor, navigate to HKEY_LOCAL_MACHINE\SYSTEM\CurrentControlSet\Control\FileSystem.
3. Create a REG_DWORD entry and name it **NtfsMftZoneReservation**.
4. Set the value of the entry to **2**.
5. Close the Registry Editor.

DISABLING DATE AND TIME STAMP UPDATING

NTFS regularly updates the date and time stamp from the last time it goes through the directory. With many directories, this process can slow your system down a bit; disabling this date and time stamping feature doesn't impact how you work with your files. Disable the dating and time stamping process by following these steps:

1. Select Start ➪ Run, type **regedit**, and click OK.
2. In the Registry Editor, navigate to HKEY_LOCAL_MACHINE\SYSTEM\CurrentControlSet\Control\FileSystem.
3. Locate the NtfsDisableLastAccessUpdate entry. (If you do not find it, create it in the entry as a REG_DWORD).
4. Change the value of the entry to **1**.
5. Close the Registry Editor.

Defragmenting the Hard Disk

Fragmentation is a normal occurrence within file systems. Windows XP attempts to store files in a contiguous format. However, as files are changed and resaved, the file system has to move data to different blocks of free space. The result is that a typical file might have pieces scattered all over the disk. When you open the file, the disk must work harder to retrieve all the pieces and reassemble them. When this happens, the disk is referred to as fragmented. Disk Defragmenter, which is also available on the Tools tab of the disk's Properties dialog box, is a tool you should run about once a month if you use your computer frequently. Disk Defragmenter helps repair normal file fragmentation that occurs over time in any file system.

The Disk Defragmenter rearranges data so that it is stored contiguously on the disk. Bear in mind that the "defrag" tool is not perfect; the drive will not be completely defragmented after the utility is run. However, for very fragmented drives, you are likely to notice significant performance improvement after running Disk Defragmenter. The following steps show you how to use this tool:

1. Open My Computer. Right-click the disk you want to defragment and select Properties.
2. On the Tools tab, click the Defragment Now button.
3. The Disk Defragmenter dialog box appears (see Figure 7-13). Click the Analyze button.
4. After the drive analysis is performed, a message tells you whether or not you should defragment the drive. You can also view a report (see Figure 7-14).
5. If the drive needs to be defragmented, click the Defragment button. The defragmentation process may take some time, depending on how badly the drive is fragmented. Once the process is complete, you can view a report again, if you like.

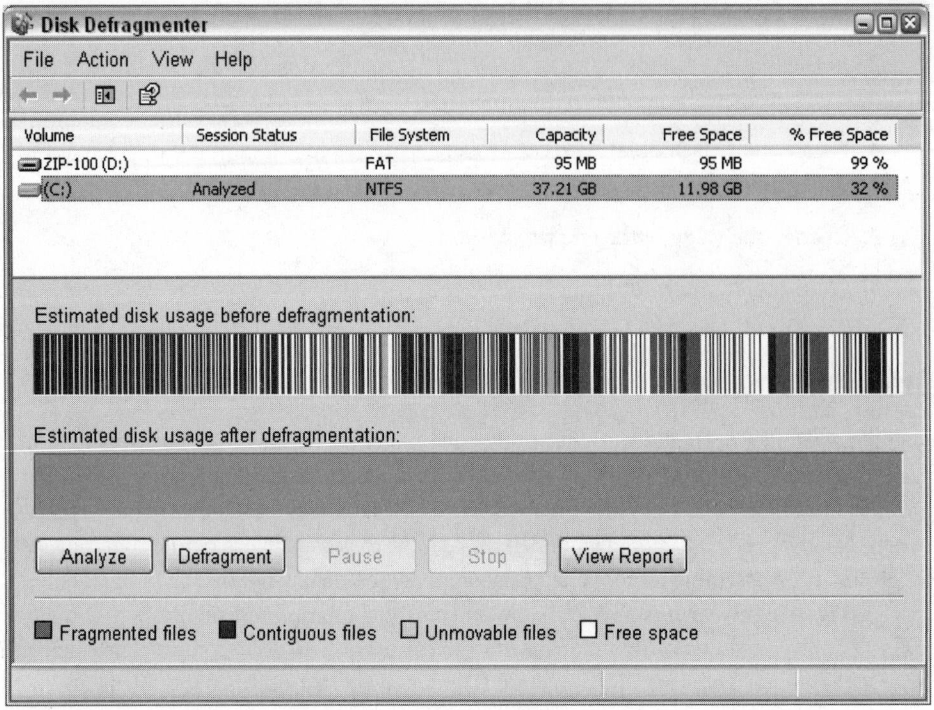

Figure 7-13: Disk Defragmenter analysis.

You can employ some other defragment options beyond the basic disk defrag process. First, you can run the Disk Defragmenter from the command line and use a few switches that you may find helpful. Select Start ➪ Run, type **CMD**, and click OK. At the command prompt, type **defrag /?** to see a list of available switches (see Figure 7-15).

Aside from this feature, note that Windows XP forces applications and boot files to the edge of the hard drive for faster access. Windows XP does this about every three days to keep these files more readily accessible, but you can force this application and boot file defragmentation manually using the command line. At the command prompt, just type **defrag C: -b**.

Checking for Disk Errors

The Error Checking tool, which is available on the Tools tab of the hard disk's Properties dialog box, gives you simple check box options to look for file system errors and recover bad sectors (see Figure 7-16). The Error Checking tool needs complete access to the disk to work properly. Applications must be closed. In some cases, Error Checking asks you to

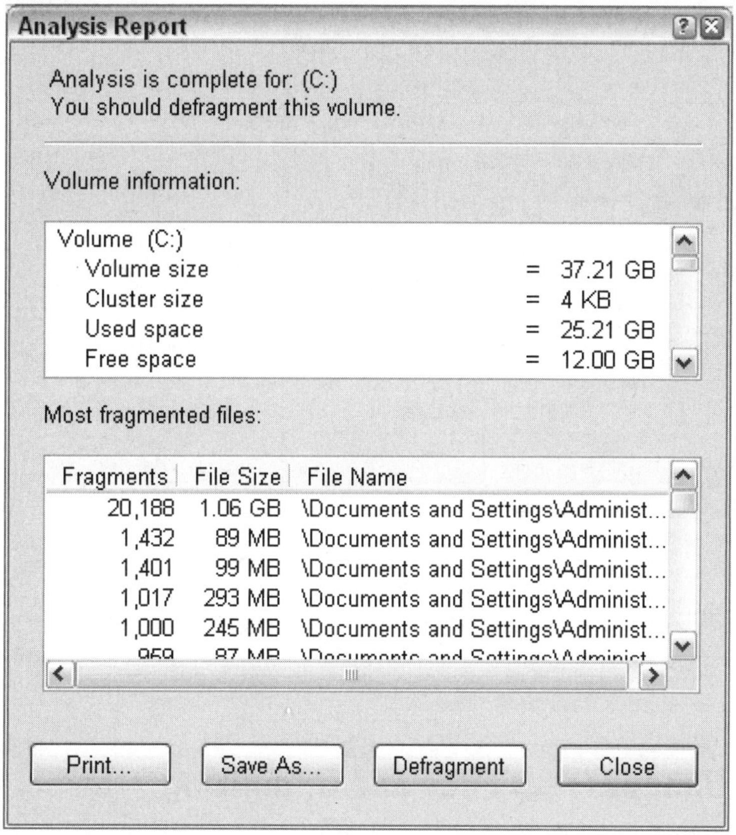

Figure 7-14: Report generated by the hard disk analysis.

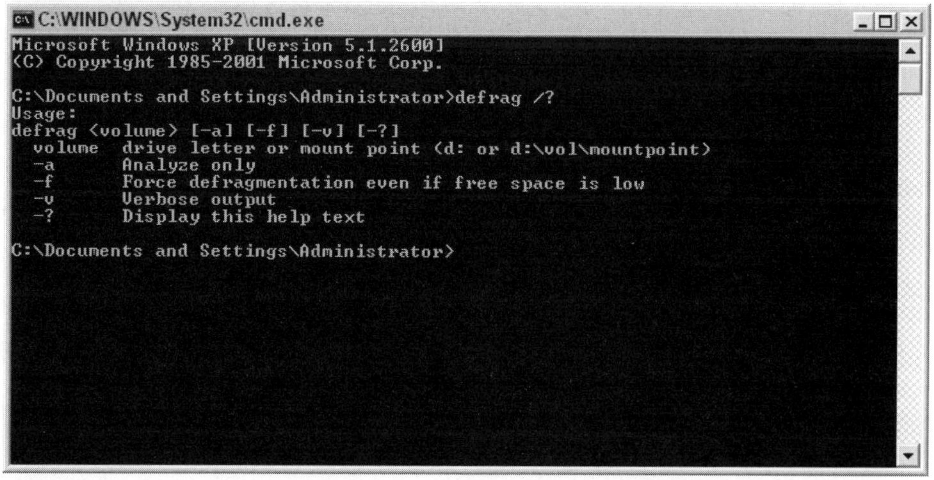

Figure 7-15: You can use various defrag switches at the command prompt.

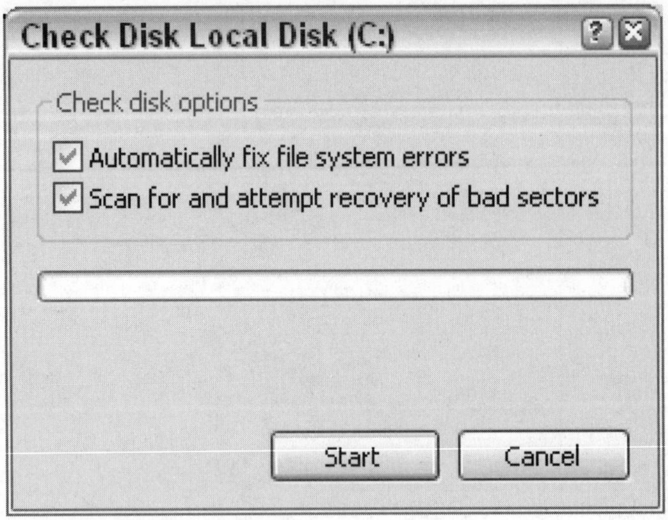

Figure 7-16: Error Checking feature.

reboot before it starts to gain complete access to the disk. If you use your computer often, it is a good idea to run this tool every six weeks or so to make sure that your disk is in good working order.

Cleaning Up Unnecessary Files and Optimizing the Recycle Bin

If you want the hard disk to work most efficiently, keep junk off of it. An overstuffed hard drive makes Windows XP work harder. Make sure you have a system in place to keep old files and junk cleaned up and removed. Also make sure you optimize the Recycle Bin so that it doesn't hold onto deleted files any longer than necessary. Refer to Chapters 1 and 2 to learn more about these issues.

How Compression and Encryption Affect Performance

With NTFS, you can compress and encrypt folders and files to stop unauthorized access to them. The compression feature works well but compressed files take longer to open and resave. If you want to squeeze as much speed as possible from your system, avoid compressing drives. Instead, keep junk off your disk in the first place by moving old files to removable storage, such as a CD or DVD.

If you still want to compress a drive, access the disk's Properties dialog box and select the "Compress drive to save disk space" check box on the General tab (see Figure 7-17).

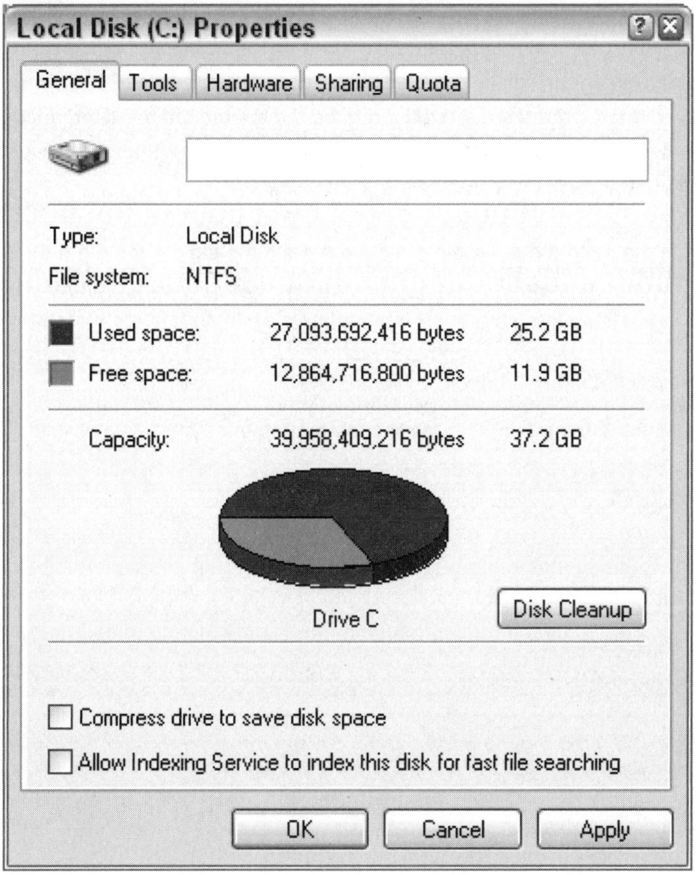

Figure 7-17: Do not compress a disk unless absolutely necessary.

Encryption also reduces performance. After all, the encryption process has to make sure you are authorized to view files. However, I don't notice much performance improvement by unencrypting files. In many cases, safe data is more important than speed when it comes to private files. The general rule to follow here is to encrypt files or folders that are necessary, but don't get in the habit of encrypting everything just because you can. Encryption is a good safety measure and has its place, but use it judiciously.

Stopping Hibernation

Hibernation is a nice feature of Windows XP—if you use it. When the computer hibernates, only a small amount of power continues to run the computer. When you bring the computer out of hibernation, you return to the desktop as you left it and see all your open applications. For Windows XP to know where everything is when it goes into hibernation, of course, it has to store that information on the hard disk. If you use hibernation, that's great. If not, you should disable it so that it does not consume system resources. To disable hibernation, open the Start menu and select Control Panel ➪ Power Options Properties. Click the Hibernate tab and clear the Enable Hibernation check box (see Figure 7-18).

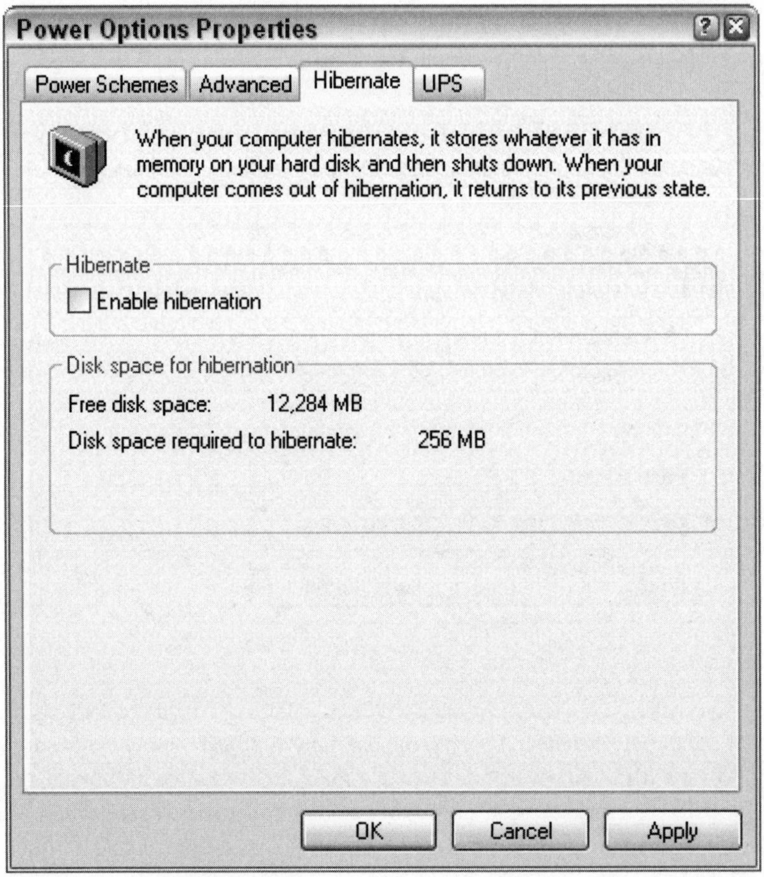

Figure 7-18: Disabling hibernation.

Using DMA Mode on IDE Drives

Direct memory access (DMA) mode works best for IDE drives in Windows XP. If the IDE drives are set up in a different mode, you may experience slower overall performance and jerky performance of digital media, such as movies and music. Make sure your IDE drives use DMA mode by following these steps:

1. Open the Start menu, right-click My Computer, and select Properties.
2. Click the Hardware tab and choose Device Manager.
3. Expand the IDE controllers and double-click the IDE primary drive.
4. If different mode options are available, you'll see an Advanced tab. Click the Advanced tab and make sure that DMA mode is selected from the drop-down box.
5. Click OK and restart your computer.

Helpful Disk Management and Performance Utilities

If you want to keep your computer's hard disk in tiptop shape, one of the best things you can do is get a free or inexpensive disk management and performance utility to help you keep things working they way they should. There are plenty to choose from. Here are my favorites.

Diskeeper

Diskeeper is a utility that defragments the hard disk. It makes several passes over the disk and is designed to improve disk performance. The automatic setup feature allows it to run automatically instead of forcing you to run it manually every time. The tool costs around $50. Find out more about it at `www.pcmag.com`.

ShowSize

ShowSize is a disk utility that examines folder contents, sends reports to you, and helps you find items that are wasting space on your PC. You can then remove and manage those items. Essentially, the software works as a good house-cleaning tool. Find out more about it at `www.showsize.com`.

Norton Speed Disk

Norton Speed Disk, a part of Symantec's SystemWorks, is an overall disk management utility. It is basically another defragmentation utility but it works very well; you'll also enjoy the other tools that come with SystemWorks. The bundle costs around $70. Find out more at www.symantec.com.

Other Free Utilities

If you want to try some free disk management and performance utilities, check out www.thefreesite.com. Search for "disk utilities" and you will find a collection of various utilities you might want to try.

Chapter 8

Dealing with Hardware Devices and Drivers

One of the most aggravating and problematic issues in the PC world has been dealing with hardware. Yet from the days of Windows 2000, and now in Windows XP, hardware and device drivers are easier to manage and configure than ever before. So why a whole chapter on the subject? As we examine speed and optimization issues, hardware becomes a primary area of concern for computer users—and hardware always has the potential to cause problems and keep your system from running at its peak condition. The same issue is doubly true for device drivers, which need to be updated from time to time and certainly need to be compatible with Windows XP. If you are a hardware pro, you can skip this chapter and move onward. If you haven't worked with hardware or device drivers much before, however, you should carefully read this chapter and become familiar with hardware configuration issues in Windows XP.

Installing and Removing Hardware

As you are probably aware by now, most modern computing systems are "plug and play"; Windows XP is no exception to this rule. Plug and play means that Windows XP can detect hardware changes and adapt to them. For example, you can install a new device and, upon reboot, Windows XP will detect the new hardware and attempt to install it automatically. If the installation is successful, the hardware is ready for use.

If Windows XP cannot automatically install a new piece of hardware, the Add Hardware wizard appears so that you can install it manually. Of course, if you are using newer hardware that is compatible with Windows XP, it should be installed automatically thanks to plug and play, but if you do have problems, the Add Hardware wizard will be of assistance to you. Windows XP has an extensive device driver database; in most cases, you can find a driver that will make the hardware device work.

Tip

Always strive to use the correct drivers for your hardware devices. This is one your greatest defenses against optimization and speed troubles. You cannot expect older drivers to do the trick. I talk more about device drivers, and updating them, later in this chapter.

Compatibility is the primary issue if you want to optimize your system so that hardware works the way it should. Simply put, hardware and device drivers that were written for Windows 98 may not work well under Windows XP. When purchasing and installing new hardware, check for compatibility. Also, check the Hardware Compatibility List (HCL) at `www.microsoft.com/whdc/hcl/`to see if the device is listed as compatible with Windows XP.

Note

The HCL only lists devices that have been tested and approved. As you might guess, not every device that actually works with Windows XP has been tested. Just because a hardware device is not listed on the HCL does not mean the device will not work with Windows XP; it just means that Microsoft has not yet tested the device. In this case, you have to reply on the manufacturer's statements about hardware compatibility. Still, the HCL is a good place to start.

Should you have problems installing a hardware device, the simple-to-use Add Hardware wizard can walk you through the steps. Essentially, this wizard seeks to identify the device and have you choose a driver that will make the device work in Windows XP.

In case you are not experienced with hardware, a *driver* is software that enables a hardware device to interact with an operating system. For example, if you install a game controller, Windows XP may require a software package to control the game controller. These little software packages must be updated and changed as new operating systems comes out. An older driver written for Windows 98 may work in Windows XP but it often will not work well and could cause problems. So with any device installation, you need to strive to get the correct driver for it. Although the Add Hardware wizard will help you install it, you should check the manufacturer's Web site to download the latest driver. Windows XP maintains a sizable database of generic drivers that may also work with your device, although the manufacturer's driver is typically better.

The following steps show you how to use the Add Hardware wizard, should the need arise:

1. Open the Start menu and select Control Panel ➪ Add Hardware.
2. Click Next on the Welcome screen.
3. The Add Hardware wizard examines the computer for any hardware that you have connected to the computer. If the hardware is not found, a dialog box appears asking you to make sure the hardware is connected. Make the correct selection and click Next.
4. You can use the Add Hardware wizard to troubleshoot a device that is not working or add a new hardware device. In the screen that appears, make a selection.
5. The wizard prompts you either to install the hardware by selecting it from a list or run a search again. Because Windows has not been able to detect the hardware up to this point, it is best to choose the "Install the hardware that I manually select from a list" option button. Click Next.
6. The hardware type screen that appears allows you to choose the kind of hardware device you want to install. Choose a desired category and click Next.
7. Windows XP creates a list of hardware from the category that you selected. In the selection screen, choose the manufacturer and the model of the hardware you want to install. If you have an installation disk or CD for the hardware, click the Have Disk button and run the hardware installation routine from the disk. Make a selection and click Next.
8. The hardware you want to install is listed. Click Next to continue the installation. Files are copied and the device is installed.
9. Click Finish to complete the installation.

Tip

If you are having problems with a device not working correctly, the Add Hardware wizard may be able to help you pinpoint the problem. Just go back through the Add Hardware wizard. Any devices not working properly appear with a yellow exclamation point next to them. Select the device and click Next to read some information about the device that may help you troubleshoot the problem.

Using the Device Manager

The Device Manager is the best tool for managing hardware in Windows XP. You can examine the devices installed on your system and immediately find out if there are any problems with them. You can also find out what driver you need for a device and make configuration changes to the device. You can access the Device Manager in two ways: using the Computer Management console or the Hardware tab of System Properties.

The Device Manager interface (see Figure 8-1) gives you a listing of hardware categories. Click the plus sign (+) for each category to expand it and see any devices that are installed.

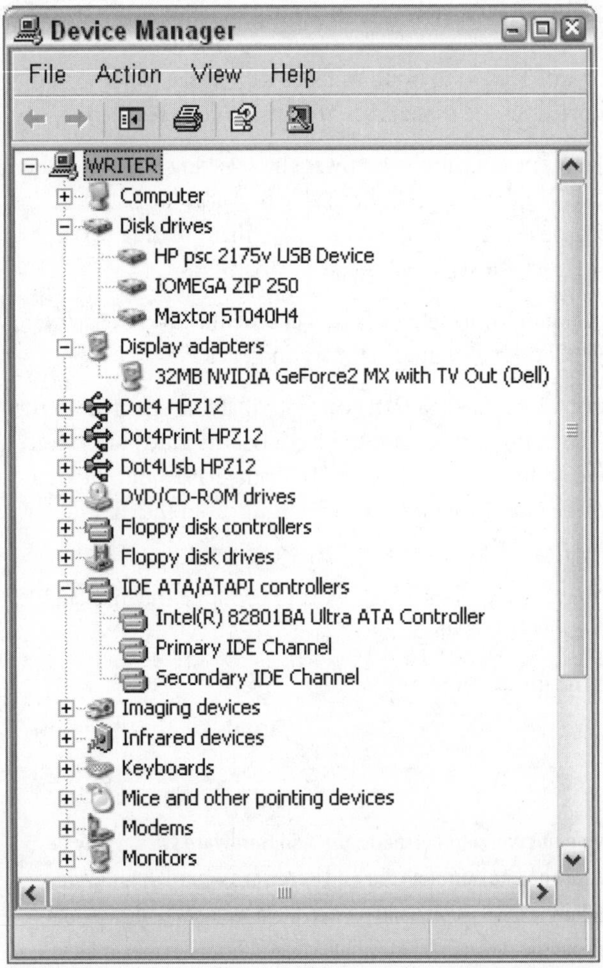

Figure 8-1: You can easily manage devices with the Device Manager.

You can easily look at all the hardware connected to your computer in this manner. If you right-click a hardware device, you'll see a context menu where you can update the driver, disable the device, uninstall it, scan for hardware changes, or access the device's properties.

You can also right-click any device and select Properties to access the Properties pages. Most devices show you a General, Driver, and Resources tab. Some specialty devices, such as printers and mice, have additional tabs that impact the configuration of those devices.

The General tab (see Figure 8-2) is a basic tab that primarily gives you information such as the device name, manufacturer, type, and where the device is installed on your system. The good thing about the General tab is that it tells you if Windows sees any problems with the device. Problems are displayed on the tab as an error message in the Device Status area. You can also disable the device by using the Device Usage drop-down list. If you want

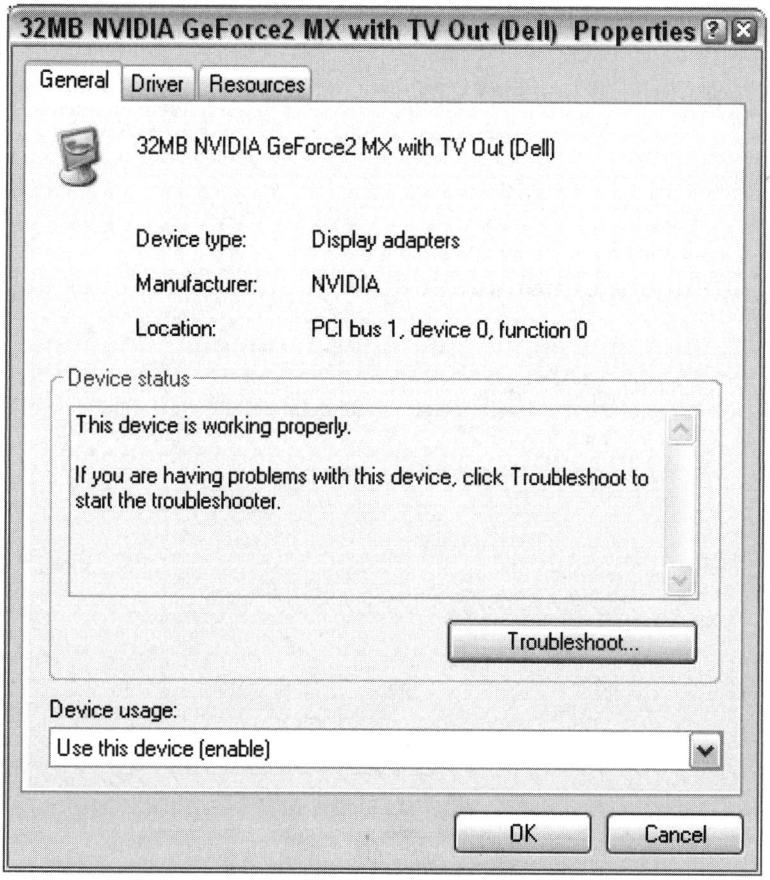

Figure 8-2: The General tab of a device's Properties page.

to disable a device, simply stop the device from working. The device remains installed on your system and you can re-enable it again from this tab, as needed.

Because driver management was such a problem in earlier versions of Windows, Windows XP seeks to relieve the difficultly of driver management with the Driver tab (also found in Windows 2000), which makes driver management much easier. I explore the management options in the next section.

On the Resources tab (see Figure 8-3) you'll see the memory ranges, I/O range, IRQ setting, and related hardware resource configuration for the device. When you install a plug and play device, the settings here are automatically configured by Windows XP and cannot be changed. This is good news because you don't have to deal with manual IRQ settings

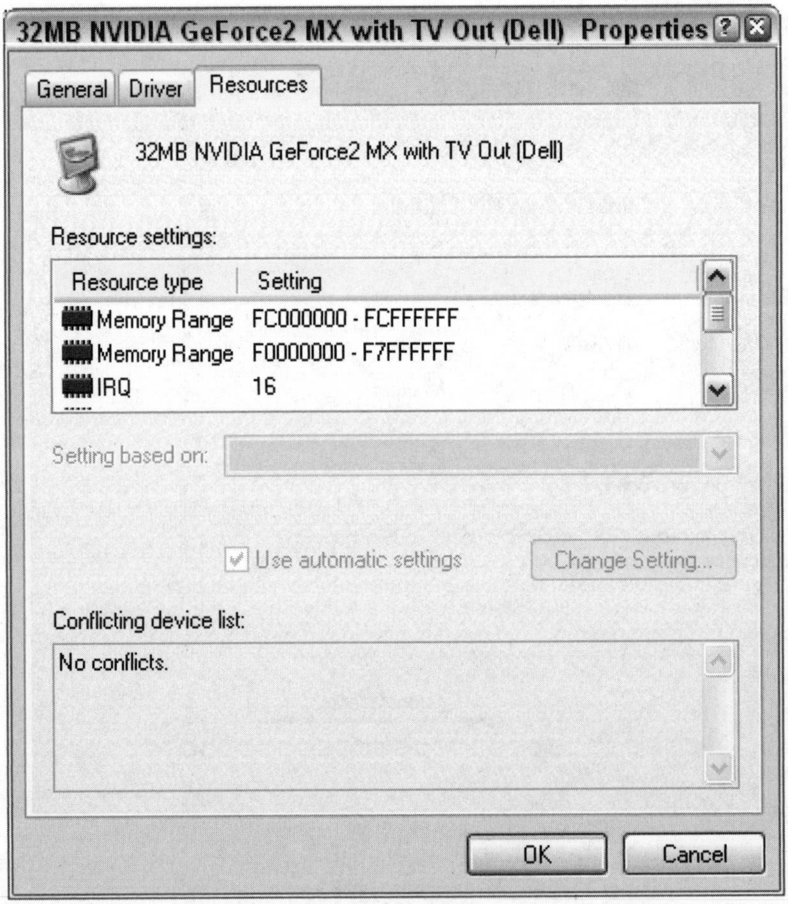

Figure 8-3: The Resources tab of a device's Properties page.

and the like. If you have manually installed a device, you may be able to make some adjustments here, as needed, but if you are using newer plug and play hardware (which you should if you want the best performance), you should not have to do anything on this tab.

Managing with Device Drivers and Driver Signing

As I've mentioned, a driver is a piece of software that enables an operating system to communicate and work with a piece of hardware. It is the hardware manufacturer's responsibility to develop drivers for their devices so that they work with Windows XP. When you purchase a new device for your computer, you typically get a disk or CD that contains the driver software to be installed. Because driver development is up to the device's manufacturer, Microsoft does not support problems with drivers—technical support will refer you to the hardware manufacturer that carries the burden of ensuring that drivers work the way they are supposed to. In most cases, the appropriate driver for Windows XP can be downloaded from the hardware device manufacturer's Web site. If not, Windows XP will try to use a generic driver in its database but there is no guarantee that the generic driver will work as expected.

The Driver tab (see Figure 8-4) gives you a few options to manage the device's driver. The design allows you to gather information quickly and update a driver (which installs new software) easily.

The Driver Details button gives you information about the driver, such as the location, provider, file version, copyright, and digital signer information. You can't do anything here but gather information about the driver, which can be helpful when you are trying to find out if the driver needs to be updated or not.

Naturally, you should use the latest driver available from the manufacturer for Windows XP. If you discover that you need to update the driver, download it from the hardware manufacturer's Web site and click the Update Driver button on this tab. This action launches the Hardware Update wizard that walks you through the steps to install the new driver.

The Driver tab also shows the Roll Back Device Driver button. When you install a new driver, the old one is kept for safety's sake. In the event that the new driver causes you problems, you can click the Roll Back button to go back to the previous driver. Essentially, this is a nice safety net for you.

Figure 8-4: The Driver tab of a device's Properties page.

If you ever want to uninstall a driver completely, click the Uninstall button. Windows XP uninstalls the driver, which also uninstalls the hardware. Then Windows XP detects the uninstalled hardware device as new hardware and attempt to reinstall it.

I should also mention the driver signing feature, which makes certain that the driver has been tested and will work with specified hardware in Windows XP, and that the driver comes from a valid source. Signed drivers have a digital signature stamp to ensure that they are from a reliable source. From a safety point of view, you should strive to use signed drivers that are actually developed by the hardware manufacturer. In some cases, you may need to use an unsigned driver. This is fine but you'll have to do a bit of research on your own to make sure the driver originates from a reliable source.

If you open System Properties and click the Hardware tab (see Figure 8-5) you see the Driver Signing button. Open the dialog box here to determine how driver signing is handled on your system.

Figure 8-5: The Driver Signing option on the Hardware tab in the System Properties dialog box.

Note

The Hardware Profiles button can be very helpful if you are using a portable computer. I discuss hardware profiles later in this chapter.

About CD/DVD-ROM Drives

CD and DVD-ROM (or combo) drives are standard on computers today. In many cases, computer systems now contain multiple CD/DVD drives and CD read/write drives. Like any hardware device, internal CD/DVD drives must be attached to the system and detected by plug and play. Windows XP typically identifies CD read/write drives as such.

The trick when installing new internal or external CD-ROM devices is to use devices that are listed on the HCL and make sure you have the most current driver. A secondary note about installation concerns audio playback. If you expand the CD/DVD category in the Device Manager, you'll see your CD/DVD drives listed. If you right-click the desired CD/DVD drive and select Properties, you'll see a Properties tab. You can adjust the overall CD volume here, as well as determine whether or not the drive is allowed to play audio CDs. If you are having problems with a CD-ROM drive not playing music, check the setting on this tab. You can also check the Volumes tab and see the partition setup of the CD, its capacity, status, and other general information about the state of the disc.

Other types of removable media drives—such as Zip, Jaz, or tape drives—function the same way. You can install them by connecting them to an appropriate port and allowing plug and play to detect the drives. From that point, you can install an appropriate driver.

Hardware Optimization and Management Tactics

The following sections point out some features and configuration that you may want to check out to optimize and manage your hardware.

Stopping the Unsigned Driver Dialog Box

The unsigned driver dialog box pops up whenever you try to install an unsigned driver is designed as a safety net for you. The warning can become rather aggravating, however, especially if you are a pro at installing hardware and drivers and are not particularly worried about whether the driver is signed or not. With Windows XP Professional, you can stop this dialog box from appearing. Follow these steps:

1. Select Start ➪ Run, type **gpedit.msc**, and click OK.
2. Navigate to User Configuration ➪ Administrative Templates ➪ System (see Figure 8-6).

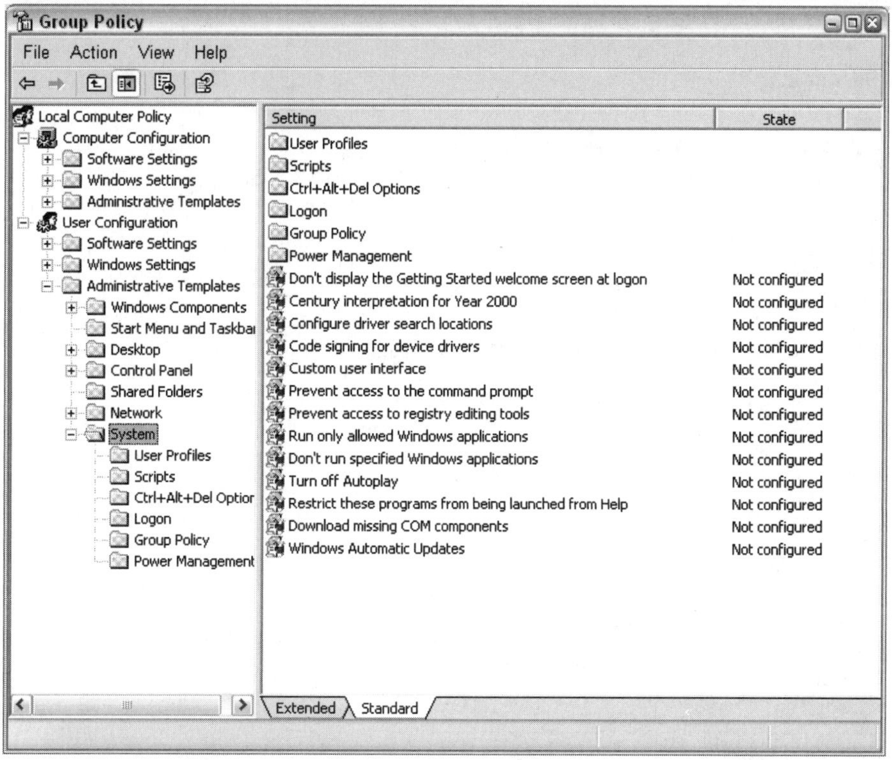

Figure 8-6: The Group Policy console.

3. In the right pane, right-click the "Code signing for device drivers" icon and select Properties.
4. Click the Enabled option button and, in the drop-down menu that appears, choose Ignore (see Figure 8-7).
5. Click OK to close the Group Policy console.

Tip

You can also configure this setting by accessing System Properties. On the Hardware tab, click the Driver Signing button and choose the Ignore option in the dialog box that appears.

Showing Hidden Devices in the Device Manager

Some devices that are actually installed on your computer may not appear in the Device Manager. In other words, the device may no longer be technically present on the computer,

Figure 8-7: Enable the setting and choose the Ignore option.

yet the drivers are still installed; therefore, the computer thinks the device is still installed. This problem may happen with older hardware installed in Windows XP. To make sure you have no "hidden" devices, open the Device Manager and select View ➪ Show Hidden Devices. This action lets you see any hidden devices so you can uninstall them from the computer, as needed.

Solving Mouse Problems in Games

If you have any problems with mouse performance, especially when you are playing computer games, two mouse settings could be the culprit. You can easily disable these settings and see if they help the mouse's performance:

1. Open the Mouse applet in the Control Panel.
2. Click the Pointer Options tab.
3. On the Pointer Options tab, uncheck "Enhance pointer precision" and "Show location of pointer when I press the CTRL key" (see Figure 8-8).
4. Click OK to close the dialog box.

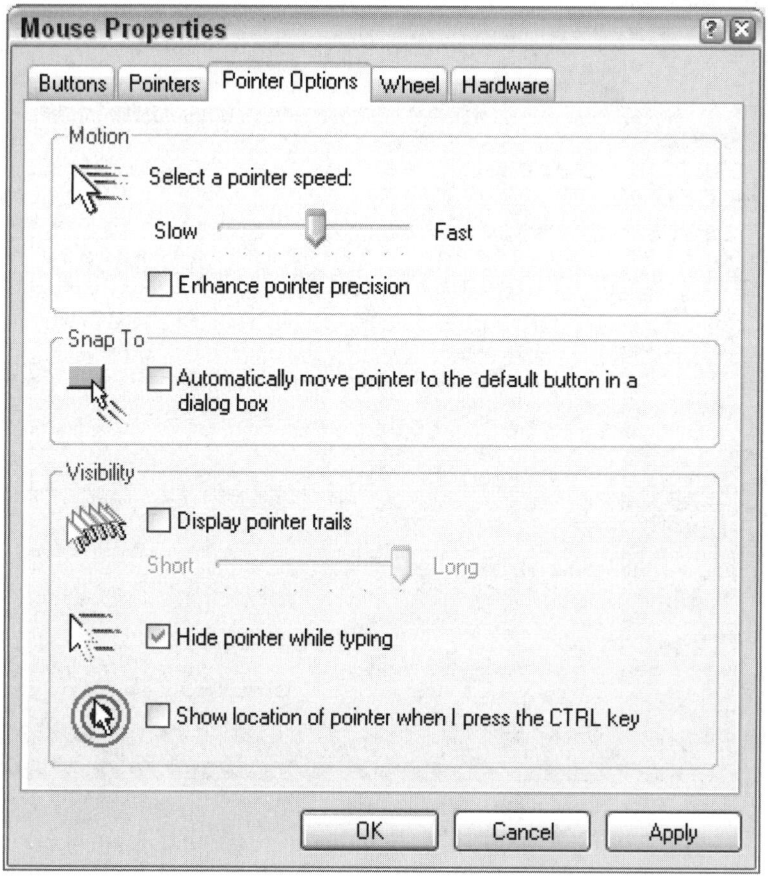

Figure 8-8: Mouse pointer options.

Using Tweak-XP Pro

There are a number of utilities that tweak various portions of Windows XP. I enjoy Tweak-XP Pro, available from `www.totalidea.com`. You can download and use this utility for

30 executions; after that, you have to pay $30 to continue using it. Tweak-XP Pro has many different settings you can easily invoke, and it has some hardware tweaks you may find helpful as well.

When you open the utility, choose the desired category and then click the desired tab to review the tweaks you can make (see Figure 8-9). Overall, the utility is very handy and easy to use, so check it out.

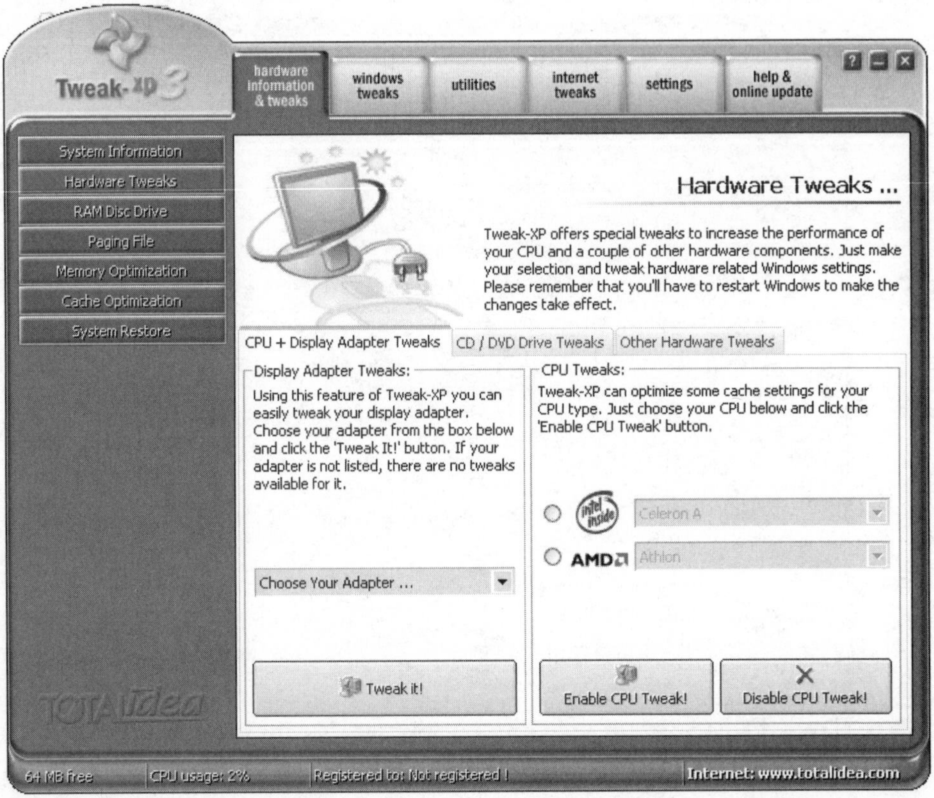
Tweak-XP 3
hardware information & tweaks
windows tweaks
utilities
internet tweaks
settings
help & online update
System Information
Hardware Tweaks
RAM Disc Drive
Paging File
Memory Optimization
Cache Optimization
System Restore
Hardware Tweaks ...
Tweak-XP offers special tweaks to increase the performance of your CPU and a couple of other hardware components. Just make your selection and tweak hardware related Windows settings. Please remember that you'll have to restart Windows to make the changes take effect.
CPU + Display Adapter Tweaks
CD / DVD Drive Tweaks
Other Hardware Tweaks
Display Adapter Tweaks:
Using this feature of Tweak-XP you can easily tweak your display adapter. Choose your adapter from the box below and click the 'Tweak It!' button. If your adapter is not listed, there are no tweaks available for it.
Choose Your Adapter ...
Tweak it!
CPU Tweaks:
Tweak-XP can optimize some cache settings for your CPU type. Just choose your CPU below and click the 'Enable CPU Tweak' button.
Celeron A
AMD
Athlon
Enable CPU Tweak!
Disable CPU Tweak!
64 MB free
CPU usage: 2%
Registered to: Not registered !
Internet: www.totalidea.com

Figure 8-9: Tweak-XP Pro for Windows XP.

Creating a Hardware Profile

If you are using a portable computer, such as a laptop, a hardware profile is one solution that can make your computer boot faster and run more quickly. It tells the computer what hardware to enable and use depending on the circumstance. For example, suppose your laptop connects to a docking station at your office. When you are at the office, you use an external keyboard, mouse, printer, and a few USB peripherals. However, when you travel, your laptop does not use any of these devices. You can create a hardware profile that you invoke when you travel so that all of those hardware devices you don't use are disabled. This should help the laptop boot more quickly and conserve system resources when you are on the road.

You can create as many hardware profiles as you need, and they are easy to create. The following steps show you how to create a hardware profile:

1. Open the Start menu and select Control Panel ➪ System Properties.
2. Click the Hardware tab and then click the Hardware Profiles button.
3. In the Hardware Profiles dialog box that appears, a default profile is listed (see Figure 8-10). Click the Properties button to see the standard configuration

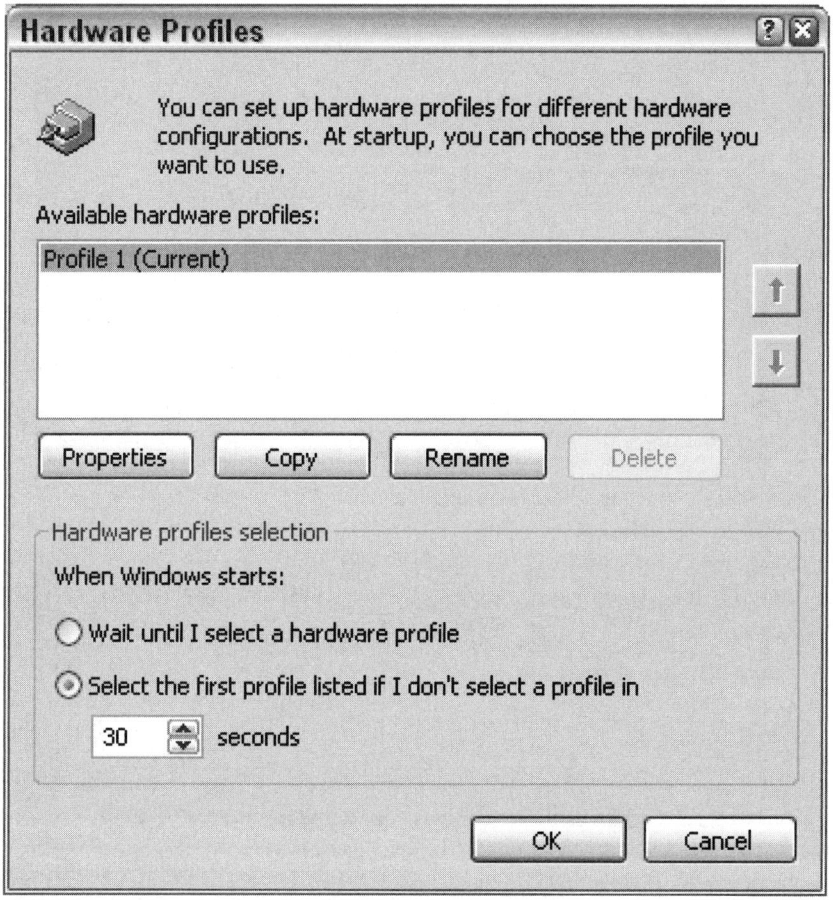

Figure 8-10: Each computer has a default hardware profile.

of the default profile. You can choose to make the default profile the docked or undocked state. Because all installed hardware is available in the default profile, keep the default profile as the docked state.

4. Click the Copy button. This action creates a duplicate of the default profile. Enter a name for the copy (such as **Undocked**) and click OK. You now have two identical profiles. But you don't want two identical profiles so now you need to reconfigure the new profiles in a way that is useful to you.

5. Select the new profile and click Properties. In the Properties dialog box, make this profile the undocked profile and click the "Always include this profile as an option when Windows starts" check box (see Figure 8-11). Click OK.

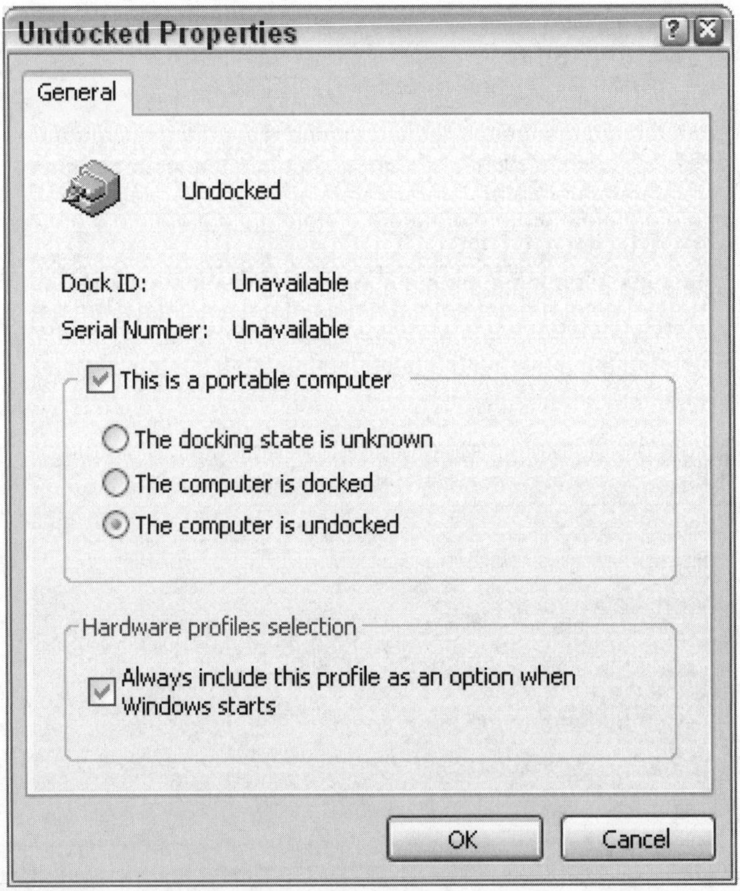

Figure 8-11: New hardware profile properties.

6. Close everything on your computer and restart it. A boot menu now appears listing the two hardware profiles. Choose the Undocked hardware profile and allow the computer to finish booting. Log on with Administrator privileges.
7. Open the Device Manager and systematically work through it, disabling devices that you do not to use when the computer is undocked. This action does not remove those devices from your computer; it simply disables them for this particular profile.
8. After you are done, you can choose the desired hardware profile each time you boot your computer. Because you have disabled unneeded devices when the computer is undocked, you should see better performance when you are mobile.

Chapter 9

Optimizing Display Performance

To optimize your monitor display so that it works the way you want it to work, you need to configure the settings within Display Properties. The settings that are available to you here may be able to fix or change issues or problems that you are currently experiencing with your display. If you are already an old pro at configuring display settings, you can skip this section and move on to the rest of the chapter, which explores other optimization features that can speed up your video display.

Display Properties

The following sections show you how to optimize your display settings, which you can access by right-clicking an empty portion of the desktop and selecting Properties to open the Display Properties dialog box.

Themes

A theme is a group of settings applied to Windows XP that make your display look a certain way. If you've used Windows before, you are familiar with the concept of themes. Windows 95 gave you some options for sounds and Windows 98 gave you a whole list of themes that completely revamped the desktop, such as "Mystery," "The 70s," and "Underwater." The Windows XP look is a theme in and of itself, which you can see selected on the Themes tab in the Display Properties dialog box (see Figure 9-1).

The Themes option is placed here in Windows XP because the default Windows XP interface is one among a number of themes from which to choose. By default, the Windows

Figure 9-1: Themes tab in the Display Properties dialog box.

XP theme is used, but you can also choose the Windows Classic theme as well. The Classic theme resembles Windows 2000, Windows Me, and Windows 9x. Of course, once you get used to Windows XP, most people opt for the default theme because it has a number of interface improvements compared to the older versions of Windows. If you want to use the Classic theme, click the drop-down menu on the Themes tab and choose Windows Classic. If you want to modify the current Windows XP theme, you can do so on other tabs available in Display Properties.

Desktop

The second tab in the Display Properties dialog box is the Desktop tab (see Figure 9-2), which determines how your Windows XP desktop area should look. Here you decide what color, style, or picture appears on your desktop.

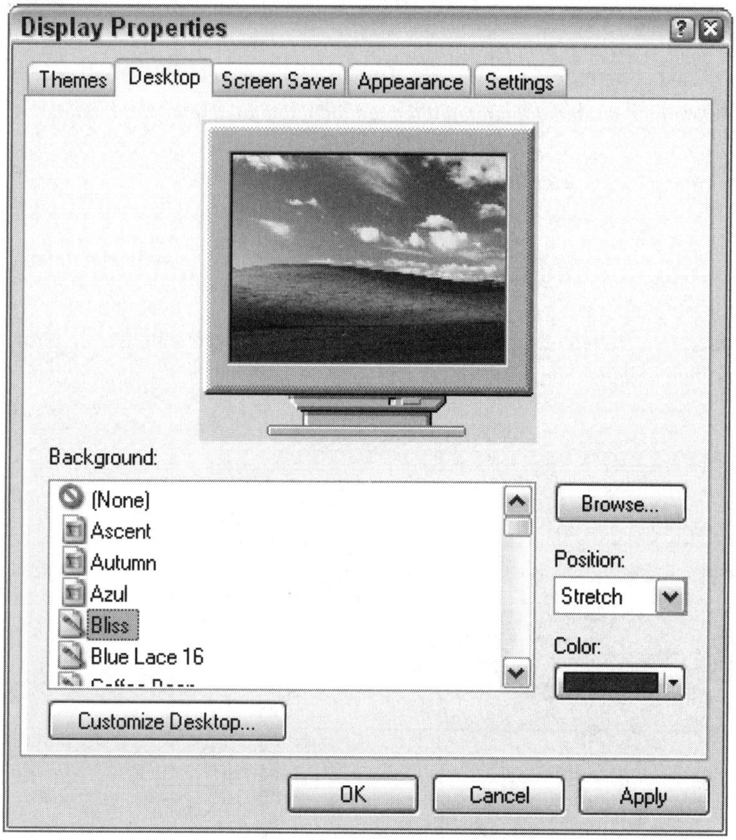

Figure 9-2: Desktop tab in the Display Properties dialog box.

Windows XP gives you several built-in options that you can choose for your background. Background patterns and pictures consist of JPEG, BMP, GIF, and related picture file formats, as well as HyperText Markup Language (HTML) files.

On the Desktop tab, you see a number of background options. Select a desired background to see a preview of it in the monitor graphic. Note that you can adjust the position and color for some of the items that you might select. Generally, you can adjust the position of patterns as well as the overall color, but the adjustments do not have any effect on the main picture.

Click the Browse button to select photos from other locations on your computer for use as your desktop photo.

Finally, clicking the Customize Desktop button at the bottom of the Desktop tab takes you to the Desktop Items properties page, which contains General and Web tabs. The several different configuration items on these pages are self-explanatory.

Screen Savers

The Screen Saver tab is easy to use. Just use the drop-down menu to select a screen saver, and a sample of it will be displayed in the test window. Once you find one you like, click the Apply button. Notice that you can also directly access Power options from this tab by clicking the Power button (you can access Power options in Control Panel, as well).

Appearance

The Appearance tab (see Figure 9-3) enables you to pick an appearance scheme for your Windows XP desktop.

Figure 9-3: Appearance tab in the Display Properties dialog box.

Essentially, these options override the theme's default settings and allow you to customize the look of Windows XP. You don't have to make any changes here, but this is a good place to adjust certain qualities in the theme that you do not like. You can use the drop-down menus to change the appearance of windows and buttons, color schemes, and font sizes. Click the Effects button to open the Effects dialog box, where you can find basic check box options, such as fade, menu shadows, and so on. Clicking the Advanced button allows you to make specific font and color changes to different Windows components, such as menus, buttons, active title bar, and so on.

Tip

Click the Effects button to turn off some of the effects you could do without. Although nice, these visual effects increase graphical display overhead and contribute to a slower system overall.

Settings

The Settings tab is where you configure the display properties and video card performance to meet your needs. These settings are important to have an optimized display:

1. In the left portion of the Settings tab is a Screen Resolution slider. Drag the slider bar (see Figure 9-4) to a different setting and then click Apply. The Monitor Settings dialog box appears, allowing you to keep the new setting or not. You have 15 seconds to confirm the change; otherwise it reverts to its previous setting.
2. Adjust the color quality settings from the drop-down menu. Use the highest color quality settings that the video card supports, such as "Highest (32 bit)".
3. Click the Advanced button on the Settings tab. Several additional tabs appear. The standard tabs you see are General, Adapter, Monitor, Troubleshoot, and Color Management. You may see additional tabs, as well. These tabs are specific to your computer's video card and are determined by the video card software you install.
4. On the General tab (see Figure 9-5), you have two sections: Display and Compatibility. Under Display, you can change the DPI (dots per inch) setting to compensate for small screen items under your current resolution. The default is 96. This feature, however, does not adjust the font or color size. Under

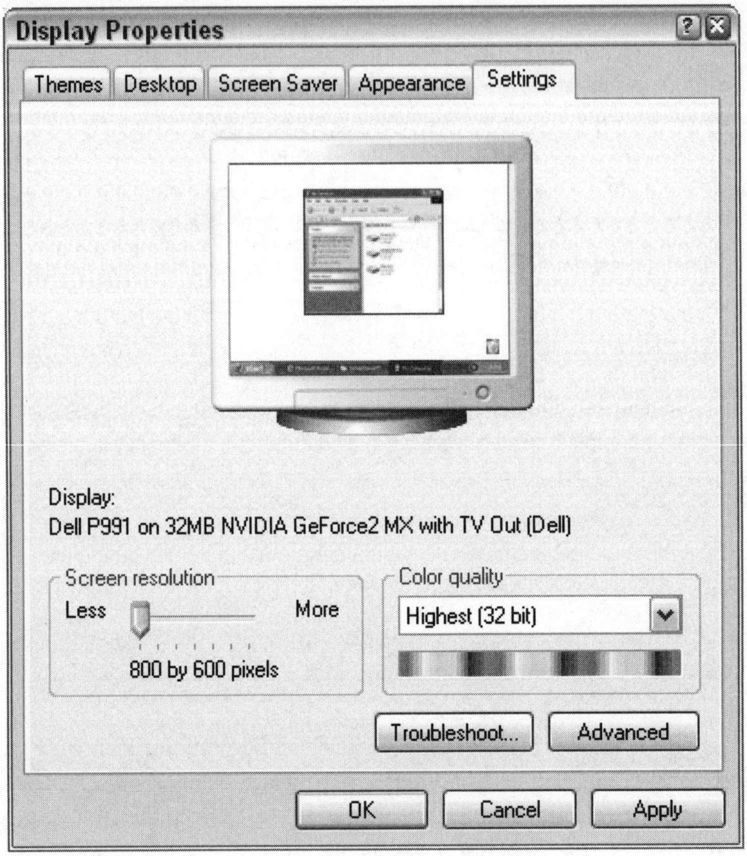

Figure 9-4: Settings tab in the Display Properties dialog box.

Compatibility, you can make the computer restart after changes are made to display settings. This feature is available because some programs may not work correctly if no reboot occurs. The default setting is "Apply the new display settings without restarting" but you can choose a different option button, depending on your needs.

5. On the Adapter tab, you can read basic information about your video adapter (see Figure 9-6). You can also click Properties to access the Device Manager's properties pages for the video card. If you click the List All Modes button, you see all screen resolution modes that are supported by the video card.

6. On the Monitor tab (see Figure 9-7) you can access the Device Manager properties for the monitor by clicking the Properties button. You can also adjust

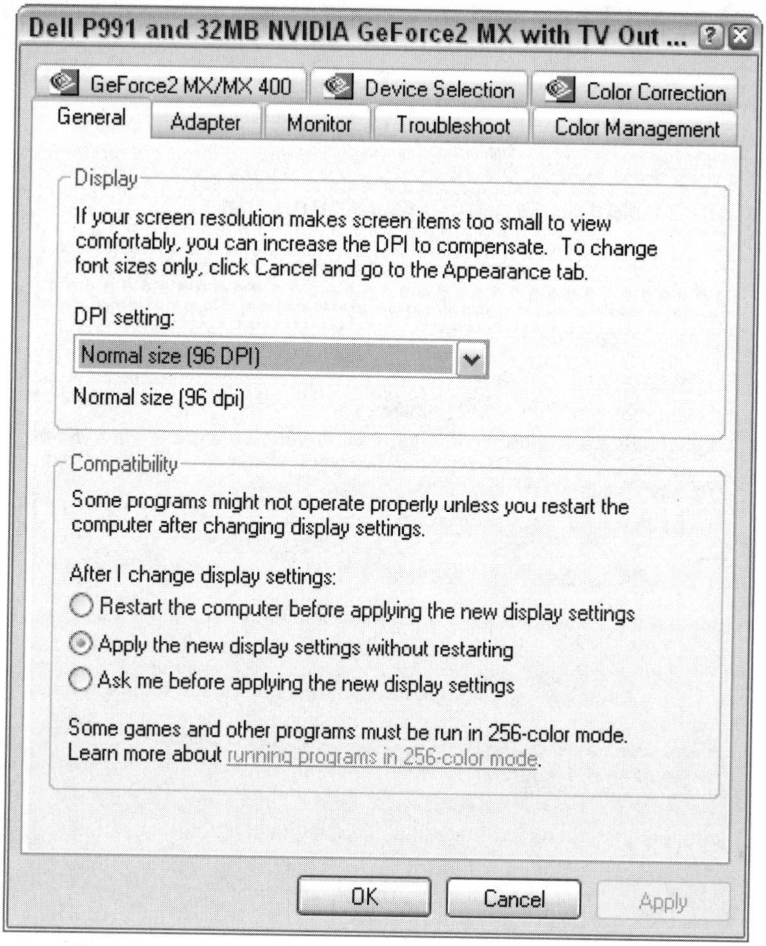

Figure 9-5: General tab in the monitor's advanced Display Properties dialog box.

the screen refresh rate. Higher refresh rates reduce screen flicker (but you'll need a quality video card to use a higher refresh rate). Default settings typically fall between 75 to 85 Hertz. Also note the setting that allows you to hide modes that are not supported by the monitor—this makes certain that an incompatible setting cannot be accidentally selected on the Settings tab.

7. On the Troubleshoot tab, you have two setting options. The first enables you to adjust the hardware acceleration of the video card. The typical setting is Full but you can gradually decrease the setting to troubleshoot performance problems with the video card. Of course, lower acceleration settings also mean lower

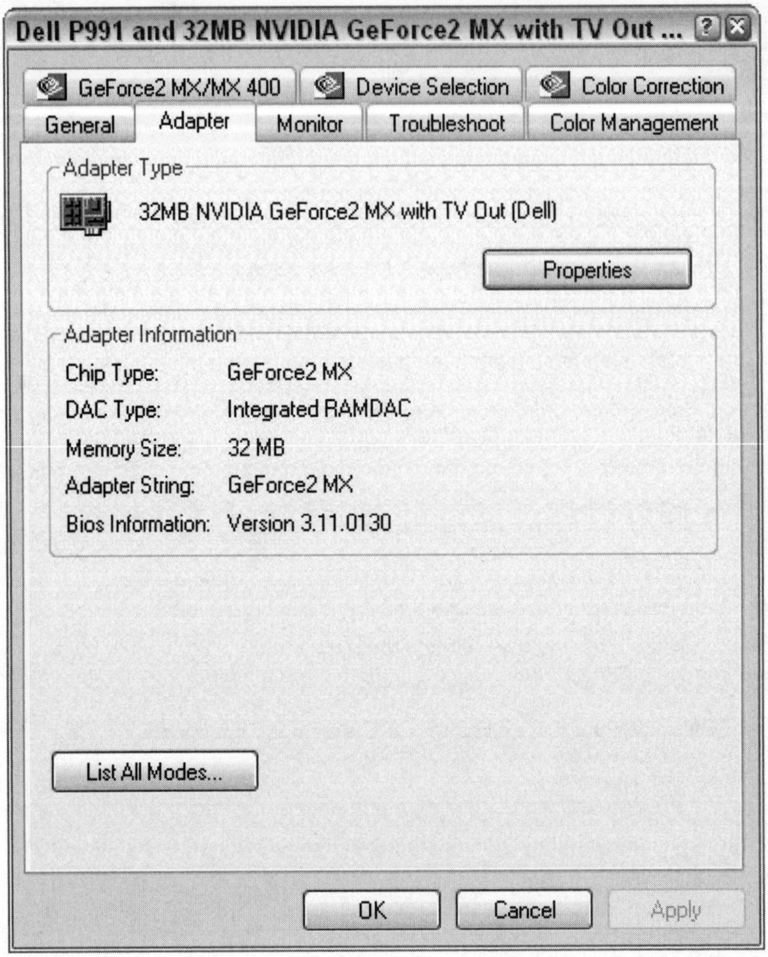

Figure 9-6: Adapter tab in the monitor's advanced Display Properties dialog box.

performance. When you move the slider bar down, you'll see a description of the impact the lower setting has on video performance. You also have the option to use Write Combining, which provides graphics data to your screen faster, thereby improving performance. However, some video cards cannot keep up with this setting. If you are having distortion problems, try clearing this check box.

8. The Color Management tab allows you to choose a color profile for your specific monitor, which determines how colors are displayed. If you click the Add button, you see a list of profiles that are available by default. Choosing a color profile

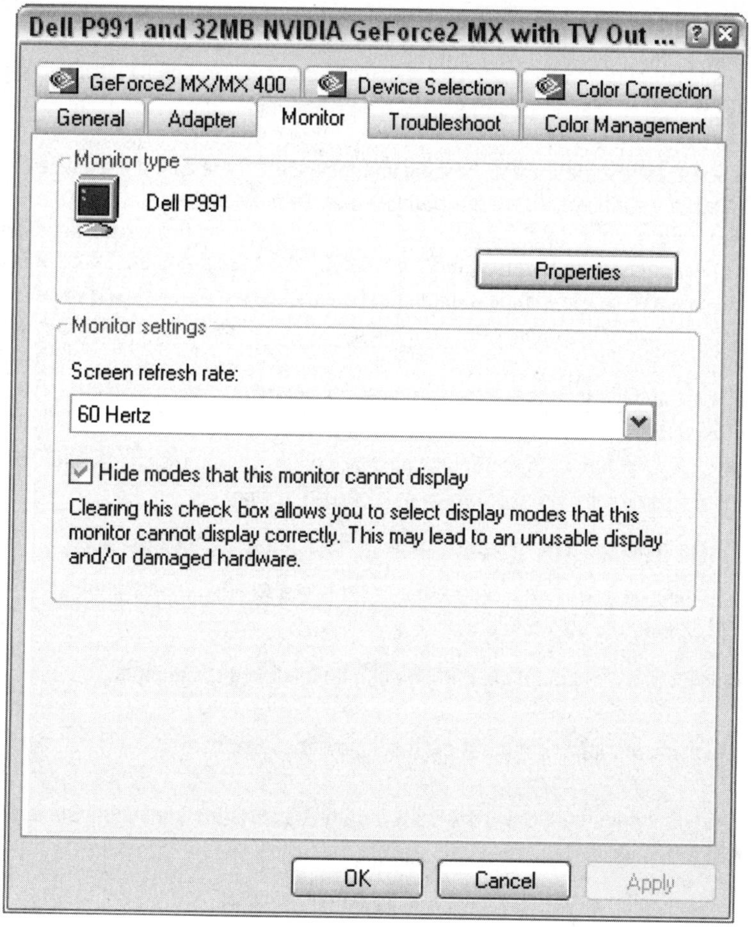

Figure 9-7: Monitor tab in the monitor's advanced Display Properties dialog box.

specific to your monitor's make and model may improve color performance. As a general rule, unless you have color-specific problems, do not use a color profile because this may limit your monitor's color capabilities.

Multiple Monitors and Windows XP

Windows XP supports multiple monitors. This means you can run different applications on different screens, essentially increasing your workspace—and your productivity. With Windows XP and the right hardware, you can connect up to 10 individual monitors to a single PC. Using multiple monitors even allows you to position items between monitors. For

Multiple Monitors and Windows XP *(Continued)*

example, suppose you have a spreadsheet with many columns. You could stretch the file among two monitors so that all columns are visible without horizontal scrolling.

When you use multiple monitors, one monitor serves as the primary monitor where the Windows logon screen appears. You can use multiple video cards with different settings or you can use a single video card that has multiple outputs to which you connect the monitors. Regardless of the configuration you choose, use Display Properties to adjust the appearance of each monitor. By the way, Windows XP also supports a dual-view feature. This does the same thing as multiple monitors but is used on laptop computers where the laptop screen is always the primary monitor and the attached desktop monitor serves as a second viewing area.

When setting up multiple monitors, there are a few basic rules to keep in mind:

- If the computer has a video adapter built into the motherboard, the built-in adapter must be used as the video graphics array (VGA) device.
- Monitors in the multiple monitor setup must use either PCI or AGP slots.
- The Peripheral Component Interconnect (PCI) and Accelerated Graphics Port (AGP) cards cannot use VGA resources.
- Only Windows XP–compatible drivers can be used on the monitors.

To set up a multiple monitor configuration, just follow these steps:

1. Turn off the computer. Follow the manufacturer's instructions to install the new PCI or AGP video card.
2. Attach a monitor to the new card and boot the computer.
3. Windows XP plug and play will detect the new card and install it.
4. Right-click an empty area of the desktop and select Properties. Click the Settings tab. You'll see two monitor icons on the tab. Select the monitor that you want to use as the secondary monitor. If the primary monitor is an onboard video adapter built into the motherboard, it must be the primary monitor.
5. Click the "Extend my Windows desktop onto this monitor" check box.
6. Adjust the resolution and color scheme settings as desired for the monitor and click OK.

To add more monitors to the configuration, repeat Steps 1–6.

Display Optimization and Speed Solutions

Once your display and video card are configured the way you want, you can turn your attention to optimization and speed. Only a few issues concerning the optimization of your video card require consideration. The following sections explore these issues.

Using Compatible Video Cards and Correct Drivers

The most important aspect of video card performance and optimization is using a video card that is compatible with Windows XP and the proper driver for the card. Most video cards you purchase are currently compatible with Windows XP, and drivers are specifically developed for the Windows XP operating system. If you upgraded to Windows XP from an older computer system, you may be using an older video card and older drivers. If the card is compatible, you should check for updated drivers at the video card manufacturer's Web site. Correct drivers will solve many issues and problems, so make sure that yours are up to date.

Cross-Reference

See Chapter 8 to learn more about device drivers and hardware.

Reducing Visual Effects

If your system tends to be a bit sluggish, one thing you can do is reduce the overall visual effects provided in Windows XP. These visual effects, while nice-looking, tend to eat up memory and processor cycles, which is noticeable if you don't have many to spare. (Refer to Chapter 2 for details.)

Making BIOS Adjustments for Faster Performance

Concerning video card performance, you may be able to adjust settings to your computer's basic input/output system (BIOS) to help speed up graphics and what you see on your screen. BIOS settings vary from computer to computer, so check your PC's specific setup instructions about accessing the BIOS settings and making changes to it. Generally, though, enabling a couple of settings may make things a bit speedier concerning graphics and display:

- **AGP Fast Write:** This setting for AGP video cards enables the processor to communicate directly with the graphics processor instead of sending data through the computer system's memory. This should give you a performance boost. Most newer video cards support the AGP Fast Write feature, and you can typically find the setting in the BIOS section for advanced chipset features.
- **AGP Master 1WS Write/Read:** This AGP BIOS setting can improve your graphics because the setting speeds up write and read performance. This setting is typically found in the BIOS under advanced chipset features. You'll see settings for both read and write. Make sure they are both enabled.
- **Video Memory Cache Mode:** This setting, if supported by the computer's BIOS, provides two different options. You should see a UC (uncacheable) setting and a UCWC (uncacheable speculative write-combining) setting. The UCWC setting typically gives you better performance because the video card is allowed to buffer information moving between the processor and the video memory. UC disables this feature, so if your BIOS supports UCWC, make sure it is enabled.

Overclocking Video Cards

Overclocking is the process of running the video card's speed at a faster rate than is published to support. In reality, most hardware devices, such as video cards and processors, can run faster than stated. Overclocking takes advantage of that feature. In many cases, you can see some performance gain by overclocking. However, you may also experience problems, so some experimentation is in order to determine whether overclocking really helps you any.

You can overclock a video card if the card supports the feature. ATI and Nvidia are two common video cards that support overclocking. Nvidia video cards natively support overclocking but you have to edit the Registry to enable the feature:

1. Select Start ⇨ Run, type **regedit**, and click OK.
2. Navigate to HKEY_LOCAL_MACHINE\Software\NVIDIA Corporation\Global\NVTweak.
3. Create a new DWORD and call it **Coolbits**. Give the DWORD a value of 3.
4. Restart your computer.

Once you do this, you'll see an additional tab found on the Advanced Properties pages accessible through Display Properties ➪ Advanced tab. You can then adjust the graphics processing unit (GPU) and memory clock speeds using this tab.

If you use an ATI video card, there is no built-in feature for overclocking but you can use the Radlinker utility, which is third-party software, to enable this feature. Download the Radlinker utility from WebTechGeek (`www.webtechgeek.com`), where you can learn more about using and configuring this utility.

Caution

Although overclocking can give you a performance boost, it is important to remember that you are squeezing more life from the hardware than it may have been designed to provide. Some hardware devices, such as display adapters, may overheat if you overclock them. Therefore, overclocking can be detrimental to your hardware. Keep this in mind if you decide to try the overclocking technique.

Part III

Internet, E-mail, and Digital Media

IN THIS PART

Chapter 10

Making the Internet Work Faster

The Internet was a most fascinating technology development that ultimately changed and continues to affect the entire world. Information barriers are broken and many of us have the ability to communicate with each other in ways never before imagined. But for all the Internet is today, the greatest complaint is that it is slow. Instead of the World Wide Web, we have the World Wide Wait. Yet Internet servers and Internet backbones are fast and have much bandwidth to offer. The problem isn't that the Internet is particularly slow but that it seems slow to us—the problem is typically on our end, in our computers and Internet connections.

The nagging question remains how to get more speed from the Internet. The answer to that question is a bit complicated because using the Internet requires different hardware and software pieces. To squeeze extra speed and power from the Internet, you have to be savvy about a variety of settings and techniques, which I explore in this chapter.

Managing Temporary Internet Files

In previous chapters I explored the concept of cleaning out junk. After all, your PC is a storehouse of information and the system can get bogged down trying to manage too many files. You need to keep that junk pile cleaned up as much as possible. Using the Internet is no exception to this rule. After all, Web pages are HTML documents that are full of other components, such as text, figures, photos, graphics, and so on. As you use the Internet, caches all the pages and objects you view. The idea is that the browser can reuse what is in the cache instead of having to download those same objects over and over. This is fine and useful but, once again, you should strive to strike a balance between downloading items and keeping too much junk on your PC that your browser has to sift through when browsing the Internet.

On one side of the scale, the Internet Explorer (IE) browser is preconfigured to manage all of this stuff without your intervention. Indeed, many users do not even know that a cache exists or that it can be managed, but IE also gives you some settings you should examine that allow you to determine how long all of the temporary Internet files and history settings are maintained. That's good news, and the settings are easy to configure.

Open the Start menu and select Control Panel ➪ Internet Options. If Internet Explorer is already open, you can just click Tools ➪ Internet Options. Either way, you arrive at the Internet Explorer properties dialog box. Select the General tab (see Figure 10-1).

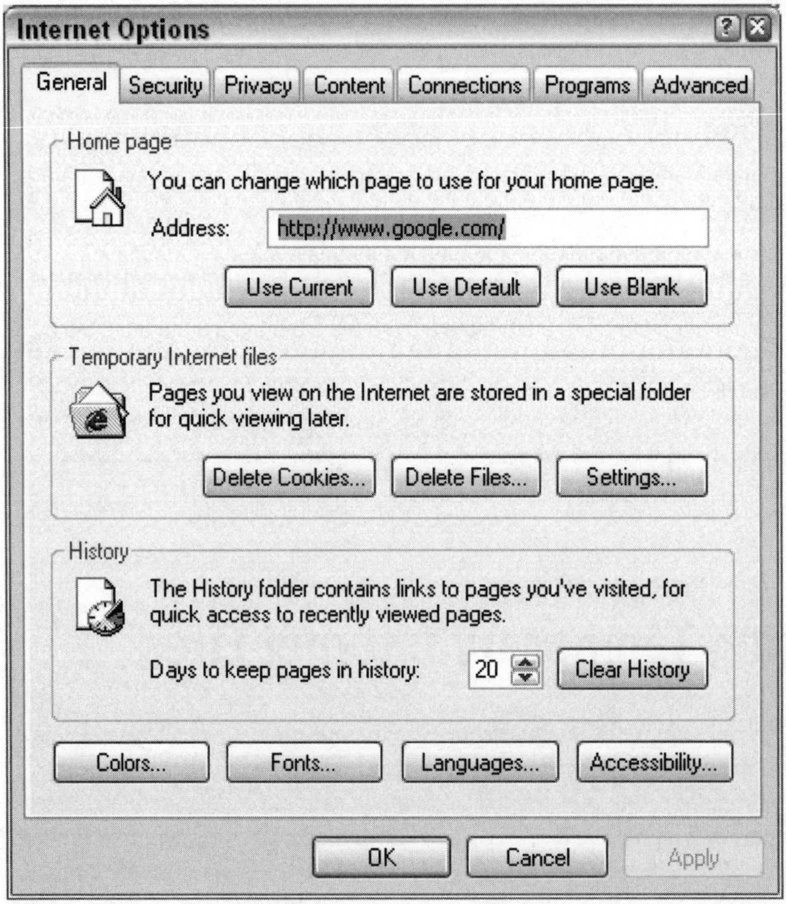

Figure 10-1: General tab of the Internet Options dialog box.

Notice the Temporary Internet Files section. Here you can delete cookies, delete files, and access settings. I discuss cookies and cookie management in Chapter 12, but notice that you can simply delete all temporary Internet files at any time by clicking the Delete Files button. Occasionally, I recommend that you come here and simply delete all temporary Internet files. Internet Explorer can manage the cached files but it doesn't hurt to lose all of them periodically and let Internet Explorer rebuild a new file cache, depending on your Web surfing needs. The important button here is the Settings button, which allows you to configure how Internet Explorer manages temporary Internet files.

Once you click Settings, the Settings dialog box appears (see Figure 10-2). By default, Internet Explorer is set to manage the temporary files automatically. As a general rule, this is your best setting. Notice that a percentage of your computer's hard disk space is used for storage purposes (generally about 10 percent). You can reduce or increase this allowance, if desired. Generally, the defaults work well but if you have a very fast Internet connection and temporary files are not that important to you in terms of speed, you can reduce the amount of disk space reserved for this purpose. If you have a slow Internet connection, you should leave these settings as they are and even bump up the disk space, if you have room to spare.

Figure 10-2: Settings tab for temporary Internet files.

You can also move the folder and view the temporary Internet files and objects. Moving the folder is not going to give you any additional speed—unless your computer has more than one hard disk and one hard disk controller. In this case, moving the temporary files folder to the second hard disk may yield some performance improvement because Internet Explorer can most likely read from the secondary disk more quickly than it can from the primary disk.

In other cases, you may not want Internet Explorer to maintain temporary files at all. You can invoke a setting that deletes all temporary files each time you exit IE. Aside from keeping clutter down to a minimum, this is also a good security feature. Suppose you manage some stocks and private accounts online. Because IE puts those pages in temporary Internet files, someone else that has access to your computer can simply use the General tab to view those pages. If they are automatically deleted each time you close IE, there will be nothing to view. If you want to enable this setting, open Internet Options and click the Advanced tab. Under the Security category, select the check box option to "Empty Temporary Internet Files when browser is closed" (see Figure 10-3).

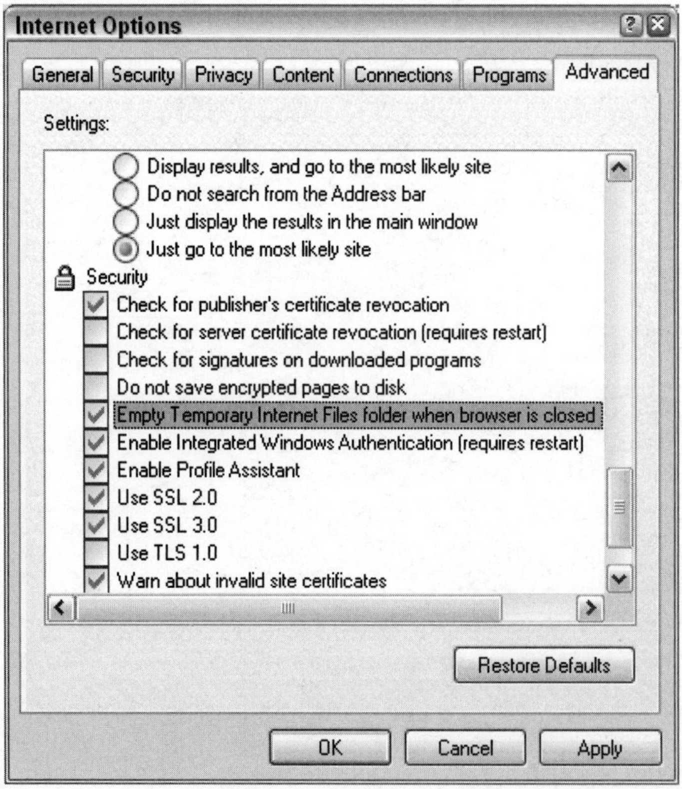

Figure 10-3: Use the Advanced tab to make sure temporary Internet files are deleted when you close the browser.

Tip

You may also want to enable the "Do not save encrypted pages to disk" setting. Any secure pages you are accessing will not be saved locally at all, which is another nice security feature.

Configuring Internet Explorer to Speed Up Internet Usage

Now that you know a few things about managing temporary Internet files, it's time to look at an assortment of settings and tricks that will help you speed up Internet Explorer. Later in this chapter I discuss fixes to help speed up the actual Internet connection itself.

Managing the Browser History

The History feature records all Web sites you visit. The idea is that you will be able to go back and see where you've been should you lose track of a URL—a good feature, but it also clutters things up and allows anyone else who is using your computer to see what you've been doing. You can easily stop the History feature from working. By default, history is maintained for 20 days and then deleted. If you are happy with that feature, just leave it alone. If you want to delete the history on a manual basis or reduce the number of days that history is maintained, go to the General tab of Internet Options (see Figure 10-1). However, if you want to stop the history from working altogether, change the day feature on the General tab to 0. This prevents the history from recording at all.

Stopping the Home Page

When you first start Internet Explorer, a default home page appears. The default home page may be the Microsoft company home page or that of your computer manufacturer. You can change the default page to something you like better or lose it completely so that you can go immediately to the page you want when you open Internet Explorer. Access the General tab; and under the Home Page section, change the URL as desired. If you don't want to see a default page at all, just clear the URL box so that it's empty, and then click OK.

Stopping FTP Folder View

If you are an FTP user, you have probably noticed the annoying FTP folder view in Internet Explorer. Besides slowing you down as you try to maneuver through an FTP site, folder view has a tendency to work more slowly as you upload and manipulate files. You can easily stop this folder view option and hopefully make FTP respond easier and faster. Return to Internet Options and click the Advanced tab. Under Browsing, clear the "Enable folder view for FTP sites" check box (see Figure 10-4).

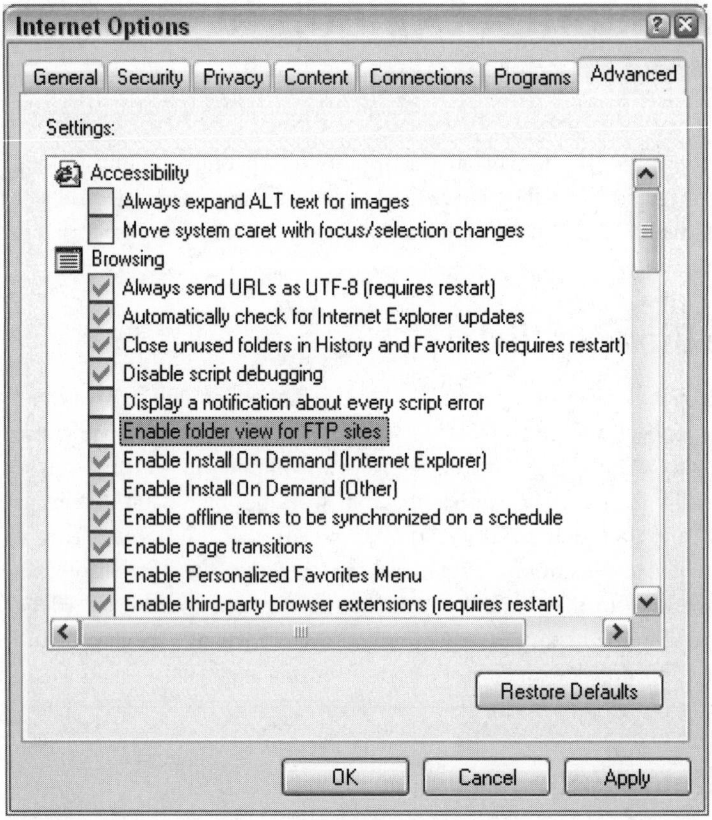

Figure 10-4: Turning off FTP folder view.

Tip

By default, Internet Explorer automatically checks `www.microsoft.com` **for updates. If you have a slow Internet connection, automatic checkup can eat up your bandwidth and make Web surfing even slower than normal. Stop this behavior by clearing the "Automatically check for**

Internet Explorer updates" option on the Advanced tab under Browsing (the option is visible in Figure 10-4).

Using Passive FTP

If your computer is behind a firewall or you use a DSL modem with a firewall feature, you may have trouble accessing FTP sites with Internet Explorer. You can quickly and easily solve this problem by enabling passive FTP. This feature allows you to connect to those sites and bypass the interference of the firewall. Essentially, this feature allows a different type of connection to the FTP server that does not violate typical firewall rules. To enable passive FTP, go to Internet Options and click the Advanced tab. Under Browsing, click the "Use Passive FTP option" option, and click OK.

Stopping Script Errors

When Internet Explorer attempts to load a page, there can be script errors. In many cases, you can use the Web page just fine but, by default, Internet Explorer is configured to tell you every time there is a script error. This can lead to those aggravating script error windows you are probably familiar with. You can easily stop this behavior. Open Internet Options and access the Advanced tab. Under Browsing, clear the option to "Display a notification about every script error" and click OK.

Increasing the DNS Cache Size

The Domain Name System (DNS) is a record of all domain names on the Internet. When you type in a URL, the URL has to be resolved to a TCP/IP address through a series of domain name servers on the Internet. As you resolve these host names to IP addresses, Windows XP maintains a DNS cache of those items. When you want to visit a Web site, the cache is first inspected to see if the domain name has already been resolved. If it has, you get faster service because Internet Explorer does not have to spend time resolving the host name. The cache is temporary; older items expire and current items are often bumped out to make room for new ones. If you tend to visit the same collection of Web sites over and over, increase the DNS cache size to help you out a bit. You need to edit the Registry to make these changes:

1. Select Start ⇨ Run, type **regedit**, and click OK.
2. Navigate to HKEY_LOCAL_MACHINE\SYSTEM\CurrentControlSet\Services\Dnscache\Parameters.

3. Create these DWORD values:

```
CacheHashTableBucketSize = 1
CacheHashTableSize = 180
MaxCacheEntryTtlLimit = ff00
MaxSOACacheEntryTtlLimit = 12d
```

4. Exit the Registry Editor.

Tip

A fun, timesaving tip you may enjoy concerns the typing of URLs. Suppose you want to visit `www.wiley.com`. Instead of typing the full address, just type **wiley** and press Ctrl-Enter. The "www" and ".com" are filled in automatically. This feature only works with Web addresses ending with .com.

Allowing More Than Two Simultaneous Downloads

By default, Internet Explorer limits you to two simultaneous downloads. However, IE supports more than two. You can change the simultaneous download value for IE from 2 to 10 with two new Registry entries:

1. Select Start ➪ Run, type **regedit**, and click OK.
2. Navigate to HKEY_CURRENT_USER\Software\Microsoft\Windows\CurrentVersion\Internet Settings.
3. Create the following two new DWORD Registry entries:

```
MaxConnectionsPer1_0Server=Dword:10
MaxConnectionsPerServer=Dword:10
```

4. Close the Registry Editor.

Stopping Pop-up Windows

Aggravating pop-ups often appear when you visit some Web sites. Instead of surfing the site, you end up spending your time closing pop-up windows containing advertisements. You can stop them, or at least greatly decrease them, in Internet Explore or using third-party software. The Internet Explorer setting is only available if you have Windows XP Service

Pack 2 installed (if you don't, use Windows Update to download and install it). To use Internet Explorer's pop-up blocking feature, follow these steps:

1. Open Internet Options and click the Privacy tab.
2. At the bottom of the tab (see Figure 10-5), click the Block Pop-ups option and click the Settings button.

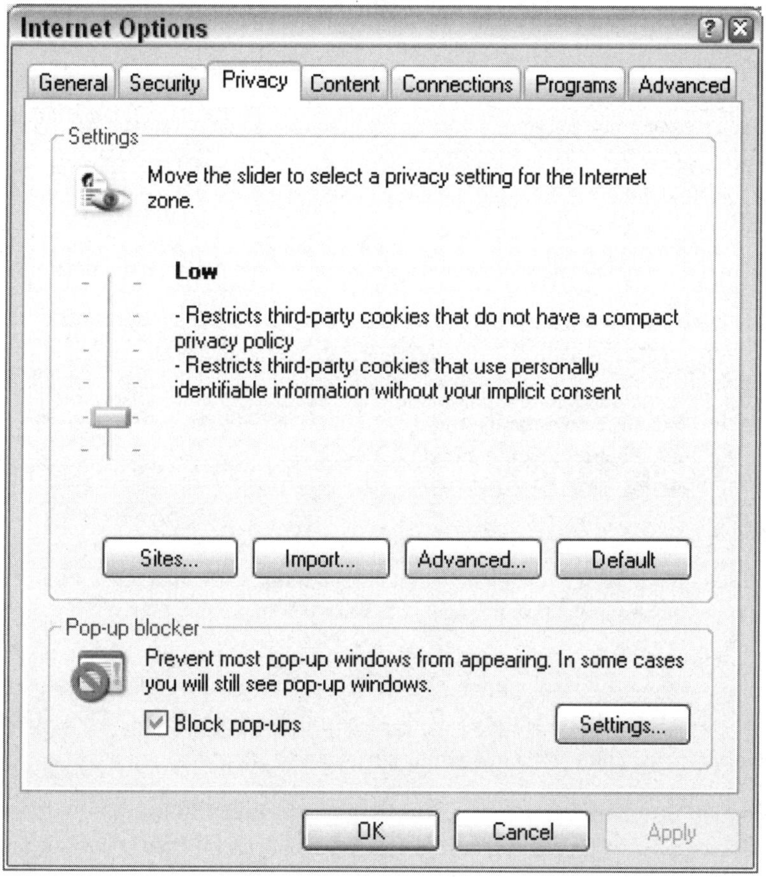

Figure 10-5: Enable the Block Pop-ups option.

3. In the Pop-up Blocker Settings dialog box (see Figure 10-6), you can choose to allow pop-ups from certain Web sites, if you like. Enter the Web site's URL and click the Add button to add it to the list of sites for which you allow pop-ups. Also note the options at the bottom of the dialog box, which you can adjust as

desired. Click Close to leave this dialog box and then OK to close the Internet Options dialog box.

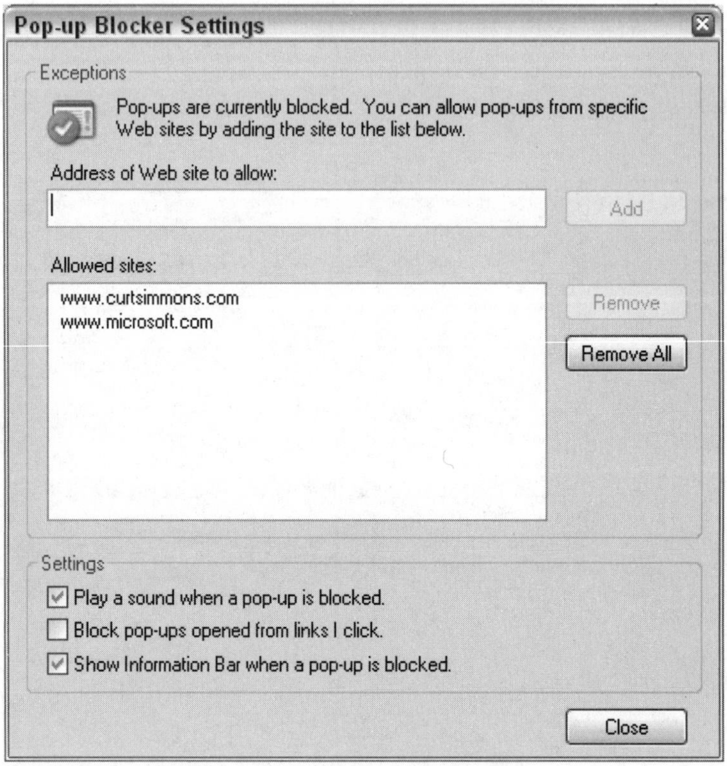

Figure 10-6: You can allow pop-ups from desired Web sites.

In addition to the pop-up blocker built into IE under Windows XP Service Pack 2, you can also download and use a number of third-party pop-up blockers. These utilities are easy to install and use; here are a few you might want to try out:

- **Pop-Up Stopper Free Edition:** This handy tool keeps an icon in the browser's notification area so you can easily see what has been blocked. Find out more and download it at `www.panicware.com`.
- **Pop-Up Blocker:** This is a good program that works well with all Web sites. Find out more at `www.synergeticsoft.com`.
- **Popup Zero Pro:** This one does a good job of blocking only advertising pop-ups but showing you other pop-up windows you might want to see. You can find this one at `www.pcworld.com`.

Other Internet Explorer Tweaks and Utilities

As I discuss configuring Internet Explorer to boost speed and reduce problems from the Internet, let me turn your attention to some valuable third-party tweaking and configuration utilities.

TWEAK-XP PRO

Tweak-XP Pro for Windows XP has several IE functions that you'll enjoy. Not only can you easily view and delete temporary Internet files and history, but you can configure some basic IE settings, run an ad-blocker and pop-up blocker, and generally make some things work a bit better (see Figure 10-7). I recommend this one. Find out more from Totalidea Software (`www.totalidea.com`).

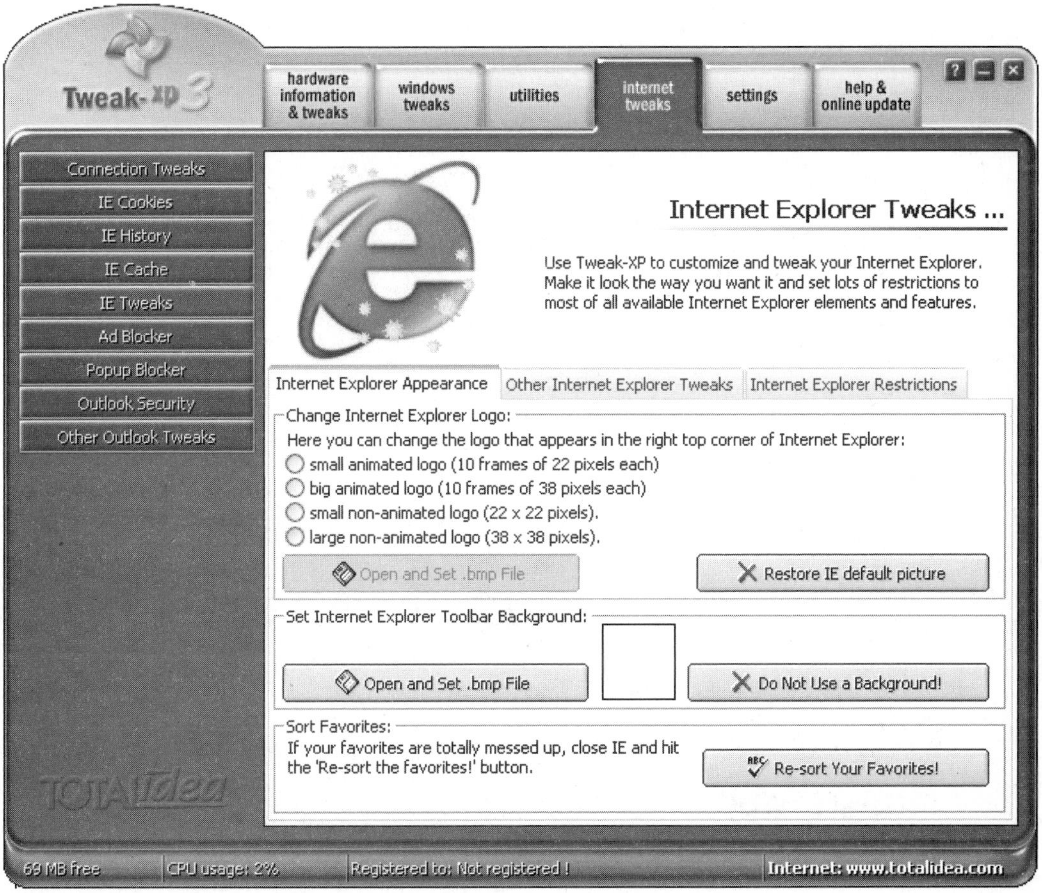

Figure 10-7: Tweak-XP Pro for Windows XP from Totalidea Software.

TWEAK UI

Tweak UI is a Microsoft-developed (although unsupported) utility that allows you to make a number of changes to Windows XP, including Internet Explorer. Tweak UI doesn't necessarily give you any settings that make Internet Explorer work more quickly, but you might enjoy some of the fixes found in the easy-to-navigate interface (see Figure 10-8). Download this free tool from the Microsoft PowerToys for Windows XP page (`www.microsoft.com/windowsxp/downloads/powertoys/xppowertoys.mspx`).

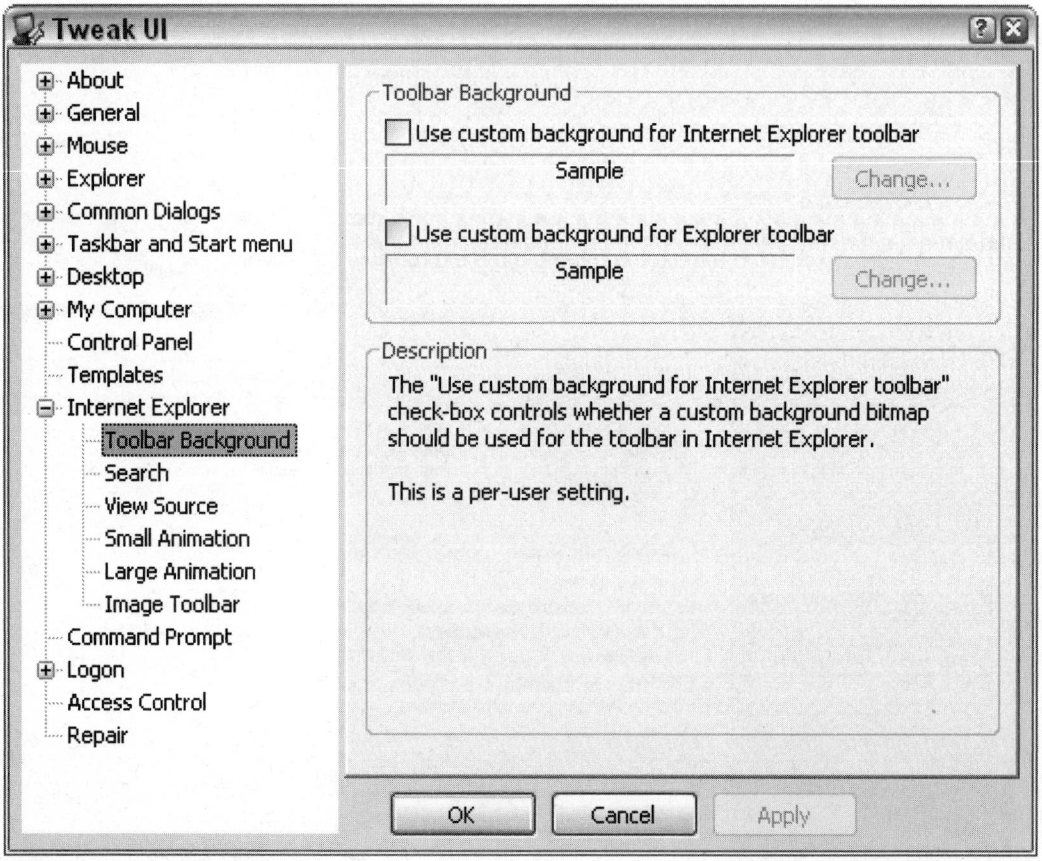

Figure 10-8: Tweak UI from Microsoft.

INTERNET TWEAK

Internet Tweak provides a number of tweaks for Internet Explorer, as well as for connection hardware and the like (see Figure 10-9). Download a trial version to see what you think. Find out more from Magellass (`www.magellass.com`).

Figure 10-9: Internet Tweak from Magellass.

OTHER HELPFUL UTILITIES

If you are a utilities nut like me, here are a few more that you'll like and can help you keep control of Internet Explorer and your Web surfing:

- **STOPZilla:** This tool gives you control over adware, spyware, cookies, and history to help make your Web surfing experience faster and easier. Find out more at `www.stopzilla.com`.
- **WebWasher:** Banner ads and cookies can certainly slow down your surfing speed. This utility helps stop all of those things and keeps the banner ads out of your way. Find this utility at `www.pcmag.com`.
- **AnalogX:** This is another pop-up window manager. Find it at `www.pcmag.com`.
- **GhostSurf Pro:** This tool allows you to surf the Internet without leaving any trail of where you have been. Find it at `www.pcmag.com`.
- **AdFree:** This is another ad-blocking tool that you'll find quite useful. Find it at `www.pcmag.com`.

Note

Going in a completely different direction, you might want to try a browser besides Internet Explorer. Other browsers are known to be faster, although they lack some of the features and configuration options. (Regardless, Internet Explorer is still overwhelmingly the most popular.) I recommend Opera (`www.opera.com`), Mozilla Firefox (`www.texturizer.net/firefox`), and Avant (`www.avantbrowser.com`).

Speeding Up Your Internet Connection

You can use some of the speed solutions explored in the first half of this chapter to help speed up Internet Explorer. After all, your perception of what is fast or not depends on how quickly you end up seeing web pages.

Yet, in the end, the Internet connection itself has the most to do with speed. For all the fixes and tweaks you can make to Internet Explorer, nothing is really going to speed up a slow Internet connection. Your computer is a fast machine and the Web pages you view are nothing in terms of data—your PC can handle it. The problem is the pipeline that gets the data to you.

Let me say categorically that dial-up connections (modems) are dreadfully slow; there isn't a whole lot you can do about it. I'll show you some tricks to squeeze every ounce of speed out of your modem, but the Internet has become a multimedia animal and the modem is only capable of a certain speed, typically around 48 Kbps with a 56 Kbps modem (you don't actually get the full 56 Kbps because of telephone company regulations). That speed is rather slow for the graphical nature of Web pages these days, and it is painfully slow when you want to download files of any noticeable size. Your best tactic for speeding up your Internet connection is to go to broadband, such as cable or DSL. Cable and DSL prices are much more affordable now than they were in years past, thanks to competition, so if you really want speed, consider an upgrade.

With that said, let's take a look at some settings and tactics you can use to help speed up your Internet connection.

Note

You may live in an area that does not offer cable or DSL Internet. I know about that all too well because I live in such an area. However, you can get a type of broadband service through satellite,

although it is a bit more expensive and there are more startup costs. Visit `www.starband.net` **to learn more.**

Modem Drivers and Your Phone Line

Make sure you have the latest drivers for your modem. Without them, you may not get the best speed possible. Check your modem manufacturer's Web site. See Chapter 8 for more information on installing new drivers. Also, check the phone line the modem is connected to. Put a phone on that line for a moment and make some calls. Listen for line noise, such as static and popping. If you hear interference, you can be certain that it will interfere with your modem's performance. Your phone company should be able to help you with this one.

Modem Connection Properties

Check out the properties dialog box for your modem connection to make sure everything is configured for the best speed possible:

1. Open the Start menu and select Connect To ➪ Show All Connections.
2. Right-click the modem connection and select Properties.
3. On the General tab, click the Configure button.
4. In the Modem Configuration dialog box (see Figure 10-10), set the modem speed to **115200**. You won't actually get this speed but it ensures the fastest connection. Make sure the hardware flow control, modem error control, and modem compression check boxes are all selected. If you don't like hearing the modem connection noise, disable it here by unchecking the appropriate option.
5. On the connection's Properties dialog box, click the Options tab. Here you can configure redial options that will enable the modem to redial automatically should you get disconnected (see Figure 10-11).
6. Click the Networking tab. If you are only using your modem to connect to the Internet and for no other networking purposes, it is a good idea to disable the check boxes for any protocols except TCP/IP. You don't use them anyway and they have a tendency to bog things down. Simply clear the check boxes next to the protocols you do not need (see Figure 10-12). Click OK when you're done.

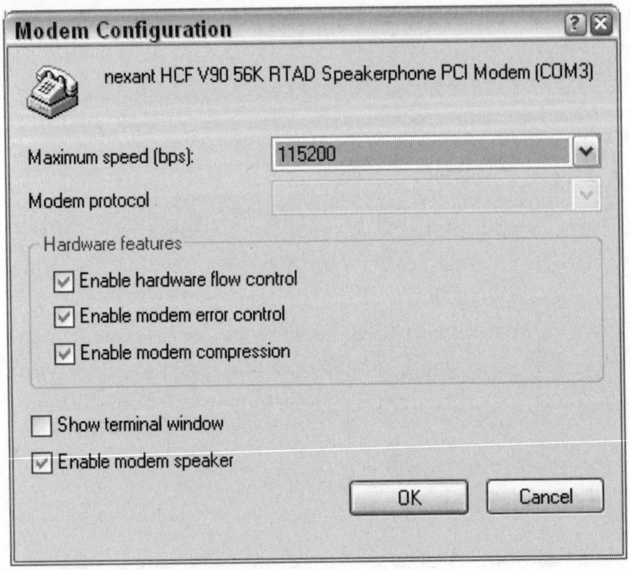

Figure 10-10: Use these settings in the Modem Configuration dialog box.

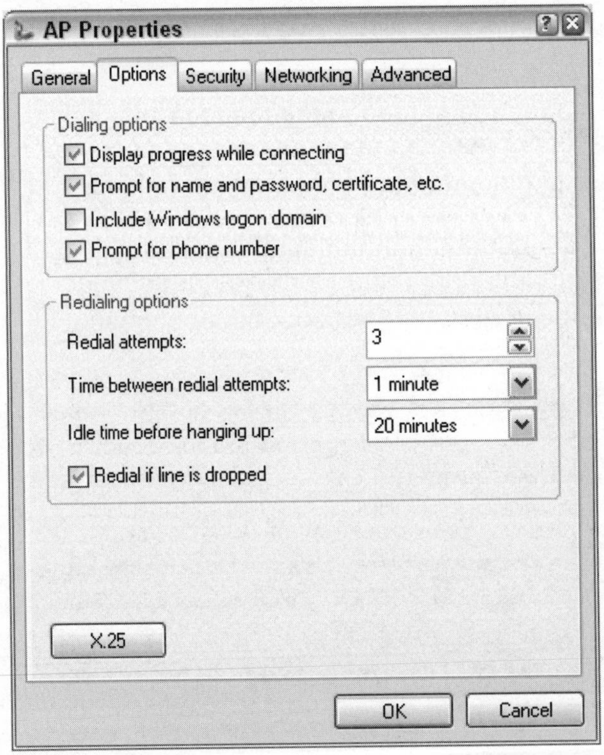

Figure 10-11: Control modem redialing on the Options tab.

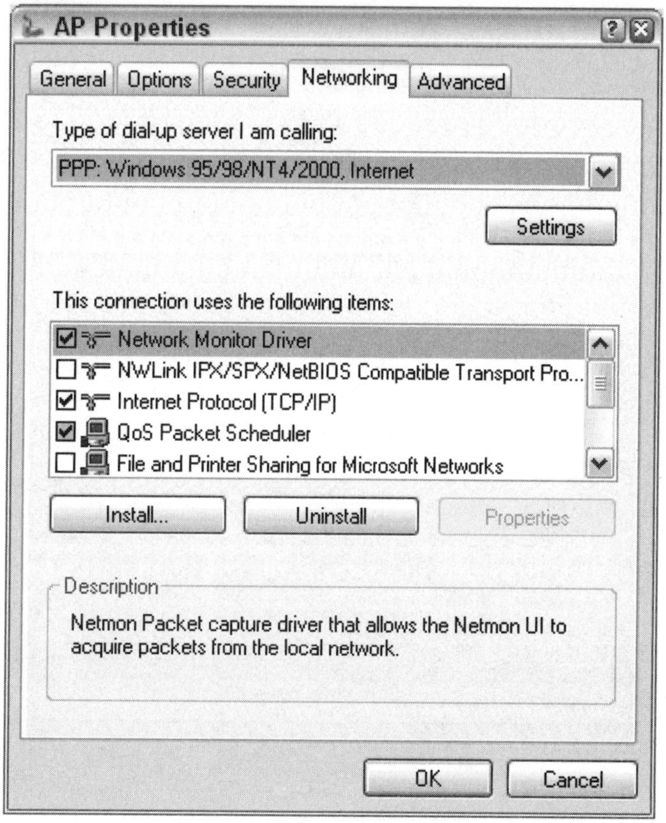

Figure 10-12: Remove any unnecessary networking protocols.

Modem Initialization Strings

Open the Control Panel and then open Phone and Modem Options. On the Modems tab, select your modem and click the Properties button. This opens the properties dialog box for the modem. On the Advanced tab (see Figure 10-13) notice that you can type in extra initialization commands. These commands are modem-specific and may help improve modem performance. Because the commands you are likely to use depend on your modem manufacturer, refer to `www.56k.com` and `www.modemhelp.org` to find out which commands you can try with your modem.

Other Advanced Modem Settings

Check out a few other modem settings. On the Advanced tab (see Figure 10-13) click the Advanced Port Settings button. In the window that appears, make sure the Use FIFO

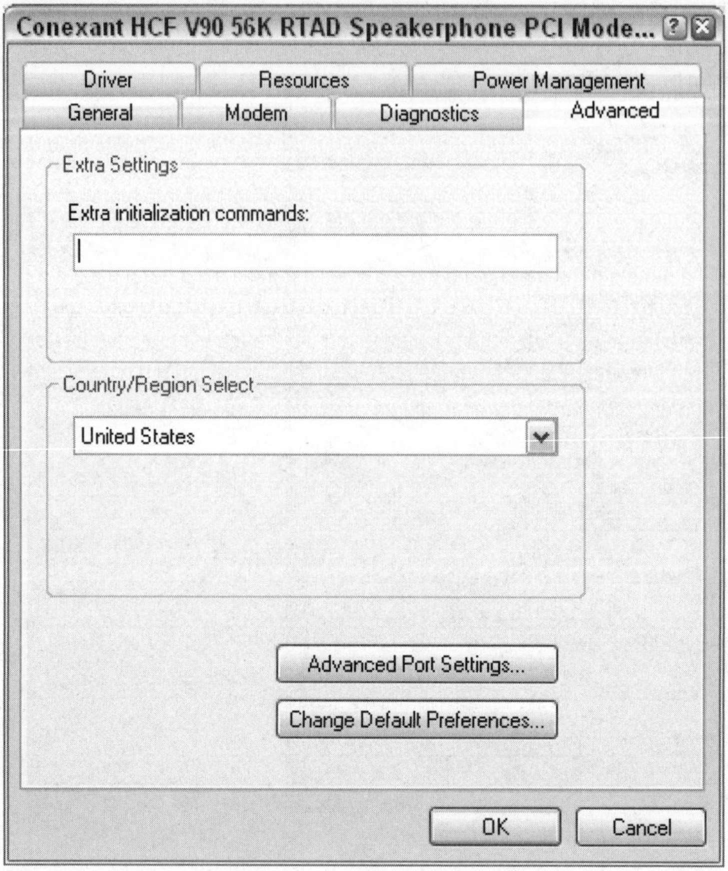

Figure 10-13: You can enter extra initialization commands for your modem.

Buffers option is selected. Then make sure both sliders are moved to the far right (see Figure 10-14).

Back on the Advanced tab, click the Change Default Preferences button. You probably have the correct settings on the two tabs available, but check them out to make sure they are configured as follows.

On the General tab:

- **Port Speed:** 115,200
- **Data Protocol:** Standard EC
- **Compression:** Enabled
- **Flow Control:** Hardware

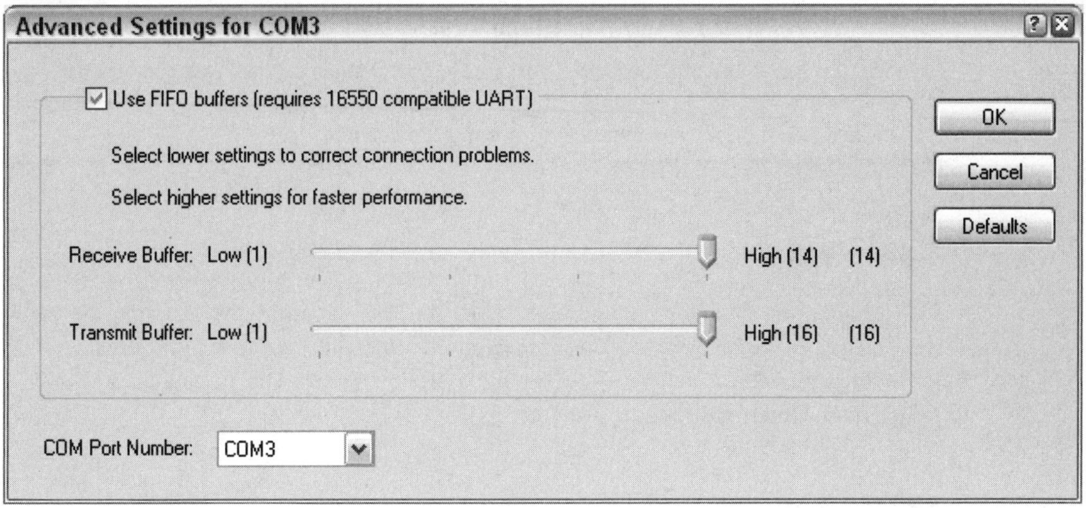

Figure 10-14: Make sure you use these advanced settings.

On the Advanced tab:

- **Data Bits:** 8
- **Parity:** None
- **Stop Bits:** 1
- **Modulation:** Standard (if it's grayed out, that's OK)

Download Manager (Modem Connections)

If you have a modem connection, you would do well to install a download manager. These programs manage lengthy downloads and can automatically reconnect you and continue the download, should you get disconnected. They are free and very helpful. I recommend Star Downloader (`www.stardownloader.com`).

Be Wary of Internet Speed Utilities

You've seen the ads: "Boost your Internet speed by 300%." Are you cautious? You should be. While some of these utilities provide boosting capabilities to the TCP/IP protocol stack and actually do help optimize Internet connections, many of them do little and some are actually fronts for adware and spyware. There is even a class-action suit against one

Be Wary of Internet Speed Utilities *(Continued)*

vendor. So, buyer beware. If you are interested in one of these utilities, I suggest you do some homework. Look for reputable reviews on sites such as `www.pcmag.com`, `www.cnet.com`, and `www.zdnet.com` before making a final decision.

CableNut

One of the best tweaking utilities for cable and DSL connections is CableNut (`www.dslnuts.com/software.shtml`). CableNut examines all of the TCP/IP stack entries in the Registry and looks for ways to optimize them. This tool is very popular and seems to help boost Internet speed. It's also free.

MTU Settings

The Maximum Transmission Unit (MTU) has to do with TCP/IP settings and how they are optimized for the Internet. You can check out the MTU settings and make sure they are optimized for the kind of Internet connection you are using with a TCP/IP analyzer test. Go to `http://forums.speedguide.net:8117/`. This site automatically runs a test and reports the Registry settings for TCP/IP, which determines whether those settings are optimized for your type of Internet connection.

Chapter 11

Dealing with Spam and E-mail Problems

If you are like me, e-mail is a very important part of your life. I use it every day for my work and to keep in touch with friends and family. Yet there are many aggravations with e-mail today. For all the great things about e-mail, unsolicited junk e-mail, or spam, has become a big problem. Some people receive hundreds of spam messages every day. Some big attempts have been made in the Internet industry to curb the tidal wave of spam, and Windows XP Service Pack 2 adds some features to Outlook Express 6 that you can configure and put in place. This chapter explores those features and some other tactics for managing junk e-mail.

Creating E-mail Rules

One of the first things you should do when using Outlook Express, or even other e-mail clients such as Outlook, is to create e-mail rules. These can help you save time by helping you manage your e-mail more effectively.

For example, suppose you tend to get a lot of junk e-mail from one particular sender. You can create a rule that sends all of that sender's e-mail directly to the Deleted Items folder so that you never have to deal with it directly. Or suppose you subscribe to a discussion list and you get 30 or so e-mails a day from that list. You can create a rule that puts all e-mail from the list into a folder within Outlook Express. You can then read those messages at your leisure, without them clogging your inbox. You can even use message rules to help reduce spam by flagging certain subject heading keywords and sending those messages directly to the trash.

While message rules can be very helpful, you also have to be careful not to overdo them. Too many rules tend to become confusing, and you'll end up rerouting mail to different folders or retrieving messages from the Deleted Items by accident. The lesson here is to think carefully about the rules you want to create and don't create so many rules that you can't manage them.

Blocking Senders

The action of blocking senders identifies the e-mail address of a particular sender and immediately puts all e-mail from that sender into the Deleted Items folder. To invoke this setting, select one of the sender's e-mails in your Inbox and select Tools ➪ Block Sender. You can edit your blocked sender's list at any time should you change your mind. Select Tools ➪ Message Rules ➪ Blocked Senders List. You can then add, remove, or modify blocked senders (see Figure 11-1).

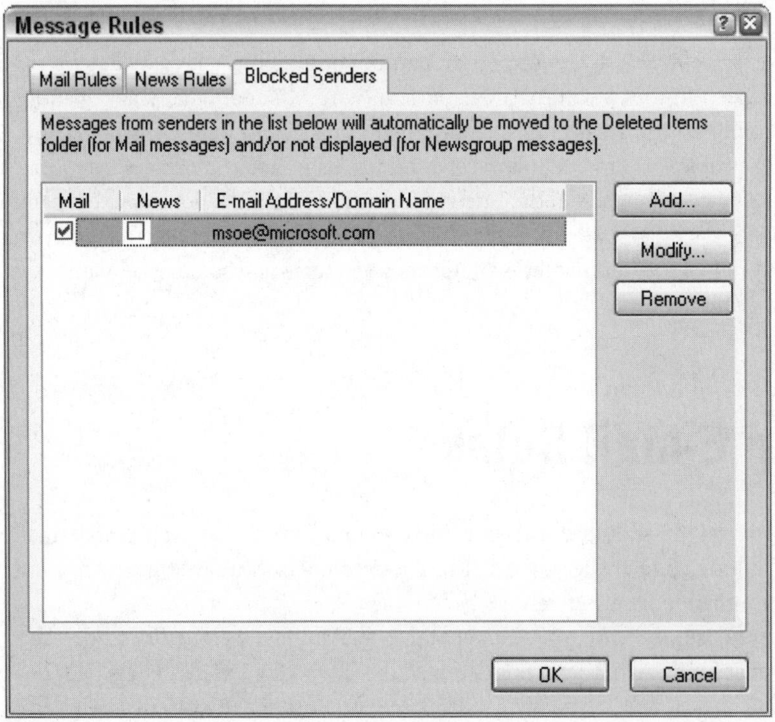

Figure 11-1: You can easily edit the Blocked Senders list in the Message Rules dialog box.

Note

The Block Sender option works for POP3 e-mail only. It does not work for HTTP or IMAP e-mail accounts.

Creating Rules

It is easy to create new message rules. You can also create a rule based on a message you receive. If you want to use the second option, select the message in your Inbox and select Tools ➪ Create Rule From Message. If you want to create generic rules, just follow these steps:

1. Select Tools ➪ Message Rules ➪ Mail.
2. This action opens the New Mail Rule dialog box (see Figure 11-2). Select a condition for a rule and an action for the rule. Once you make your selections, the rule description appears in the third step. Name the rule and save it by clicking OK.

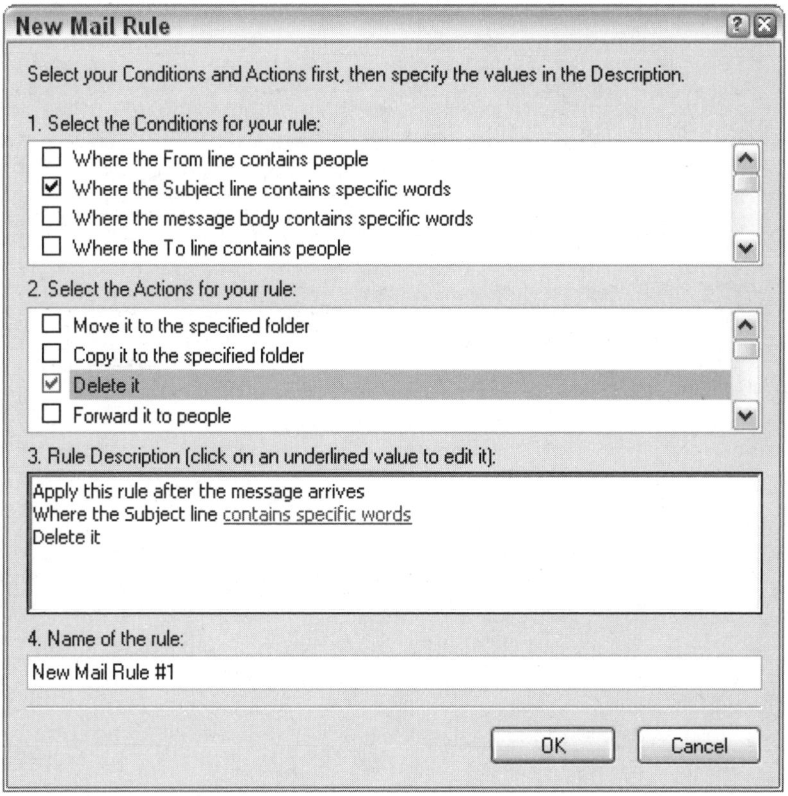

Figure 11-2: New Mail Rule dialog box.

3. Notice the hyperlinked words or phrases in the third step. These works or phrases lead you to additional configuration options. For example, Figure 11-2

shows that I have chosen to filter subject line words in Step 1 and delete the messages in Step 2. In Step 3, "contains specific words" is hyperlinked. If I click the link, I can create the word list in the Type Specific Words dialog box that Outlook Express uses to determine if the message should be deleted or not (see Figure 11-3). Click OK when you are done.

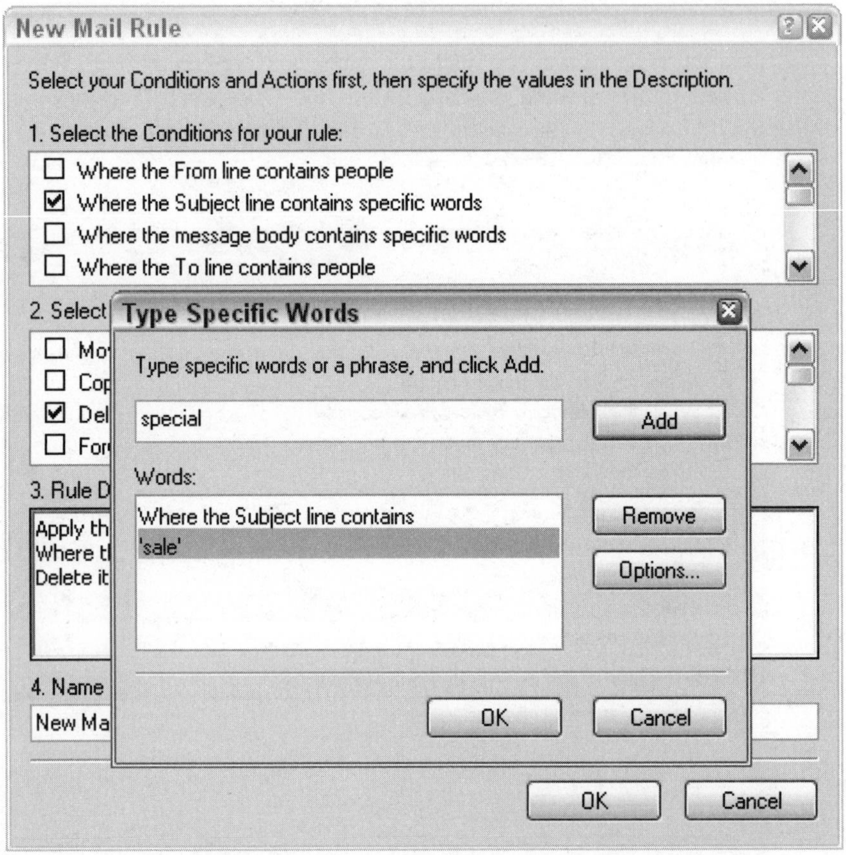

Figure 11-3: Creating the filter word list in the Type Specific Words dialog box.

Tip

Click the Options button in the Type Specific Words dialog box to adjust the filtering process. The options you see here vary depending on the kind of filter you are creating.

You can perform this process over and over again to create as many rules as you like. Just remember that the judicious use of rules can help you manage incoming e-mail and junk e-mail, but be careful about creating too many rules because you may experience problems with valid messages getting shuffled around. You can always adjust rules as needed.

Setting Security

If you select Tools ➪ Options and then click the Security tab, you'll see a few additional security settings. Notice the section for Virus Protection (see Figure 11-4). In reality, Outlook Express does not provide "virus protection" per se. You still need to use antivirus software, but it does provide some features that can reduce the likelihood that you will get a virus through e-mail. These settings are a preventative method that can help somewhat.

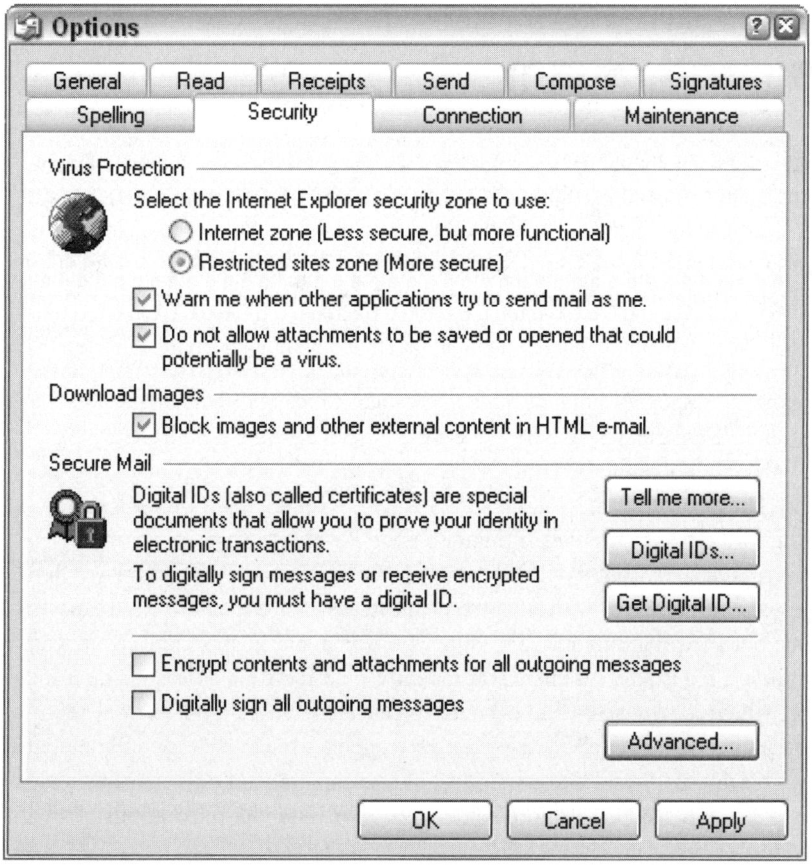

Figure 11-4: The Security tab in the Options dialog box.

Notice that you can choose the Internet Explorer zone to use for these settings, such as the Internet zone or the Restricted Sites zone. You can then choose check box options that warn you when an application tries to e-mail you. You also have a setting that blocks attachments from being opened that could be infected with a virus. The problem, of course, is that Internet Explorer could potentially block valid attachments, but experiment with this setting to see if it helps. Again, your best bet is to allow an antivirus program to manage this for you.

By default, HTML e-mail that contains images will appear without the images because images can carry viruses. This method of photo blocking has become common in many e-mail programs and it is helpful. You can also use this tab to set up digitally secure mail, assuming that others who communicate with you over e-mail can support these features. See the Outlook Express help files to learn more about digital IDs and security.

Dealing with Spam

Like virtually all other e-mail clients, Outlook Express has good filters for managing spam. However, spam in and of itself is difficult to control. Spam is a wide-encompassing term that generally refers to any e-mail you don't want to get. This includes advertisements, solicitations, and unwanted e-mail such as porn teasers. Depending on your e-mail address and activity on the Internet, you can get hundreds of spam messages every day. I maintain a public e-mail address, `curt_simmons@hotmail.com`, so that my readers can contact me. But because this address is listed in my books and on my Web site, I get tons of spam messages. Although I welcome e-mail from you, my readers, I end up having to filter and delete the vast majority of e-mail I receive at that account.

In terms of speed, you cannot effectively manage e-mail if you have to contend with spam every day. Unfortunately, there is no direct way to stop all spam but you can do a number of things to help slow it down and filter a good bit of it to spam neverland.

Most spam is generated by "bots"—little programs that guess your e-mail address or flood a domain, such as hotmail.com, with attempted addresses. No one is directly managing these programs, but the program's job is to hunt you down and keep sending you spam. Most of the stuff you see is advertisements; apparently spammers get at least some results from these ads, which is why spam has become so prevalent. In fact, the current reports I've seen say that spammers get about 15 positive responses for every one million spam messages sent. This doesn't sound like great odds, but spammers send millions of messages every day. The following sections explore some tactics for reducing the amount of spam you get.

Spammer Tactics

Spammers are always sending out junk mail and always looking for ways around current software and tactics to stop spam. For the most part, filtering is the best way to control spam. Filtering software looks at a message's subject header and tries to determine if the message is spam or not. Based on keywords and other indicators, filtering works well. However, spammers know that filtering is used, which is why you get so many e-mails from spammers with misspelled words, odd characters, and odd spacing, such as the one shown in Figure 11-5. This indicates a spammer trying to outsmart the word list in filtering software and get their message to you. Unfortunately, their tactics often work.

!	✉	🔗	☐	From	Subject	∨ Date	Size
			☐	Lifedirec.t	Listings of foreclosed properties	Jul 6	1KB
			☐	Bernice Fullerton	Strong Buy on Growth sector	Jul 6	9KB
			☐	Men's Health	M:ale En:hanc:ement	Jul 6	2KB
			☐	Angelita	at the foot of	Jul 6	4KB

Figure 11-5: Spam message subject header examples.

Using Common Sense

The first tactic is to use some common sense. In other words, you do not want to attract spam. Avoid giving out your e-mail address to a Web site unless it is one you do business with. Avoid answering online surveys that require you to submit your e-mail address or any other personally identifiable information. When you receive spam, do not reply to it; delete it. When you reply to a spam message or click the "opt out" option many of these messages provide, you are actually confirming that you are a real person with a real e-mail address. These tactics are only likely to increase the amount of spam you get. Guard your e-mail address carefully. This is your first line of defense.

Using Separate E-mail Accounts

A great way to ward off spam from your personal e-mail is to use a different e-mail address for all online activity. When you are accessing sites that require your e-mail address or purchasing items online, use the secondary e-mail address. As I mentioned, I have a Hotmail account that I use on the Internet. However, I also have a primary e-mail address that I share with business associates and family and friends only. I don't use this e-mail address for anything I do online. This keeps spam directed toward my Hotmail account instead of my business and personal e-mail accounts, thereby reducing the time it takes me to address the e-mails I want to receive. If you maintain a Web presence, do not put your e-mail address on the site. If you must, use a separate account for the Web site.

Configuring Filters

You can and should use e-mail filters, such as the filtering option in Outlook Express explored earlier in this chapter. However, the filtering works on word associations or e-mail/domain associations. You can reduce some spam this way, but keep in mind that spammers constantly change their e-mail address and use odd spellings, characters, and spacing to try and trick the filtering system. You'll get some results with filters, but don't expect it to be great. If you create too many filters, you will likely start filtering legitimate messages you actually want to read.

Using Third-Party Software

A number of third-party software tools can help you reduce spam, some better than others. In this section, allow me to introduce to you some of my favorites that you may wish to try out.

Understanding Spam Bayesian Filtering

In the past, all spam filters were based on keywords, which isn't the most effective method. However, a new kind of filtering called Bayesian filtering is becoming a more popular standard. Rather than randomly examining keywords, Bayesian filtering uses a statistical formula to gather information about junk e-mails. Rather than examining just the subject line, Bayesian filters examine the entire content of a message and use data that has been collected to determine if the message is spam or not. The success rate is very high but Bayesian filters can be more difficult to configure. You essentially have to teach the software for a period of time what is spam and what is not. If you are serious about controlling spam, it is a great filtering system to use. Some of the tools explored in this section use Bayesian filters. I'll point those out to you as we go.

SPAMPAL

SpamPal is a great program that uses a blacklist feature to help identify spam e-mail and put it in its place (see Figure 11-6). This tool uses both Bayesian and scoring filters to identify spam and catch spam automatically as it arrives to your Inbox. SpamPal can identify domains that tend to send out spam and block them, as well. Overall, SpamPal works well and easily

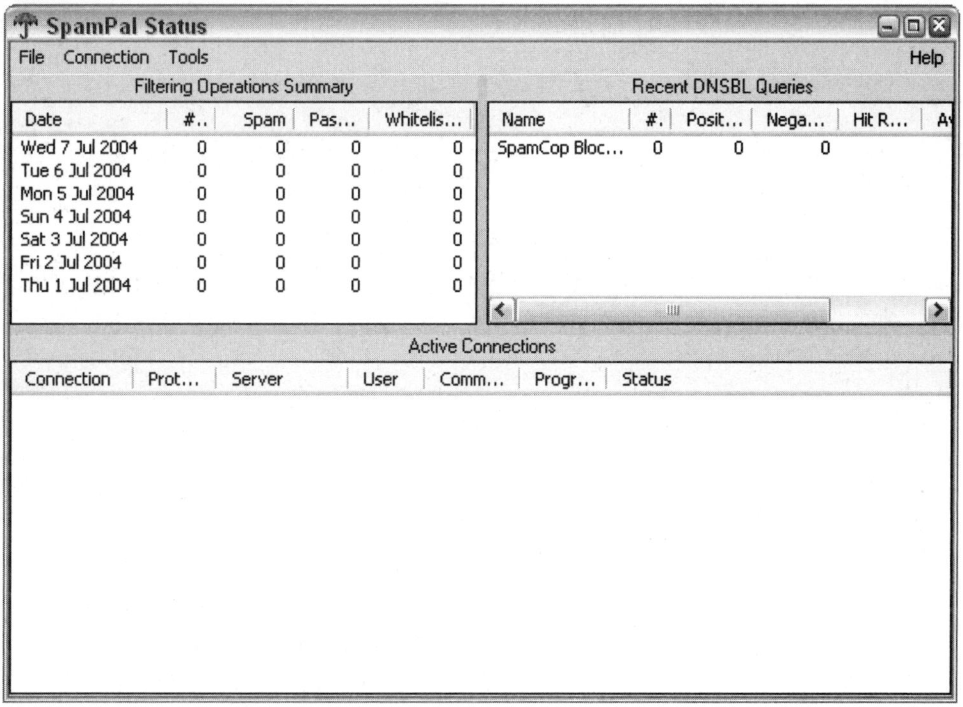

Figure 11-6: SpamPal for Windows by James Farmer.

with POP and IMAP mail accounts. However, SpamPal does not work with proprietary mail systems, such as AOL, Hotmail, Yahoo, Juno, and so on. SpamPal is a free utility that is easy to use. Find out more about it at `www.spampal.org`.

K9

K9 uses Bayesian filtering and learns quickly what kind of e-mail needs to be stopped (see Figure 11-7). You don't have to try to maintain a bunch of rules or worry about a lot of updates. However, the software only works with POP3 e-mail. The software is very trainable and it tends to get better at identifying your spam the longer you use it. Learn more about K9 and download it freely from `www.keir.net/k9.html`.

MAILWASHER PRO

MailWasher Pro by Nick Bolton uses several different filtering approaches to help you identify and reduce spam. The software maintains a friends list and a blacklist that also help you customize the program. It works with POP3 mail, IMAP, AOL, Hotmail, MSN, and other systems for more flexibility. Download a trial version from `www.mailwasher.net`. After 30 days it costs $40.

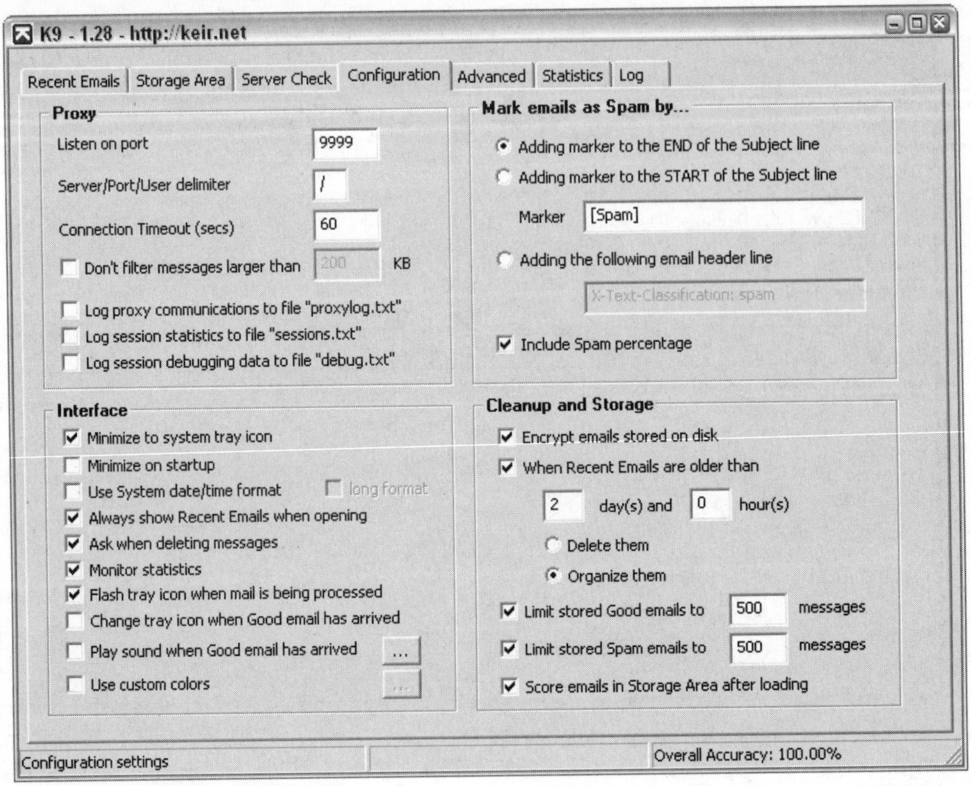

Figure 11-7: K9 by Robin Keir.

SPAM BULLY

Spam Bully is very efficient at removing spam, although you need to train it. Spam Bully uses a pre-trained Bayesian system so it may not be as effective as pure Bayesian filters. Spam Bully works with Outlook or Outlook Express only. Find out more and download a trial version of the software ($30 to keep it) at `www.spambully.com`.

SPAMIHILATOR

Spamihilator by Michel Krämer is an easy-to-use program that works with Bayesian filters and with any e-mail client. However, it only works with POP3 e-mail. Deleted spam is held in the Spamihilator, so you can actually view and browse it if you want. Spamihilator is freeware and available at `www.spamihilator.com`.

SPAM SLEUTH

Spam Sleuth by Blue Squirrel is comprehensive in its antispam techniques through Bayesian filtering. However, configuring it can be a bit trying because the program is so complicated.

It uses blacklists, challenge/response filtering, and other filtering features. It only works with POP3 mail and there are lots of configuration options, which can be quite intimidating. Find out more about Spam Sleuth at `www.bluesquirrel.com`. It costs $30.

POPFILE

POPFile is a handy spam-filtering program that can also help you organize your e-mail. The program scans all mail as it arrives and determines what to do with that mail. It can organize the mail into folders and filter out the spam. Download this free utility from `http://popfile.sourceforge.net`.

MCAFEE SPAMKILLER

McAfee SpamKiller is a great program that helps you locate and kill spam. Its success rate is very good. The software works with POP3, IMAP, or Hotmail. As it runs, it puts spam in folders for deletion and even supports a "Suspected Spam" folder within your mail client. You can easily preview what is being deleted so that you keep control of the process. Spamkiller costs around $40. Learn more about it at `www.mcafee.com`.

Chapter 12

Working with Cookies and Internet Security Settings

Have you ever spent time trying to rid your computer of a virus or fix a security breach? As you think about speed solutions, one of the more frustrating issues is Internet security; a lack of it can cost you a lot of personal time. I mentioned it in Chapter 11 in relation to Outlook Express e-mail, and the problem is certainly real when you use a Web browser such as Internet Explorer. For all the positive things the Internet provides us, it certainly has some big negatives. Keeping yourself private and your computer secure from Internet threats is no laughing matter. Each year, thousands upon thousands of unsuspecting users have their computers attacked by hackers (technically, “crackers”) and other threats, and many people have information about them stolen and sold to unscrupulous people. This chapter focuses on two security-related issues: cookies and Internet security settings. These two issues and the configuration settings that accompany them can certainly help you stay protected and keep Internet Explorer in top working condition.

Managing Cookies

Cookies are little text files that Web sites use. Let me say categorically that cookies are not bad. In fact, they help provide the kind of fast and efficient Web surfing experience everybody wants. Suppose you log on to your favorite Internet bookstore. The site knows who you are and what books you have bought and tries to guess what books you might like. This identifiable aspect of the site makes it enjoyable to use. This is just one example of a cookie; many sites use cookies when you access the site, and there are even different kinds of cookies, depending on what you are doing. Without them, you would feel like you were using the Internet of the mid-1990s.

However, because cookies can gain information about you, they can also be used in an unscrupulous manner to invade your privacy. Internet Explorer 6 was the first version of Microsoft's browser to provide a way to manage cookies, at least somewhat, to alleviate privacy concerns.

You can probably find some cookies in your Temporary Internet Files folder. Access the Internet Options dialog box. On the General tab, click the Settings button and then click View Files. Depending on what you have been doing on the Internet, you may be able to see some cookie files that you can open and read.

As a matter of security and management, you need to configure a cookie setting in Internet Explorer that tells the browser how to manage cookies so that it can implement the level of protection you want. You may also want to use a third-party cookie management utility; there are plenty to pick from. The following sections explore cookie management in Windows XP.

Internet Explorer Privacy Settings

Internet Explorer contains a Privacy tab found in the Internet Options dialog box (see Figure 12-1). As you can see, the privacy options really have to do with cookie management. You move the slider up or down to determine the level of security you want to invoke. Before doing that, however, you need to understand a few concepts that will make the selection easier.

Cookies are necessary on some Web sites. Your goal should be to manage cookies at the level of security with which you feel most comfortable. The more restrictive your settings, the more restricted your ability to surf the Web will be. The settings that Internet Explorer provides enable the browser software to inspect cookies, determine how they will be used, and determine whether or not to allow them. This feature works under the Platform for Privacy Preferences (P3P), which is an industry standard. It's not perfect but it does a good job overall.

As you examine the settings, you'll see a compact privacy statement and a statement from the Web site that explains how the cookies are used and how long a particular cookie is used. When you access the site, the compact privacy statement is contained in the HTTP header. Internet Explorer reads this statement and determines whether the compact privacy statement adheres to the standard.

There are also three kinds of cookies:

- **First-party cookie:** This cookie is generated at the site you are currently using and contains information about you and your browser. Sites use first-party cookies to tailor the content of the site to your specific needs.

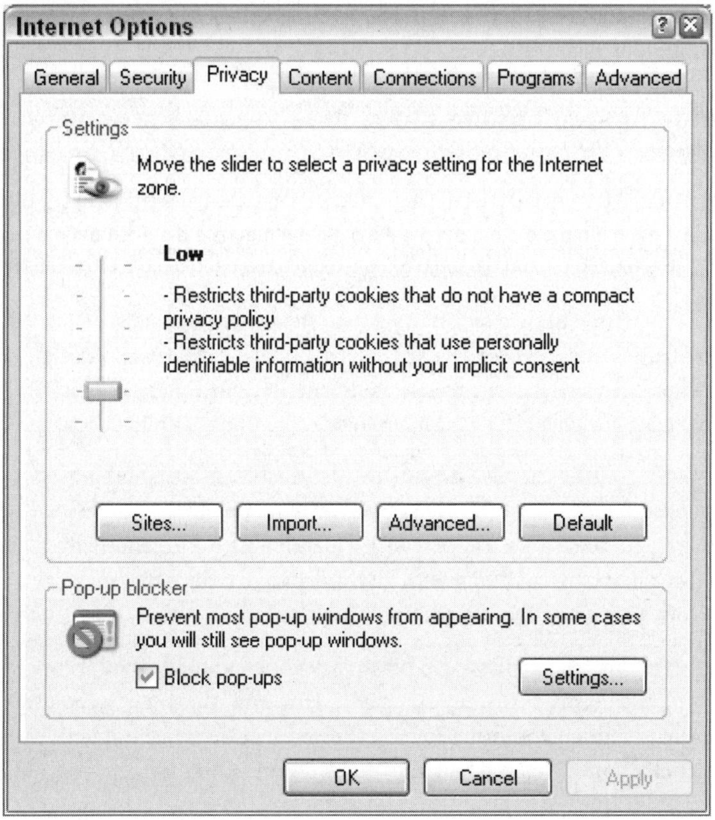

Figure 12-1: Move the slider to adjust the cookie policy.

- **Third-party cookie:** This cookie is generated on a site other than the one you are currently accessing. Banner ads are a good example of third-party cookies. As you might guess, these cookies are more worrisome because you don't really know who is using them and what information they are gaining about you.
- **Session cookies:** These cookies are generated during a session with the Web server for interactivity purposes. Session cookies are deleted once you leave the Web site. They are common and necessary. You cannot even use some sites without a session cookie.

Finally, concerning security settings, there is the issue of implicit and explicit consent. Implicit consent means that you have not directly given permission for a cookie to be used, but you have not blocked the site from doing so. Explicit consent means that you have interactively allowed the Web site to gain information about you.

The security setting you choose allows you different levels of control. If you move the slider, you'll see a description of each setting:

- **Block All Cookies:** All cookies are blocked and Web sites will not be able to generate new cookies. This setting will prevent access to some sites.
- **High:** This setting does not use any cookies that have personally identifiable information unless explicit consent is given. Also, Web sites that do not have a compact privacy statement are not allowed to generate cookies.
- **Medium-High:** This setting allows first-party cookies that use personally identifiable information only if you give explicit consent. Third-party cookies are blocked that do not have a compact privacy statement and third-party cookies that use personally identifiable information are blocked without explicit consent.
- **Medium:** First-party cookies that use personally identifiable information are allowed with implicit consent, but they are deleted when you close Internet Explorer. Third-party cookies that use personally identifiable information are blocked without explicit consent along with all third-party cookies that do not have a compact privacy policy. Medium is the default setting.
- **Low:** All First-Party cookies are allowed. Third-party cookies are blocked from sites that do not have a compact privacy statement. However, third-party cookies that use personally identifiable information are allowed without your implicit consent. These cookies are deleted when you close Internet Explorer.
- **Accept All Cookies:** All cookies are allowed and all Web sites can read any existing cookies.

The Sites button makes it easy to allow some Web sites to override your policy. For example, if you have a particular site you completely trust, you can add it to the list so it won't be restricted by your current policy. You can also use the Import button to import a third-party cookie policy that is compatible. Clicking the Advanced button overrides the settings for the Internet zone (covered in the next section). In this dialog box you can determine what to do with first-party, third-party, and session cookies. Essentially, this feature allows you to customize the default settings for the Internet zone (see Figure 12-2).

Cookie Management Software

Plenty of additional third-party tools can help you manage and control cookies. Although the cookie management feature in Internet Explorer works well, it doesn't give you the

Figure 12-2: You can customize settings for the Internet zone.

flexibility or some of the options found in some third-party tools. Like most utilities, some of these are free or require a modest fee. Here are some of the best ones you may want to try out:

- **Cookie Pal:** This software package comes recommended by *PC Magazine*. Download a trial version from `www.kburra.com`. Cookie Pal allows you to view cookies, create filters, view sessions, and basically configure the software in a way that works for you (see Figure 12-3). This software also works with Netscape and Opera.
- **Cookie Master:** This utility lives in the browser's notification area and allows you to view and manage cookies. This is a free and handy utility. Find it at `www.freedownloadscenter.com` by navigating to E-mail Tools ➪ Mail Signature Tools ➪ Cookie Master.
- **Cookie Crusher:** This tool is recommended by *PC Magazine*. Available at `www.thelimitsoft.com`, this software allows you to view, accept, and reject cookies; create rejection lists; and more. This is a good choice for a really customized cookie management program.
- **Cookie Cruncher:** This management tool enables you to manage and view cookies. Find out more at `www.rbaworld.com/Programs/CookieCruncher/`.

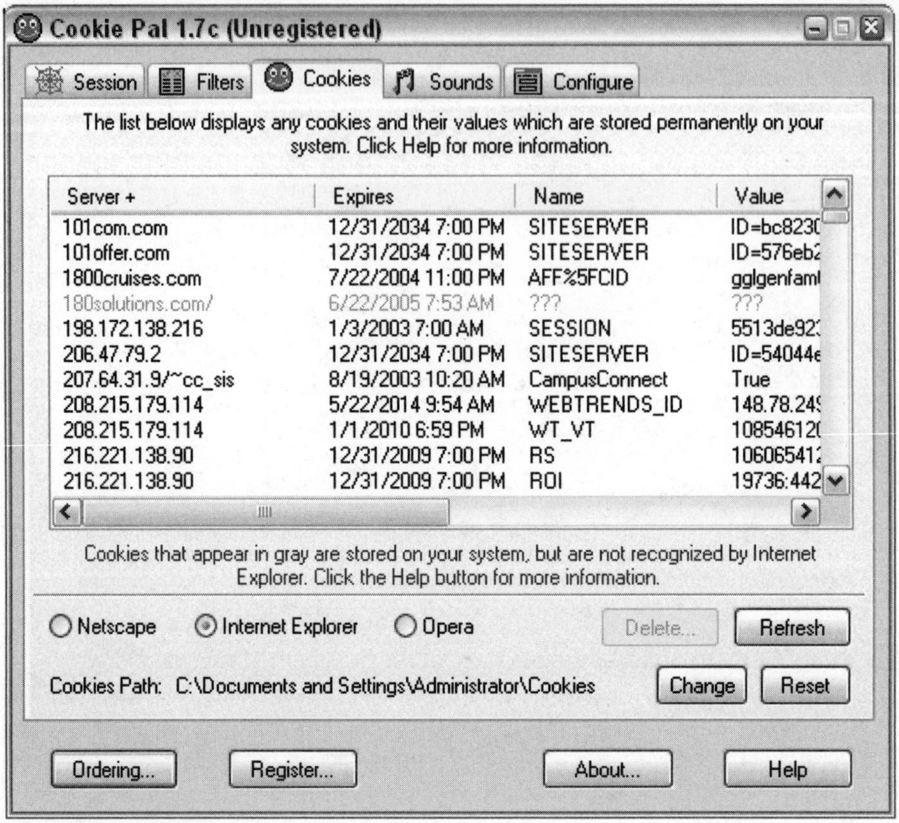

Figure 12-3: Cookie Pal.

Configuring Internet Explorer Zones

Internet Explorer uses the concept of "zones" to configure security. To understand the necessity of zones, it is important to remember that Internet Explorer is designed to function on the Internet or on an intranet. Because Internet Explorer can function in either environment, security needs for each zone are typically different. For example, on an intranet you are generally not worried about security (if at all on a small network), while on the Internet you are always concerned about security.

With this in mind, Internet Explorer allows you to configure security settings differently for both the Internet and an intranet. It also enables you to override settings by configuring trusted sites and restricted sites for specific purposes.

Zone configuration is rather easy. Simply open Internet Options and click the Security tab. Then click the security zone button you want to configure, such as Internet. Move the slider bar to the desired level and you'll be able to read the impact of the security settings next to it (see Figure 12-4). The more securely you configure a zone, the more restrictive it will be to surf it. As a general rule, a Medium setting works well and tends to meet the needs of most people. If you want to override settings for particular sites, click the Trusted Sites or Restricted Sites buttons. Follow the instructions you see to configure trusted or restricted sites.

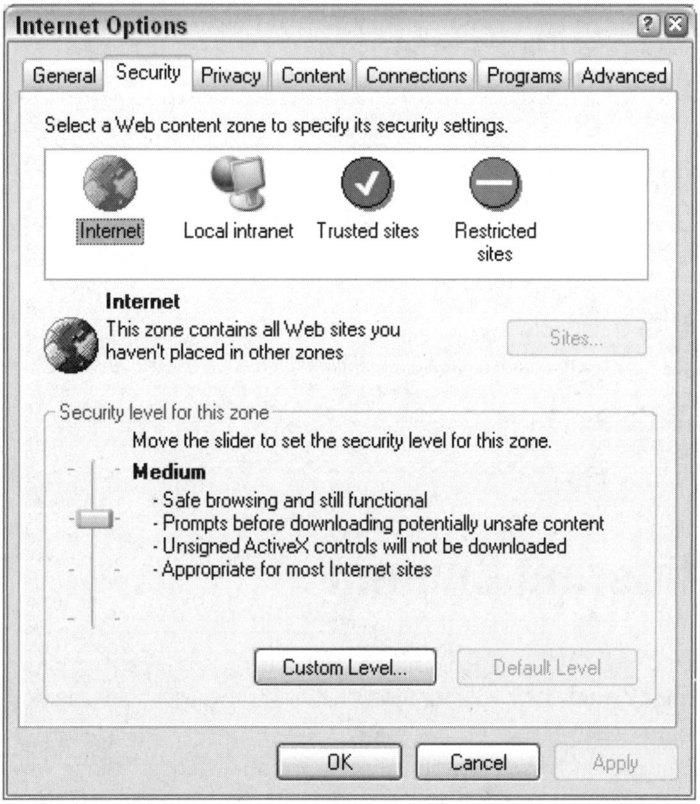

Figure 12-4: Security tab in the Internet Options dialog box.

If you don't like the particular settings you see for a security level, you can easily create one. Click the Custom Level button to open the Custom Settings dialog box (see Figure 12-5). Review the various option buttons to enable, disable, or prompt for each security item. This feature allows you to override settings of various security options. Choose the ones you want and click OK.

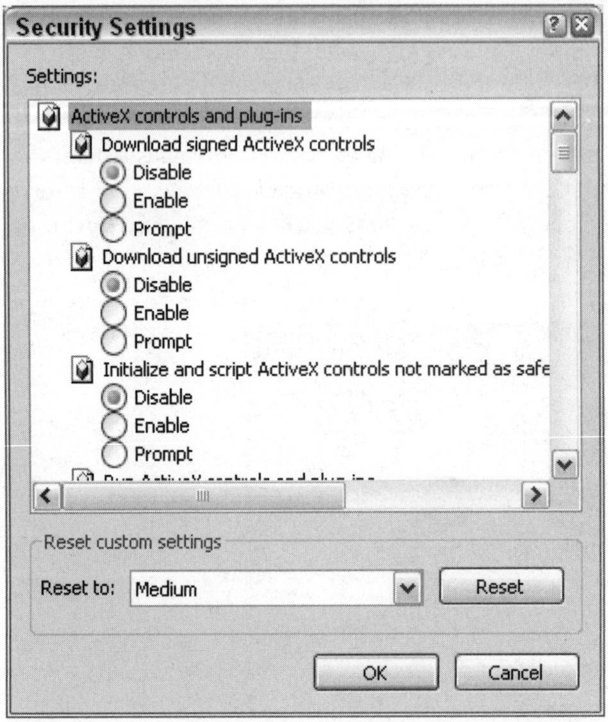

Figure 12-5: You can customize security settings to your liking.

Managing Internet Content

Internet Explorer provides you a way to help manage content. This feature enables you to block certain kinds of potentially offensive content from the Internet. The Content Advisor gives you the tools to do just that. Plenty of third-party software can also help manage Internet content. None of these options is completely foolproof, but they go a long way toward blocking content you do not want viewable. You'll find this feature particularly helpful if you have children who surf the Web.

The Content Advisor works through sites that have voluntarily provided information to the Internet Content Rating Association (ICRA) concerning site content. Because this is a voluntary rating, you may not be able to filter out all sites that you do not want to appear, but Content Advisor can still help you. Additional third-party products, such as Net Nanny (`www.netnanny.com`) or CyberSitter (`www.cybersitter.com`), may be able to provide you with additional protection.

Configuring Content Advisor is easy:

1. Open Internet Options and click the Content tab. Click the Enable button in the Content Advisor area (see Figure 12-6).

Figure 12-6: Click the Enable button to use Content Advisor.

2. On the Ratings tab (see Figure 12-7) you see a listing of content categories. Select the desired category and then move the slider to the desired level of content you want users to be able to see. Each category begins at the default level of 0, which is the least offensive setting. When you are done, click the Approved Sites tab.

3. On the Approved Sites tab, you can override the settings that you configured on the Ratings tab by entering specific URLs and clicking the Always or Never button. This gives you the ability to allow or reject certain sites completely, regardless of the other settings you configured. Click the General tab.

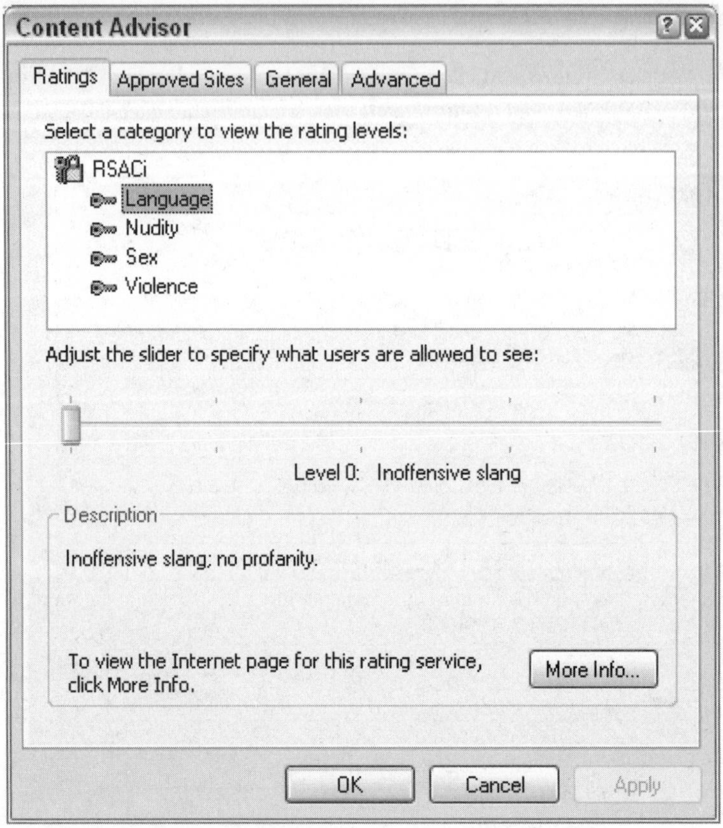

Figure 12-7: Adjust each category level as desired.

4. The General tab (see Figure 12-8) presents you with a few different access options. You can allow users to see sites that have no rating at all, or you can block all sites that do not have a rating. You can also require a password to be entered to override access to blocked sites. The Create Password button enables you to create a password that you can use to turn off or adjust the Content Advisor settings and override a blocked site. Finally, you can view information about rating systems on this tab.

5. The Advanced tab contains information about ratings bureaus and the PICSRules specification. A ratings bureau is an Internet site that can check the rating of a site to make sure it is protected under the ICRA rating. However, activating the ratings system will probably slow your browsing so you'll probably want to skip this option. Click OK when you're done.

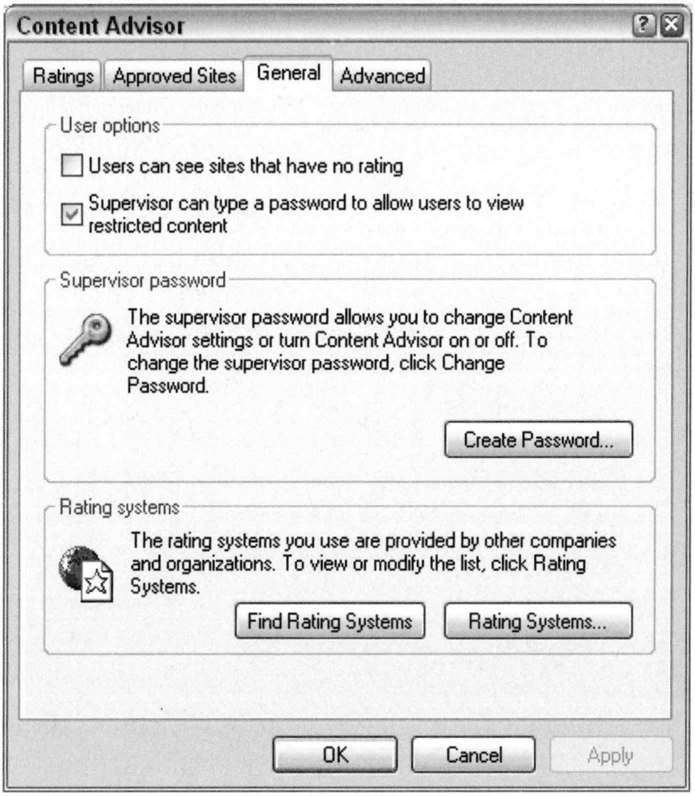
Content Advisor
Ratings
Approved Sites
General
Advanced
User options
Users can see sites that have no rating
Supervisor can type a password to allow users to view restricted content
Supervisor password
The supervisor password allows you to change Content Advisor settings or turn Content Advisor on or off. To change the supervisor password, click Change Password.
Create Password...
Rating systems
The rating systems you use are provided by other companies and organizations. To view or modify the list, click Rating Systems.
Find Rating Systems
Rating Systems...
OK
Cancel
Apply

Figure 12-8: The General tab of Content Advisor.

6. If at any time you want to disable Content Advisor, return to the Content tab and click the Disable button. You'll need to provide the supervisor password you configured originally to disable the feature.

Tip

If you are overly concerned about security, third-party programs such as Norton Internet Security can help. However, these programs have a tendency to slow things down. Speed and security tend to be a balancing act. Think carefully about how to achieve a balance that is right for you.

Chapter 13

Making Digital Media Faster and Easier

Digital photography and digital photo editing have become extremely popular over the past few years. Indeed, sales of digital cameras have virtually surpassed that of film cameras. Thousands upon thousands of songs are purchased and downloaded from the Internet every day. Digital media is here to stay, and PC users now demand more power from their computers than ever before.

How can you improve the experience of working with digital media? Whether you want to keep things working more quickly or organize everything so that using digital media doesn't drive you crazy, this chapter explores some positive actions you can take to improve speed and efficiency.

Organizing Digital Media

You must keep your digital media organized in some way or else you'll spend all your time trying to find it. Digital photos are often the culprits when it comes to organization. For example, I use my digital camera all the time. That's great, but over time my computer has become a storehouse of photos—hundreds and hundreds of them. Finding the right one takes time without proper organization.

You may feel organized for a while by keeping your digital photos and other media files inside various folders and subfolders. Even then, managing them will become overwhelming. As far as Windows XP is concerned, digital media files are just like any other files on your computer. Although the My Documents and My Pictures and other premade folders are helpful, you may quickly outgrow them. Instead of dwelling on organizing digital media by folders—you can do that on your own—I'll discuss some organizational solutions that may prove to be more helpful.

One of the things you can do is find software that catalogs all your digital media files and keeps track of them. These software packages are great because they enable you to keep up with everything in one library and search it quickly and easily for the particular file you need, rather than wading through endless folders. Most of these programs are inexpensive. I encourage you to try one of them if you are swimming in a virtual sea of digital media files. The following sections introduce you to some of my favorite applications.

Adobe Photoshop Album

Photoshop Album is a great program that enables you to import photos and other digital files into a library. You can then manage and work with that library from one interface and easily locate files you want. You can even create tags and keywords for faster searching. Photo Album even helps you do some minor photo editing and some fun things, such as create slide shows, Web galleries, and more. Overall, it's a great way to organize digital media and make your digital life easy to manage. You can often get Photoshop Album for free if you buy Photoshop Elements. Otherwise, the software costs around $50. `www.adobe.com` to learn more. There's also a free Starter Edition available (see Figure 13-1).

Jasc Paint Shop Photo Album

Jasc, the makers of the popular Paint Shop Pro, offers a photo album that provides cataloguing and searching features. You can easily store, find, and manipulate photos and create a variety of products with your photos, such as slide shows, calendars, and so forth. Paint Shop Photo Album (see Figure 13-2) costs around $50. Find out more and download the trial version at `www.jasc.com`.

ACD Systems ACDSee

ACDSee is a popular photo management program that provides cataloguing and searching features (see Figure 13-3). It also contains some great print, editing, and sharing features. Besides burning CDs, the software makes it easy to catalog video and audio files. Overall, this is a very nice program. ACDSee costs around $50. Download a trial version at `www.acdsystems.com`.

Photools IMatch

IMatch is powerful database software that leans toward the high end of digital photography (see Figure 13-4). Professional photographers often use it to keep everything in order but

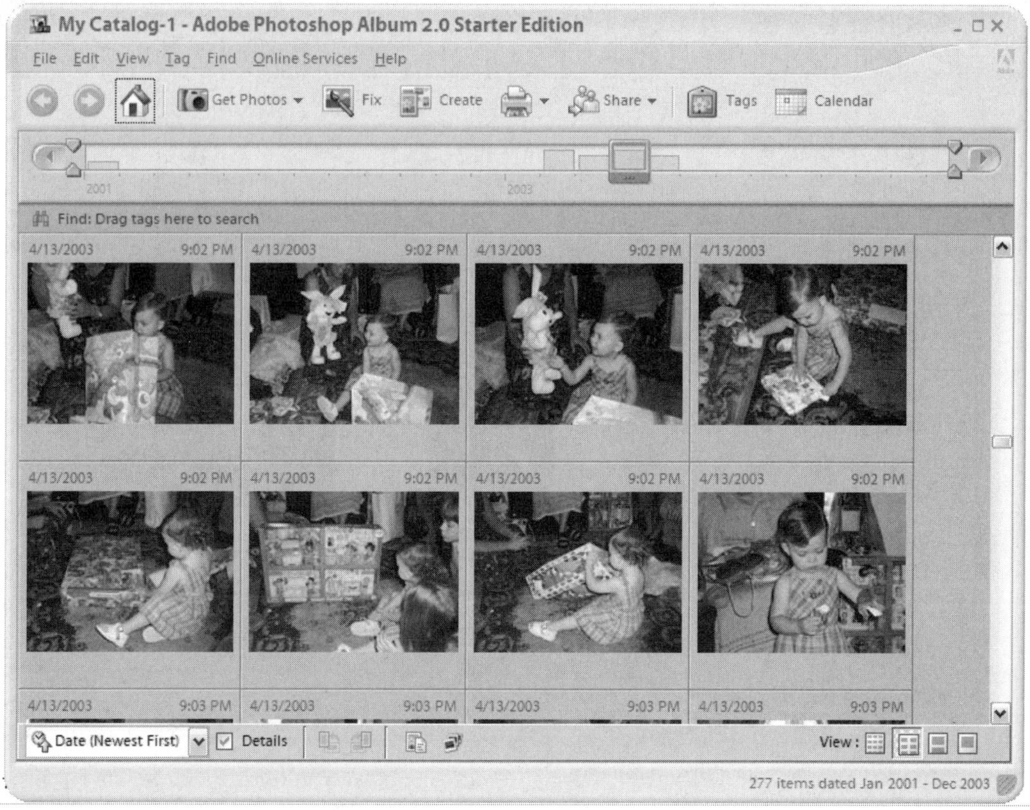

Figure 13-1: Adobe Photoshop Album Starter Edition.

you can enjoy it too. It has great cataloguing features and helps you find photos that you want quickly and easily. It also provides basic editing capabilities and supports all camera formats, including RAW. Learn more about IMatch at www.photools.com. The software costs around $50 but you can download a trial version.

Photodex CompuPic Pro

CompuPic Pro is a great management program that provides a number of helpful features for cataloguing and managing your photos (shown in Figure 13-5). You can easily add borders, use special-effect filters, convert from one file type to another, and so on. This software gathers your photos in an organized manner. Find out more about CompuPic Pro at www.photodex.com. It costs around $80 and you can download a trial version from the company's Web site.

Figure 13-2: Jasc Paint Shop Photo Albumc

iView Media

iView Media doesn't have as many bells and whistles as other photo and media management software, but for organizing media files and easy of use, iView Media is all you need. You can easily work with different kinds of multimedia files, edit them, and change file types, as needed. Find out more at `www.iview-multimedia.com`. The software costs $50.

Adjusting AutoPlay

Working with digital media means using many CDs and DVDs. As you have probably noticed, Windows XP has an AutoPlay feature that, by default, prompts for an action whenever you insert some type of media disk into the CD/DVD drive. Although this AutoPlay function is nice, the prompt can really get on your nerves, especially if you tend to do the

Figure 13-3: ACDSee.

same thing each time. For example, if you want to use Media Player each time you insert a CD, you really don't need a prompt asking every time. Fortunately, you can set a default action so you bypass the prompt, saving you time and irritation. Here's how you can do it:

1. Open the Start menu and select My Computer.
2. Right-click your CD/DVD ROM drive and select Properties.
3. Select the AutoPlay tab (see Figure 13-6).
4. By default, the "Prompt me each time to choose an action" option button is selected. Change this behavior by clicking the "Select an action to perform" option. Use the drop-down menu to determine the media type (such as "music files") and then choose an action from the provided area, such as "Play using Windows Media Player." Repeat this process for other types of media so that AutoPlay knows what to do with each type.
5. When you are done, click OK.

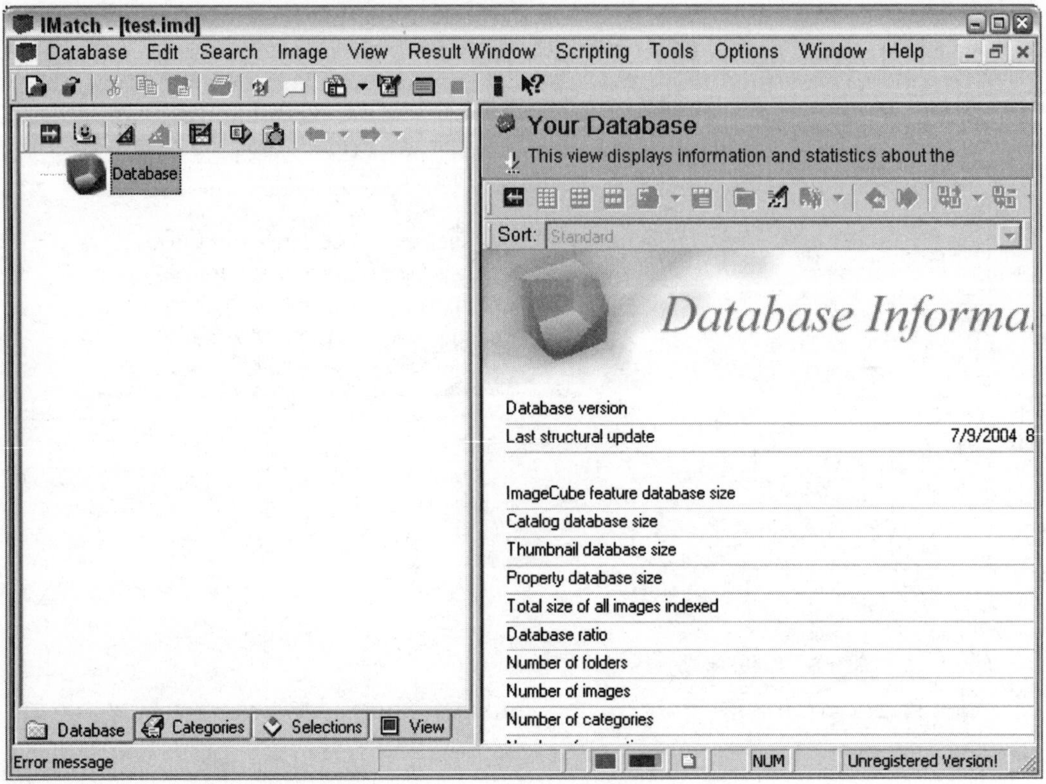

Figure 13-4: Photools IMatch.

Tip

If you have multiple CD or DVD drives installed on your PC, open My Computer and access the Properties dialog boxes for each one. You must configure the AutoPlay tab for each drive. The configuration settings apply to a specific drive only, not all drives on your computer.

Speed and Digital Media

I know what you really want. You want to edit digital video, work with numerous photos, and happily do all of those fun digital media things at the same time. However, when you try to do that, you notice an incredible slowdown on your system. It may even come to a screeching halt.

The reality is that digital media consumes a lot of processor cycles and RAM. There is no workaround for the problem except to install a fast processor and enough RAM to handle the workload. If you love digital media and you are in the market for a new PC, you should get the fastest processor available and the most RAM you can afford. These two hardware solutions are the only real speed solution when it comes to performance and digital media. Your PC will have to be a "workhorse" machine to handle lots of digital media work gracefully.

The same is true for all of your other equipment, such as a digital camera or video camcorder. You can transfer data to your computer, but the transfer will only work as fast as the USB or FireWire connection allows. There aren't any specific operating system tweaks that will help here; the lesson is always use the fastest hardware you can afford. When you need to upgrade, do so with an eye on performance and speed.

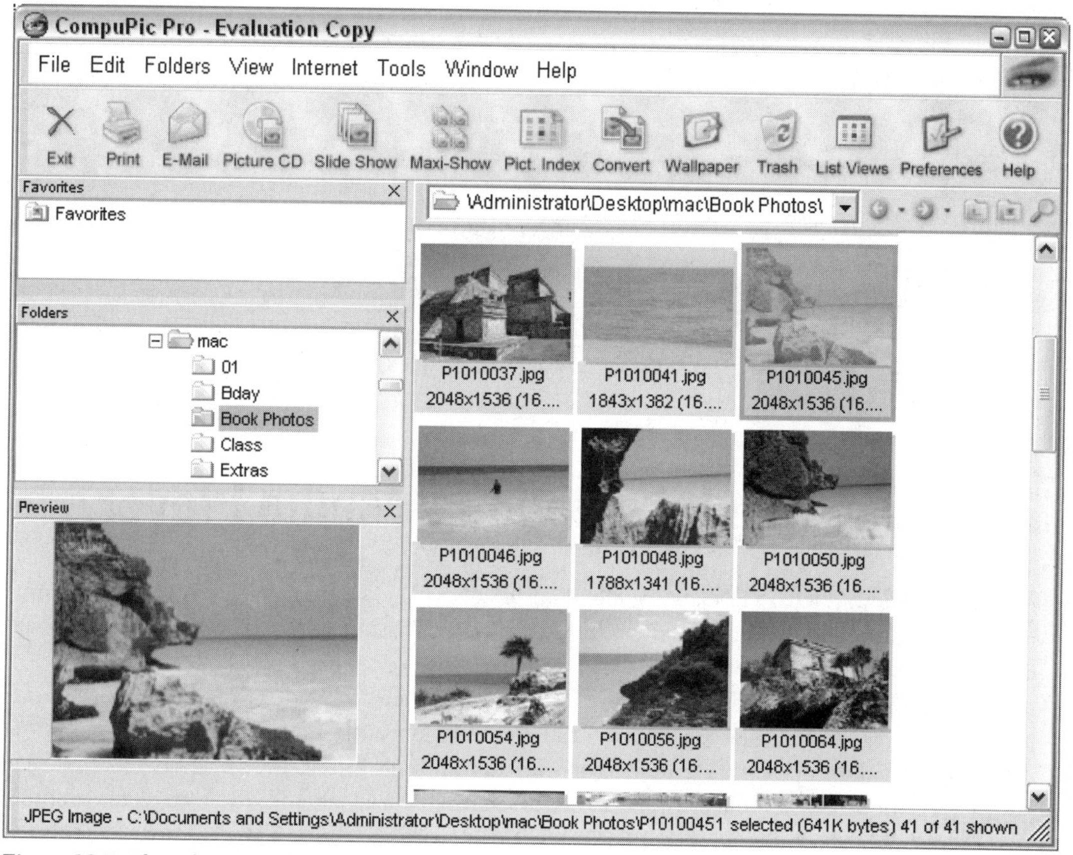

Figure 13-5: Photodex CompuPic Pro.

Figure 13-6: The AutoPlay tab in the CD/DVD drive Properties dialog box.

Speeding Up Windows Media Player

Windows Media Player is the standard for digital media playback in Windows XP. You can download and install other media players in Windows XP, but because Media Player 10 meets most of your digital media needs, I'll focus on it first.

As with all media players, the latest version of Media Player enables you to play music and movies and view photos. You can create libraries, make play lists, and rip and burn CDs. All of this comes in an easy-to-use, customizable interface (see Figure 13-7). Media Player 10 has a number of helpful improvements over Media Player 9, so if you are not using Media Player 10, I recommend that you download the new version from Microsoft.

I won't concern you here with the use and basic configuration of Media Player. If you have used Media Player 9, you will not find Media Player 10 to be radically different. Even

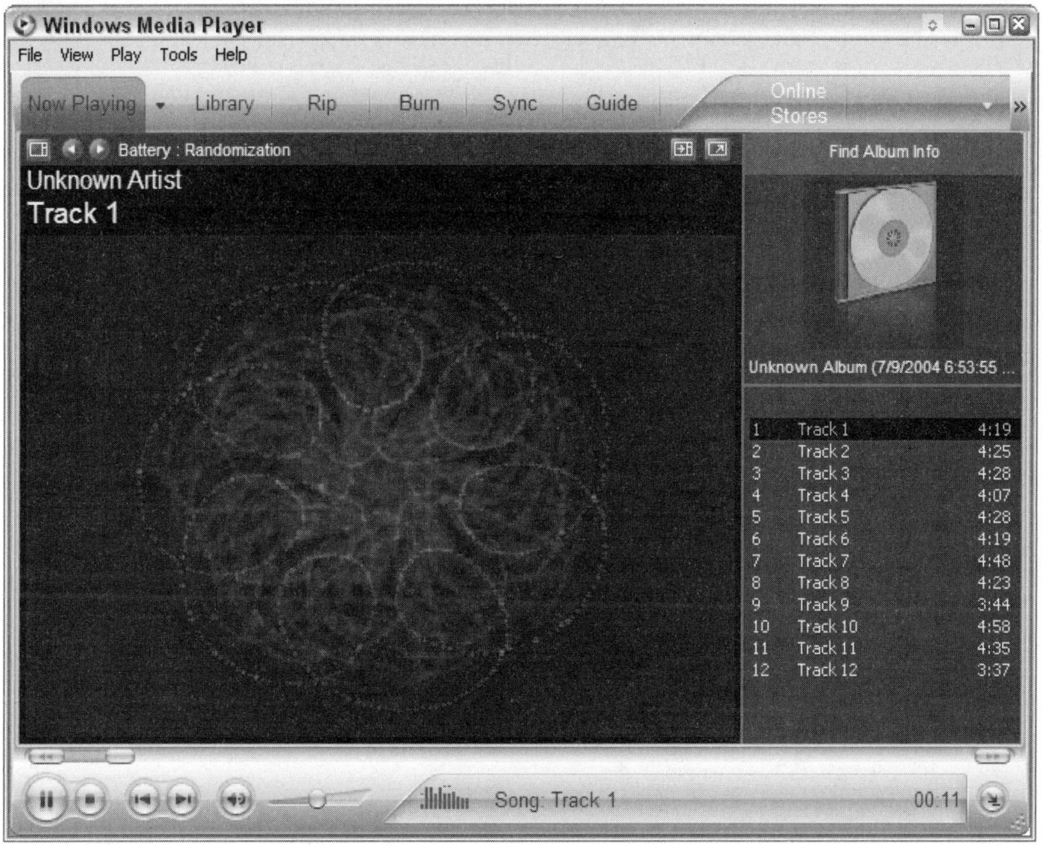

Figure 13-7: Windows Media Player 10.

if you have never used Media Player, the interface is intuitive and easy to learn, so start exploring. However, I do want to point out some configuration options you might want to make. These options may give you a bit of a speed boost and stop some of the overhead of Media Player. Typically, a good tactic is to disable features that you do not want to use, and the same holds true with this version of Media Player. You can access all of Media Player's features by selecting Tools ➪ Options. The following sections point out some settings you might want to examine.

Player Tab

The Player tab (see Figure 13-8) provides some standard settings for Media Player. One thing you can do here is adjust the Automatic Updates section. By default, Media Player

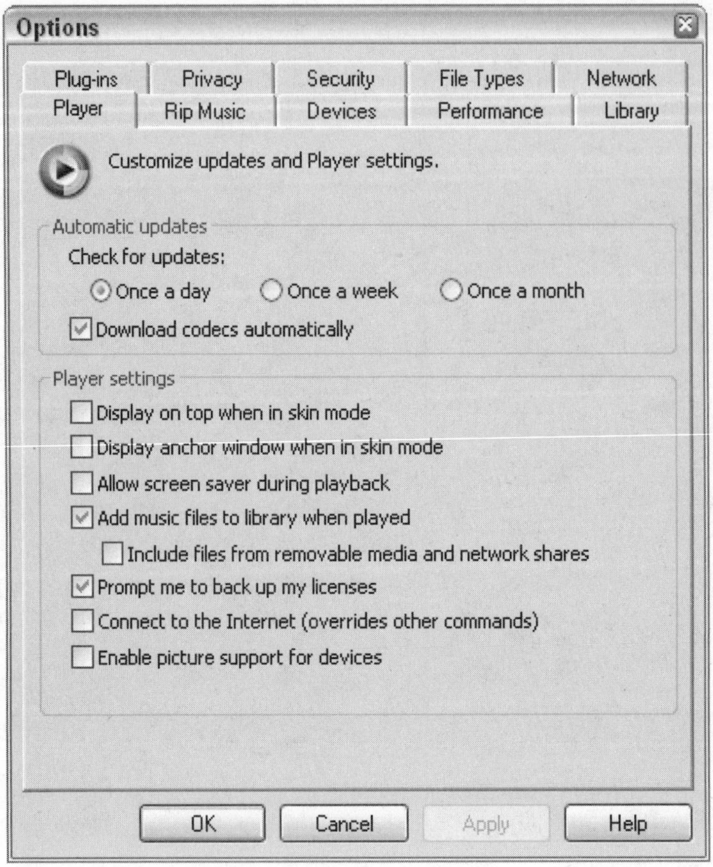

Figure 13-8: The Player tab of the Windows Media Player Options dialog box.

checks for updates every day. That's fine if you have a broadband connection but, even so, the everyday check is a bit excessive. Change this to once a week and you should be fine. Check the other settings here as well. These do not directly impact speed but they do impact the functionality of Media Player and how it behaves, so remove anything you don't like.

Rip Music Tab

The Rip Music tab enables you to set basic settings for ripping music from a CD. One item of interest concerns the audio quality slider setting. The higher the quality, the slower the ripping speed tends to be, so you need to strike a balance here between speed and the quality you want. Just move the slider to the desired position. The higher the quality, the greater the file size, as well.

Performance Tab

The Performance tab (see Figure 13-9) contains a few important settings that can affect the performance of Media Player. By default, the connection speed is detected automatically. Leave this default as is unless you want to specify a certain connection speed. Network buffering is also configured by default. This one can stay at the default level—you typically get the best performance with the default setting. In the Video Acceleration area, make sure you use the Full setting (see Figure 13-9).

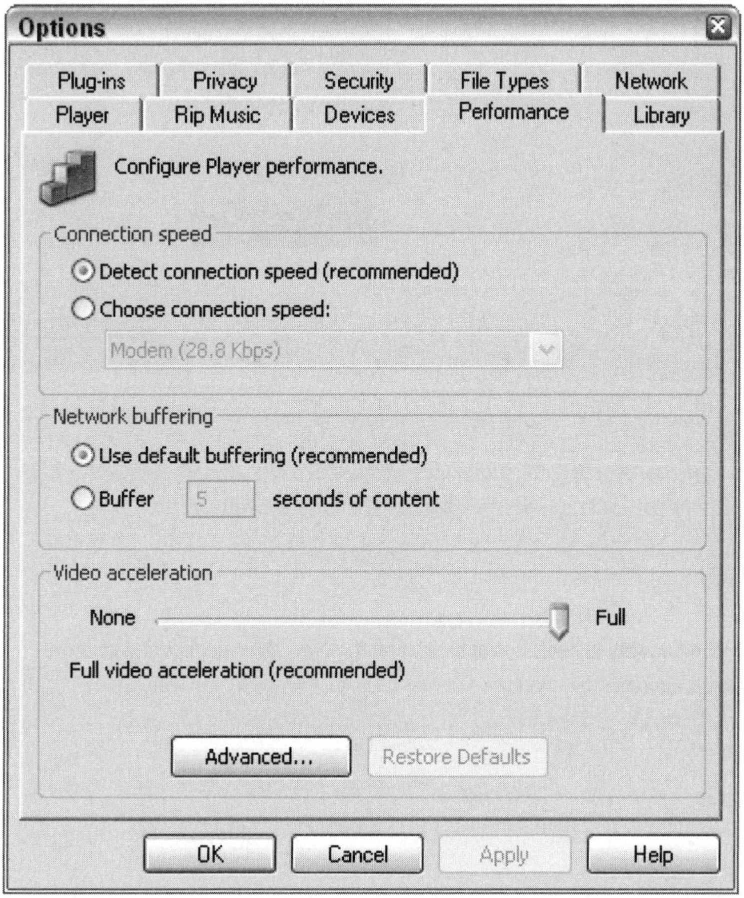

Figure 13-9: The Performance tab of the Windows Media Player Options dialog box.

Click the Advanced button to open the Video Acceleration Settings dialog box (see Figure 13-10). Check these settings. For the most part, the selections you see in Figure 13-10

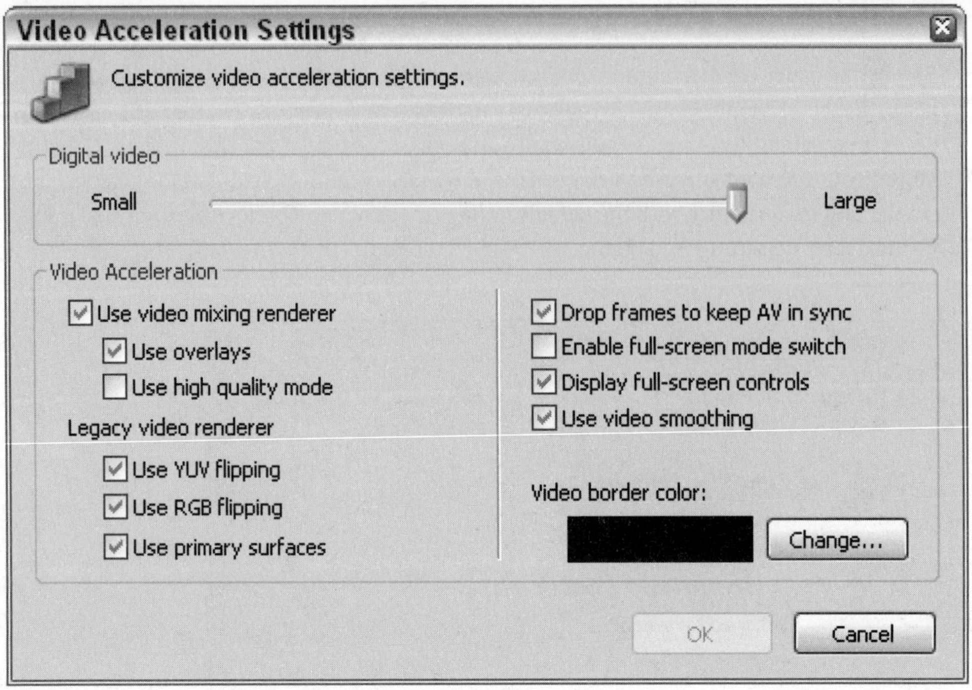

Figure 13-10: The Video Acceleration Settings dialog box.

are best. These give you the best digital video performance. Note that the Video Border Color setting is black; you can change this by clicking the Change button next to it.

Tip

As a general rule, leave the Security tab settings at their default values. Over-configuring security settings tends to slow performance.

Part IV

Keeping Your PC Healthy and Happy

IN THIS PART

Chapter 14

Automating the Health of Your System

Slowdowns in Windows XP generally occur over time—as files build up and you install and remove applications or services. In other words, as you make changes to your system and your system collects more and more clutter, Windows XP works more slowly. Beyond the speed solutions I've already explored in this book, there are a few additional things you can do to help keep Windows XP healthy and running satisfactorily. The solutions explored in this chapter all revolve around the idea of automating processes that help keep Windows XP running the way it should. You still need to tweak some things manually from time to time to keep everything running optimally, but the speed solutions in this chapter can certainly help you stay closer to that goal.

Creating Scheduled Tasks

Scheduled Tasks are one of the great features of Windows XP that users often ignore. Yet if you want to place some automation at your fingertips, Scheduled Tasks give you a way to set up some Windows XP management features to run automatically when you want. I've mentioned Scheduled Tasks a few times throughout the book, but I want to give you a solid walkthrough here.

Scheduled Tasks can be an effective way to run certain programs in Windows XP. For example, suppose you want to run Disk Defragmenter each month. You could manually start Disk Defragmenter and then wait endlessly for the process to finish, or you could use Scheduled Tasks to run Disk Defragmenter once a month in the middle of the night (provided you don't turn off the computer). This way, Disk Defragmenter won't interrupted your daytime computer usage and you won't forget to run the utility. You can run Error Checking or Disk Cleanup this way as well.

Scheduled Tasks are easy to create and manage. You simply configure them and they run when they are supposed to. If you no longer want to run a Scheduled Task, you can just delete it. The following steps walk you through the configuration of a Scheduled Task:

1. Open the Start menu and select Control Panel ➪ Scheduled Tasks.
2. Click the Add Scheduled Task option to start the Scheduled Task Wizard.
3. Click Next to go past the Welcome screen.
4. Select the application or utility you want to schedule (see Figure 14-1) or click the Browse button to locate it.

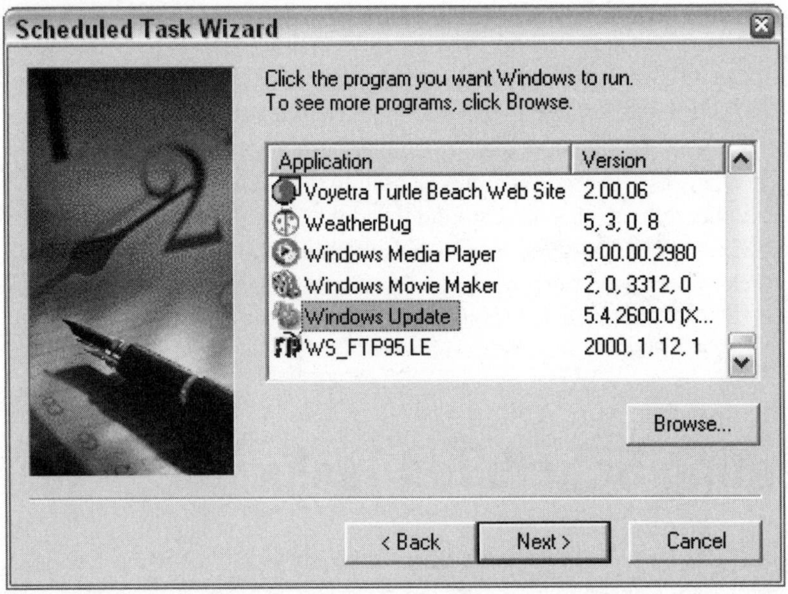

Figure 14-1: Choose a task to schedule in the Scheduled Task Wizard.

5. Enter a name for the task and determine how often it should run. You can choose daily, monthly, one time only, when the computer starts, or when you log on (see Figure 14-2). Make a selection and click Next.
6. Select a start time and day of the week, if applicable (see Figure 14-3). Be sure to choose a day and time when you will not be using your computer so as not to

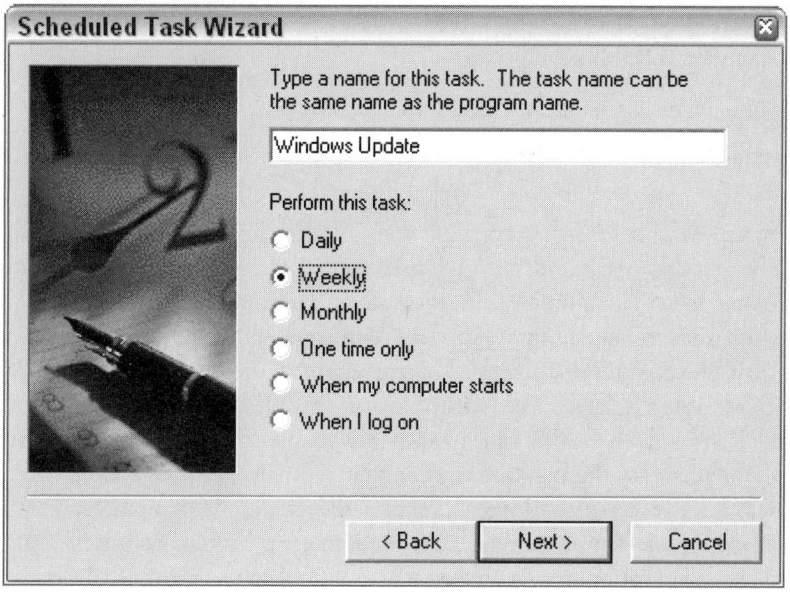

Figure 14-2: Choose a name and runtime.

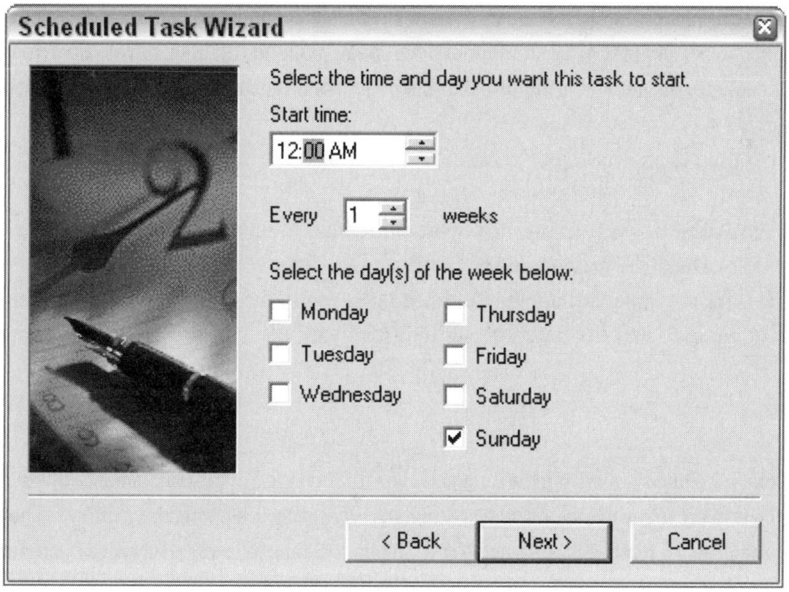

Figure 14-3: Choose a start time and day for the Scheduled Task.

interrupt your work. Here I have set Windows Update to run at midnight on Sundays. Click Next.

7. Enter your username and password and then click Next.
8. Click Finish.

Repeat this wizard to configure additional tasks to run. Naturally, you should think through the process and avoid stacking tasks so that they do not run at the same time, because some tasks may interfere with each other. For example, I have Windows Update run at midnight each Sunday, but I have Disk Defragmenter run once a month at midnight on Saturday. This ensures that the two tasks never run at the same time.

Once you create a task, you'll see it listed in the Scheduled Tasks folder. You can see when the task will run and when it last ran. You can also double-click a task to open its properties and adjust anything for the task that you configured originally in the wizard. You can even configure more advanced schedules and create some additional limitations. For example, you could stop a task from running in case the computer is running on batteries and you do not want to expend battery power on the task. You can delete a Scheduled Task at any time.

Note

Your computer must be turned on when a Scheduled Task is supposed to run. Scheduled Tasks cannot boot your computer or bring it out of hibernation mode to run themselves. So if you have items scheduled to run during the night, leave your computer on and turn off the power management options.

Now you may be wondering how you can create a Scheduled Task such as Disk Defragmenter or Disk Cleanup when they ordinarily require some human interaction in order to run. It turns out you can automate those tasks easily by creating a batch file and using Scheduled Tasks to run the batch file. I describe batch files at the end of the chapter.

Tip

You can run Scheduled Tasks from the command line through the Schtasks command. Although it's powerful, there are many command-line switches to work with, which can be a bit overwhelming and more time-consuming than just using the Scheduled Task Wizard. However, if you need to configure something very specific, you may find that the Schtasks command works well for us. Visit the Windows XP Help and Support Center to learn more about this feature.

Automating Clean-Up Tasks

As you configure options in Windows XP, keep an eye on how you could automate things. For example, you could configure Internet Explorer to delete temporary Internet files automatically every so often so that you do not have to perform the task manually (see Chapter 10). Other tools, such as Temp folder cleaners and Registry cleaners, generally include options to automate periodic cleaning. These features save you time and effort and help give you a scheduled process for keeping your Windows XP computer clean and in good working order.

Automatically Downloading Web Pages

One helpful feature you can invoke is the automatic downloading of Web pages and content. For example, suppose you like to read the latest news each day while you get ready for work. Rather than visit the Web pages yourself, have Internet Explorer grab the page and download it for you just before you need it, so it's waiting for you after you shower. You need an Internet connection for this to work, but even a modem connection will work if it is configured for autodialing.

This feature works through the offline Web pages list. Add the Web page to your list of Favorites and configure a Scheduled Task for when Internet Explorer should retrieve it for you. Follow these steps:

1. Open Internet Explorer and access the desired Web page.
2. Select Favorites ➪ Add to Favorites. The Add Favorite dialog box appears. Give the site a name and click the Make Available Offline option (see Figure 14-4).

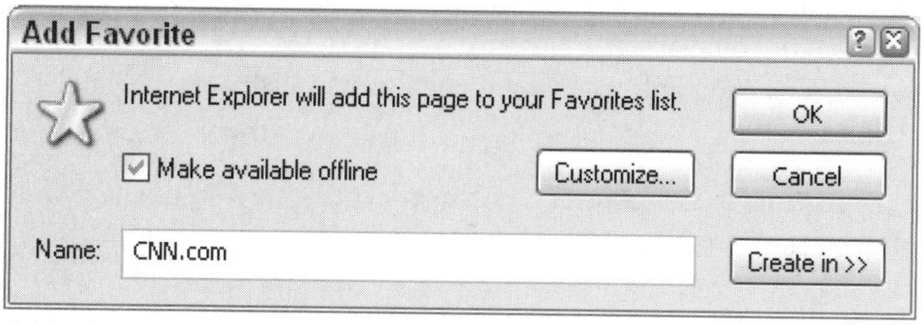

Figure 14-4: Make a site available offline.

3. Click the Customize button. This starts the Offline Favorite Wizard. Click Next on the Welcome screen.

4. On the Setup screen (see Figure 14-5) you can choose to make just the selected page available offline or make all links from the page available as well. Your selection here depends entirely on your needs. Notice that you can also determine how deep the download links should go, such as one page, two pages, and so on. Start with one page and see if you like the results. Make a selection and click Next.

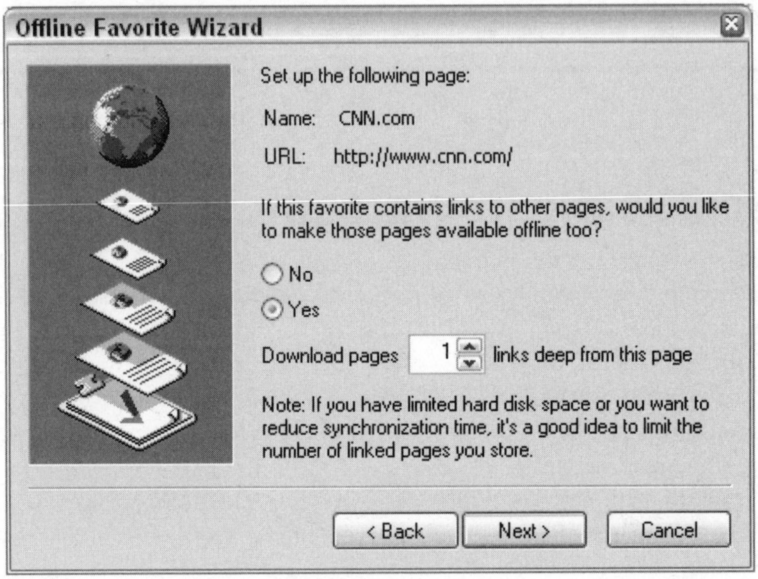
Offline Favorite Wizard
Set up the following page:
Name: CNN.com
URL: http://www.cnn.com/
If this favorite contains links to other pages, would you like to make those pages available offline too?
No
Yes
Download pages 1 links deep from this page
Note: If you have limited hard disk space or you want to reduce synchronization time, it's a good idea to limit the number of linked pages you store.
< Back
Next >
Cancel

Figure 14-5: Choose the links download option as needed.

5. On the next screen, select the option to create a new schedule and click Next.

6. On the schedule window, determine how often (number of days) and at what time you want the offline Web favorite to be updated. Figure 14-6 shows that I am downloading this Web page every day at 5:00 AM. Also notice that you can generate a connection automatically if one is not available. Make your selections and click Next.

7. If the site requires a username and password, configure it in the next window. If not, click Finish.

You can make changes any time in Internet Explorer by opening the Favorites menu, right-clicking the name of the offline Favorite, and selecting Properties. In the Properties dialog box, you can adjust the schedule and download options, and even have an e-mail sent to you when the page is updated. These options are self-explanatory.

Offline Favorite Wizard
When would you like to synchronize this page?
Every 1 days at 5:00 AM
Name: CNN Update
If my computer is not connected when this scheduled synchronization begins, automatically connect for me
< Back
Next >
Cancel

Figure 14-6: Determine a schedule.

Using Batch Files

A batch file is a text file that contains one or more commands that Windows XP can execute. You can run several commands in one file—hence the name "batch"—and you can use batch files to automate a number of things in Windows XP.

Batch files can be rather simple or they can be extremely complex. I won't explore everything you can do with batch files, but this section will get you started and show you how to automate a few common tasks that you might be interested in automating.

Most programs in Windows XP can be run from the command-line interface without the graphical portion of Windows XP. You can execute these commands and use a variety of switches that determine how the program should run. In a nutshell, the batch file holds those commands and Windows XP simply runs the batch file and executes the commands. As you can imagine, batch files can be very helpful in a variety of ways. The following sections show you how to create batch files to automate some common items.

Tip

Learn more about batch-file commands at `www.microsoft.com/resources/documentation/windows/xp/all/proddocs/en-us/batch.mspx`.

Automating Disk Defragmenter

As I mentioned previously, Scheduled Tasks are very helpful. However, if you must interact with a program that you want to run automatically, Scheduled Tasks alone will do no good. Disk Defragmenter is a good example of a program you want to automate but cannot schedule because of the need to interact with the graphical user interface. To bypass the user interface, create a batch file that tells Disk Defragmenter how to run without your intervention. Fortunately, this action is quick and easy. Just follow these steps:

1. Select Start ➪ Run, type **notepad**, and click OK.
2. In Notepad, type the following:

```
DEFRAG C:
```

   If you want to defragment other drives as well, just list them. For example, Figure 14-7 shows me creating a batch file that defragments my C, D, E, and F drives.

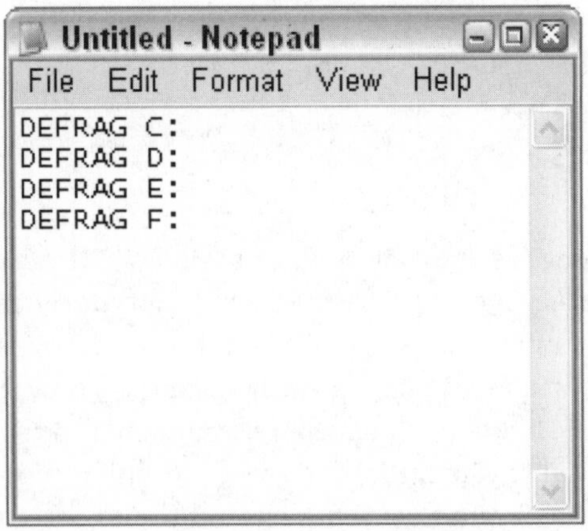

Figure 14-7: Commands to defrag the C, D, E, and F drives.

3. Select File ➪ Save As and name the file **defrag.bat**. You must use the .bat extension when you save the file, and you must change the file type to All Files (otherwise, it will be saved as a text file, which will not work).
4. Run Scheduled Tasks in Control Panel. When you are prompted to select the Scheduled Task, click Browse and locate the defrag.bat file. Finish the wizard and select the desired day and time you want defrag command to run.

You have now automated Disk Defragmenter. It will run automatically as a Scheduled Task.

Automating Disk Cleanup

You can automate Disk Cleanup and use it as a Scheduled Task, as well. However, rather than creating a batch file for it, you have to set the parameters for Disk Cleanup so that it can be automated. Once again, this process is rather easy, and the following steps show you how.

1. Select Start ➪ Run and type the following:

   ```
   CLEANMGR / SAGESET:50
   ```

   Click OK.

2. The Disk Cleanup dialog box appears. Select the items you want to clean up automatically, such as downloaded program files, temporary Internet files, and so on (see Figure 14-8). What you are doing here is creating the settings that will be automatically used. Click OK.

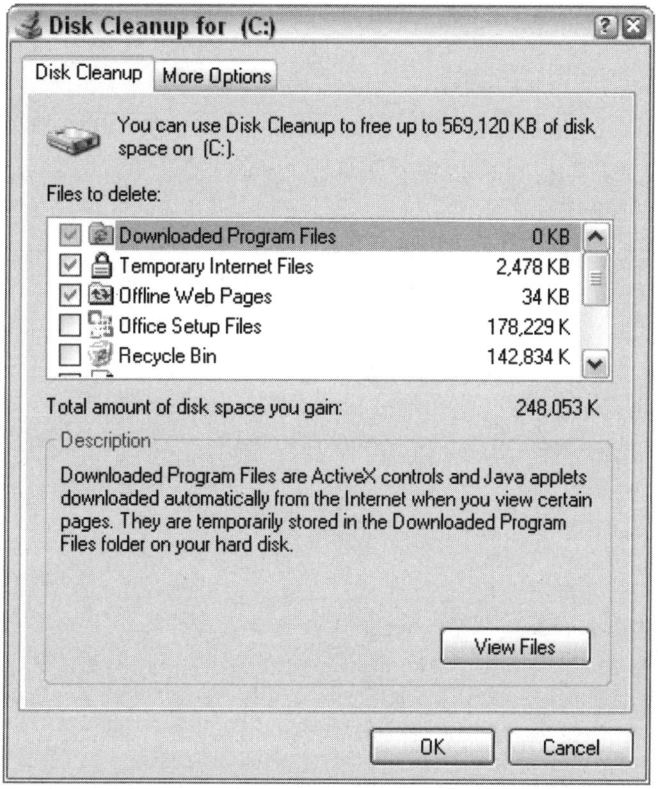

Figure 14-8: Choose the items you want to clean up automatically.

3. Run Scheduled Tasks in Control Panel and start the Add Scheduled Task wizard. Click Next on the Welcome screen.
4. On the selection screen, select Disk Cleanup and click Next.
5. Complete the rest of the wizard and configure the day and time you want the task to run.
6. On the last wizard page, select the "Open advanced properties for this task when I click Finish" option and then click Finish.
7. Notice on the Task tab (see Figure 14-9) that the path to the Disk Cleanup tool is listed—most likely as "C:\WINDOWS\SYSTEM32\CLEANMGR.EXE." All you

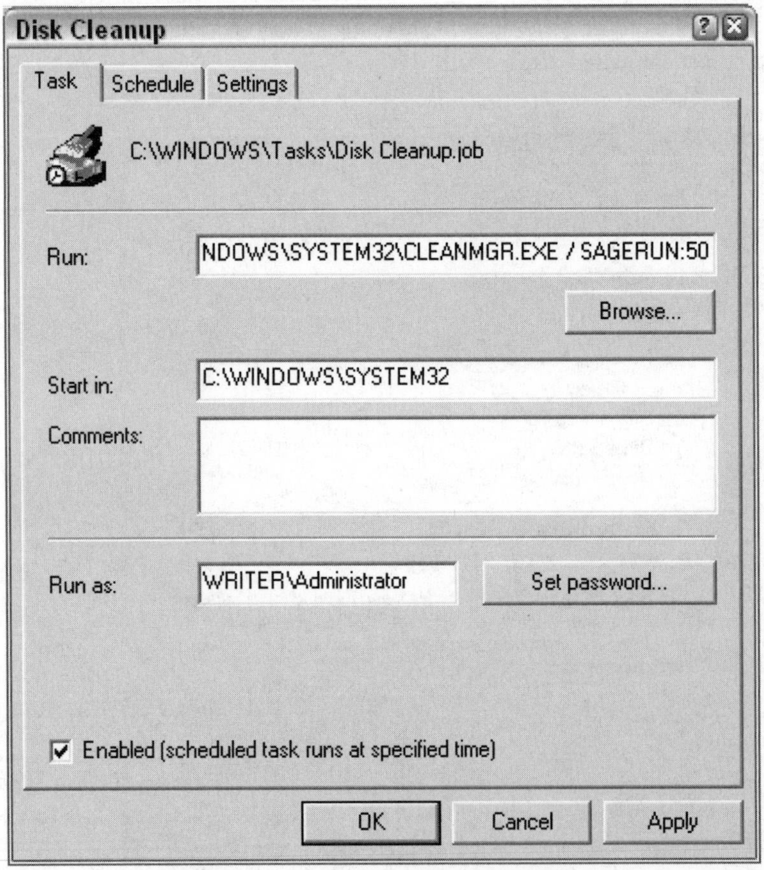

Figure 14-9: Adding "/ SAGERUN:50" to the Disk Cleanup tool's command line.

need to do is add this to the end of the line:

```
/ SAGERUN:50
```

It should now read as "C:\WINDOWS\SYSTEM32\CLEANMGR.EXE/ SAGERUN:50."

8. Click OK. The task is now complete and will run automatically.

Automatically Deleting Content from the Prefetch Folder

As I mentioned in Chapter 1, the Prefetch folder holds portions of programs that you use commonly so that they can start more quickly. Of course, the Prefetch folder can end up holding a lot of junk as well. You can easily create a batch file that empties the Prefetch folder's contents automatically whenever you want using a Scheduled Task for the batch file.

To do this, open Notepad and type the following:

```
DEL C:\WINDOWS\PREFETCH\*.* /Q
```

Save the Notepad file as a BAT file, such as **prefetch.bat**. Finally, use Scheduled Tasks to create a schedule for the batch file to run.

Chapter 15

Keeping a Check on Your System

Like all advanced computer operating systems, Windows XP can experience performance problems, despite your best intentions to keep the system working at its peak. You should get in the habit of taking note when things do not work the way they should. Windows XP provides a few tools to help you keep tabs on what is going on. Fortunately, Windows XP gives you a Task Manager, an actual Performance monitoring tool, and good error reporting so you can keep track of any potential problems or issues that might come your way. These tools can give you valuable information about your system and help you identify performance problems quickly and easily.

Using the Windows Task Manager

Suppose you are working with your computer and you realize that things seem a bit sluggish. You can take a quick look at the computer's overall performance and see what is slowing down, such as the processor or memory. The Windows Task Manager provides a quick chart of common performance data. Press Ctrl-Alt-Del to access the Windows Task Manager and then click the Performance tab (see Figure 15-1). You can get a quick look at CPU usage and page file usage, along with some other information about memory. The great thing about the Performance tab is that it can speedily tell you whether the CPU is the problem or memory is the problem. Obviously, you don't have any configuration options here, but this feature is a great way to get a fast rundown on your computer's performance.

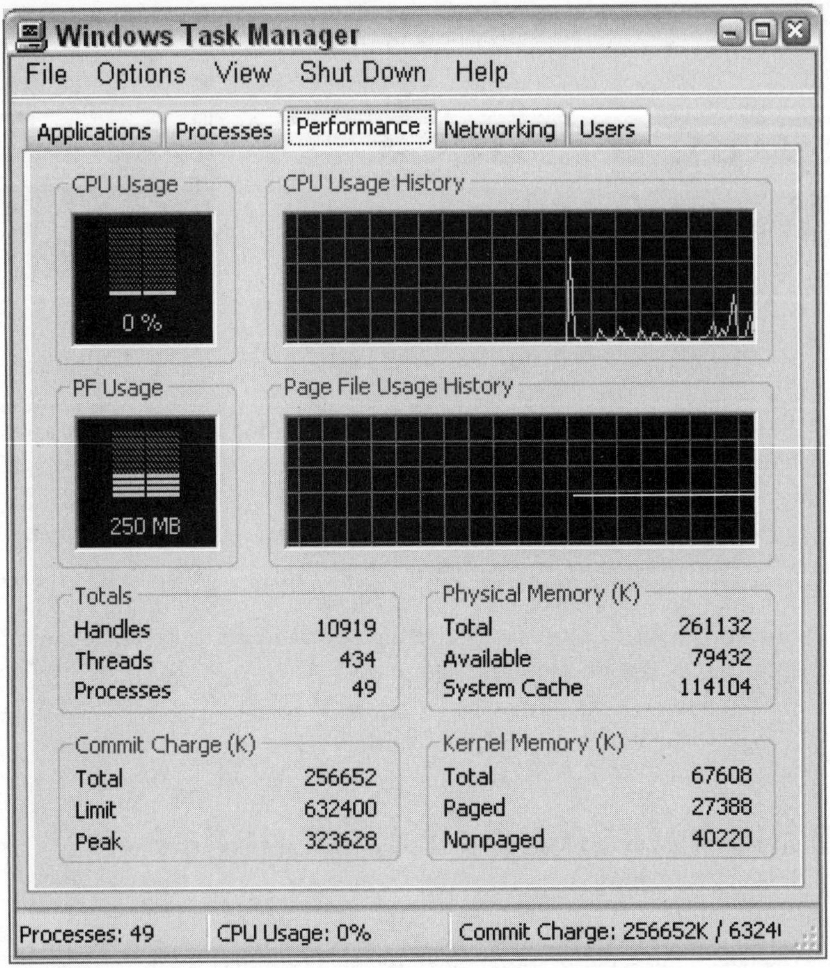

Figure 15-1: The Performance tab in the Windows XP Task Manager.

Using the Performance Tool

The Performance tool you see in Windows XP, once called Performance Monitor, has been around since the days of Windows NT—and hasn't changed much. The tool works well and can be helpful in providing you with specific information about the performance levels of various services and hardware running in Windows XP.

Performance provides you with useful information as a chart, report, or histogram. You can also log data to a log file and configure administrative alerts. Administrative alerts can be sent in the form of making an entry to the application's event log, sending a network message, starting a performance data log, or running a program. Because Performance works on a counter basis, you can individually choose what you want to monitor. This way you can try to isolate any specific performance problems you experience.

As the name implies, Performance doesn't fix any problems; it simply monitors your system in a way that you can discover the cause of existing problems. The purpose of monitoring performance is to gain information about the functioning of various system components and hardware, such as memory and processor utilization. Monitoring is best used with a performance baseline. This means using Performance over a long period—during peak and nonpeak times—to determine the baseline under which the component functions. After you see high and low peaks of performance, you can determine more effectively what constitutes "normal," satisfactory operation for that component. Once you have a baseline, you can use Performance later to see whether the component is functioning within normal parameters. If it is not, you know either that a problem exists with the component or that the load placed on the component has increased. Either way, you can effectively identify the component that is unable to keep up with the demands placed on it—commonly called a *bottleneck*.

Performance functions through the use of objects, counters, and instances. In Performance, "objects" represent certain performance categories, such as memory, physical disk, processor, and related categories of system components and hardware that the tool can monitor. Under each object are specific counters that represent what you are actually monitoring, such as "bytes per second."

Some objects have only a few counters, depending on what can be monitored, while others may have 10 or more. The idea is to provide you with specific counters so that you can monitor specific actions of the object. For example, you could monitor the "memory" object, the "available bytes" counter, and the "pages/sec" counter to gain information about memory availability and current usage, or you could use a combination of memory counters. When you choose to monitor a counter, you monitor an "instance" of that counter.

Exploring the Performance Tool

To run the Performance tool (see Figure 15-2), open the Start menu and select Control Panel ➪ Administrative Tools ➪ Performance.

The left pane contains the System Monitor node and the Performance Logs and Alerts node. You interact primarily with Performance in the right pane. There are three basic divisions of this pane, starting at the top.

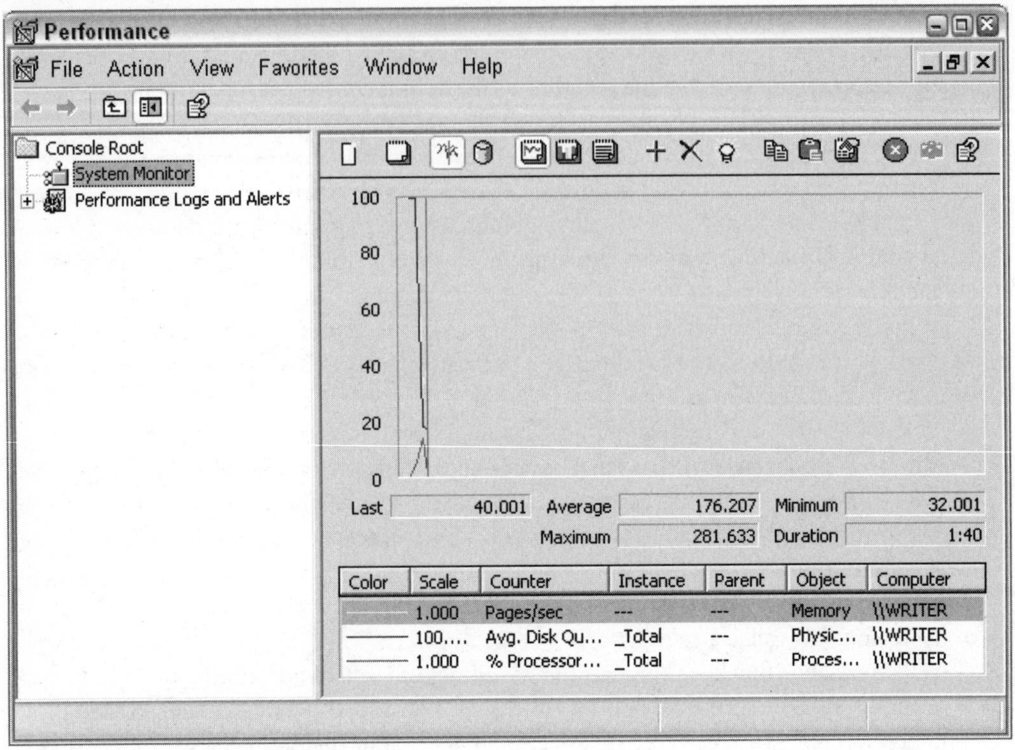

Figure 15-2: The Performance tool.

First, you see a toolbar. It contains icons you use regularly to generate the types of charts and information you want. The toolbar contains the following options, shown from left to right in Figure 15-3:

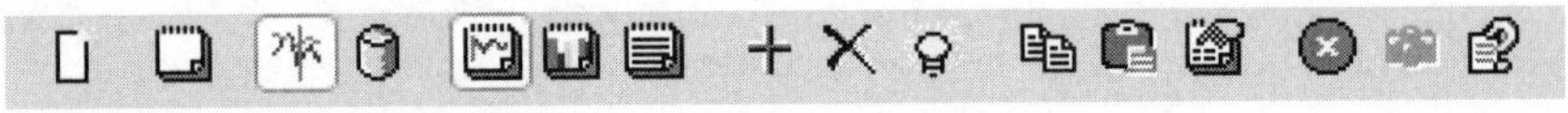

Figure 15-3: Performance toolbar.

- New Counter Set
- Clear Display
- View Current Activity
- View Log Data
- View Graph
- View Histogram

- View Report
- Add
- Delete
- Highlight
- Copy Properties
- Paste Counter List
- Properties
- Freeze Display
- Update Data
- Help

The second division is the information area, containing the chart, histogram, or report you want to view (see Figure 15-4). Click the desired button on the toolbar to view counter information in the desired format.

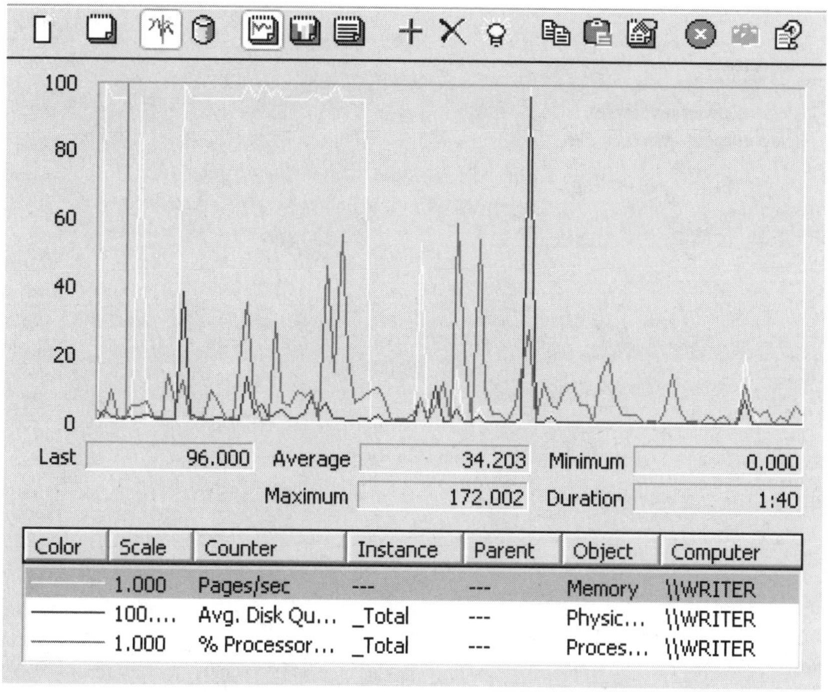

Figure 15-4: Information area.

Finally, the Counter list appears at the bottom of the information area (see also Figure 15-4). All counters displayed in the list are currently being reported in the information area. You can easily remove or add counters to the list using the toolbar. Each counter in the Counter list is given a different color for charting and histogram purposes.

Adding Counters

You primarily use Performance by accessing objects and choosing counters. You choose the counters you want to monitor and then view those counters as a chart, report, or histogram. The following steps show you how to add counters to the Performance monitor interface:

1. Open the Start menu and select Control Panel ➪ Administrative Tools ➪ Performance.
2. In the Performance window, click the New Counter Set button on the toolbar. Then click the Add button on the toolbar.
3. In the Add Counters dialog box (see Figure 15-5), use the drop-down menu to choose a Performance object. As you can see, I have chosen the "Processor Time" counter.

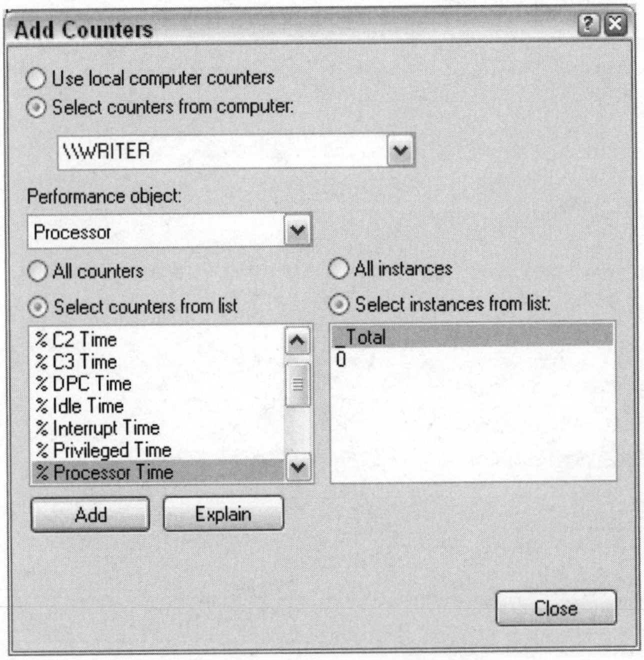

Figure 15-5: Adding counters for the Performance tool.

4. You can choose to monitor all counters under the object you selected or just select desired counters from the list. To select an individual counter, select it and click the Add button. Notice that the Instances dialog box may be active, depending on your selection. The Instances dialog box allows you to choose certain instances, if they are available.

5. Repeat the counter-adding process until you have added all desired counters, then click Close.

You can see that the counters you are adding are being monitored. You can always change the chart, histogram, or report view by clicking a different option button on the toolbar.

Logging Data

As you monitor various counters, you can gain information about the performance of the system processes and components you selected. Generally speaking, consistent, high readings mean that the component or hardware is not able to meet the burden placed on it by the operating system's processes. Although high spikes are normal, consistent high readings on counters usually mean that a problem exists. This is where your baseline data is important. Using the baseline, you can tell whether a component has higher readings than normal and what those reading might mean for system performance.

So if baseline performance is important to establish, how can you gain that data without sitting in front of a screen all day? If a particular object seems to be causing problems, how can you monitor that object during an entire day's operations without physically watching the screen? Performance gives you the ability to log data over a period of time, which is a great way to gain performance data without having to sit physically at the machine. The performance data for the desired object(s) and counter(s) can be sampled over a period of time and then recorded in a log file. You can then use the log file to examine the data at a time that is convenient for you. Fortunately, using the log file is rather easy; the following exercise walks you through the process:

1. In Performance, expand Performance Logs and Alerts in the left pane. Right-click Counter Logs and select New Log Settings.

2. In the New Log Settings dialog box, give the log file a name and click OK.

3. The test dialog box for the log file appears. On the General tab (see Figure 15-6) change the default log filename and storage location if you like. Next, click the Add Objects and Add Counters buttons to add the desired objects or counters you want to log. Figure 15-6 shows me logging several memory counters. Under the sample data heading, choose how often you want the log file to sample data. For example, in the figure I am sampling memory data every 15 seconds.

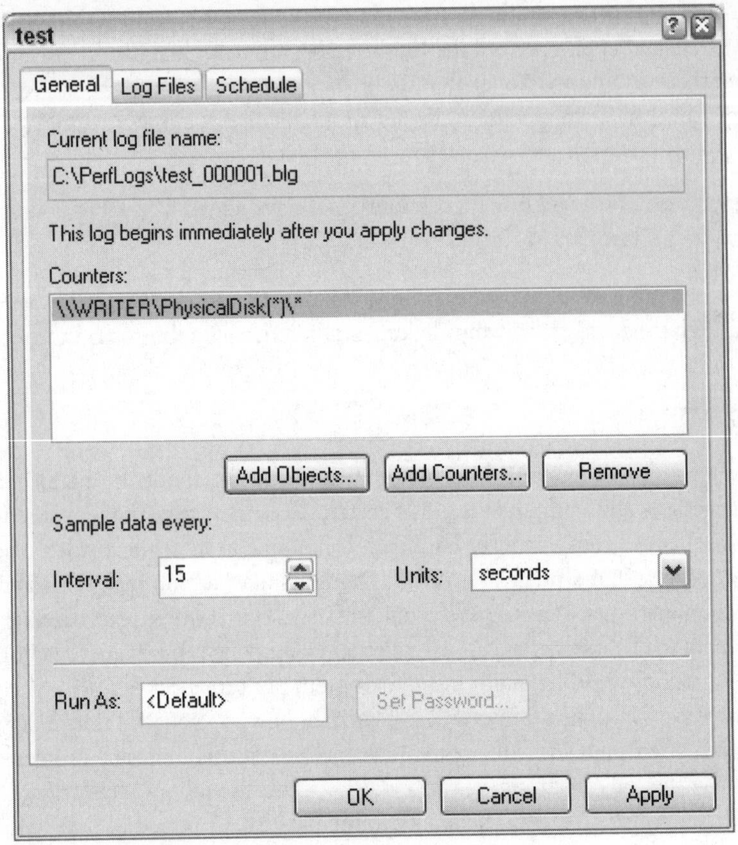

Figure 15-6: General tab of the test dialog box for the log file.

4. On the Log Files tab (see Figure 15-7) you can choose the type of log file you want to produce, which is set to Binary File by default. You can configure this as a text file, binary circular file, or even a SQL database file. Use the rest of the Log Files tab to adjust the filenaming scheme.

5. The Schedule tab allows you to configure how the log file is started or stopped (see Figure 15-8). The settings here are self-explanatory. When you are done with all of the settings for the log file, click OK.

Creating Alerts

The Performance tool has the capability of alerting you whenever a certain component falls below a performance baseline you set. An alert is simply an action that Performance

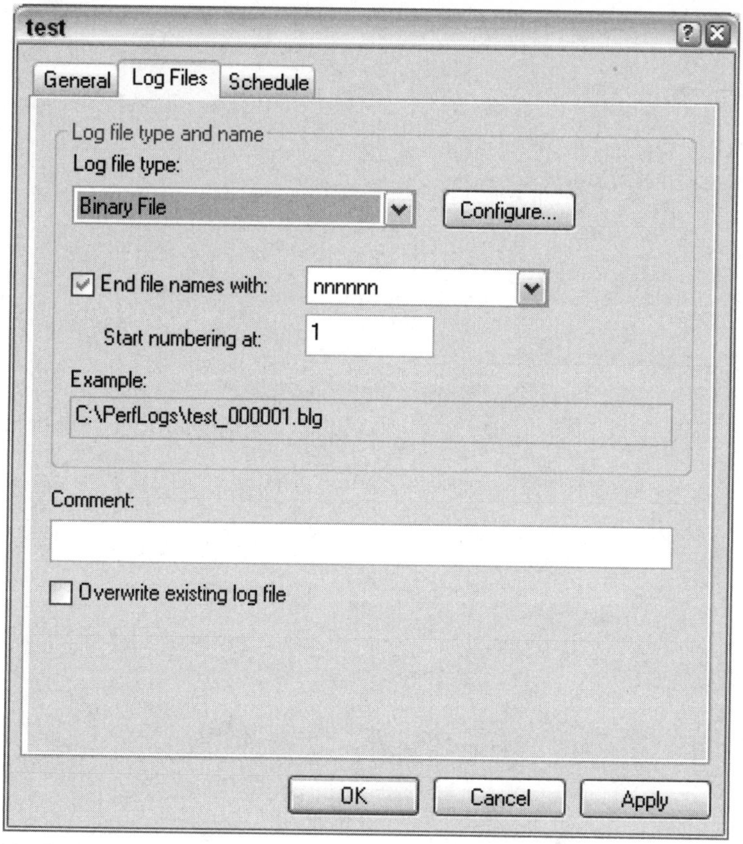

Figure 15-7: Log Files tab of the test dialog box for the log file.

carries out when it's triggered. You configure the alert to carry out a particular action, such as sending a network message or recording an event to the event log, when the alert is triggered. This is one way to keep track of objects that fall below baseline standards. In critical scenarios, it is a great way to find out about baseline failures as they occur. Like log files, alerts are rather easy to configure; the following exercise shows you how:

1. In Performance, expand Performance Logs and Alerts in the left pane. Right-click Alerts and select New Alert Settings.
2. Give the new alert setting a name in the dialog box that appears and click OK.
3. The test dialog box for the alert appears. On the General tab (see Figure 15-9) add counters to the alert, just as you would for a log file. Once the counters are added to the list, choose a baseline limit and data sample rate.

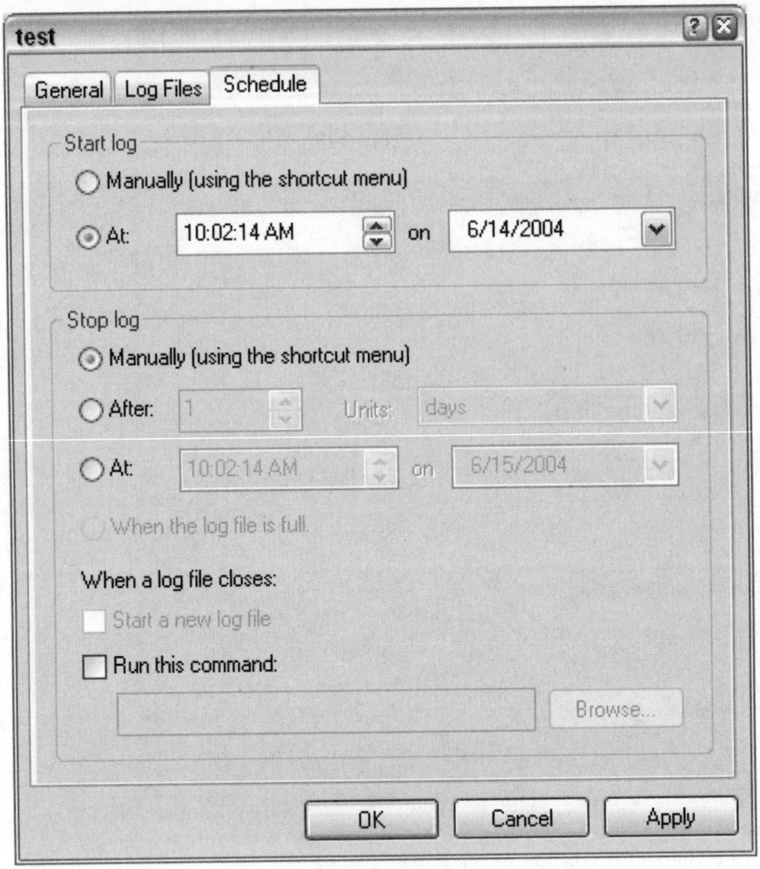

Figure 15-8: Schedule tab of the test dialog box for the log file.

4. On the Action tab (see Figure 15-10), choose an action that occurs when the event is triggered.
5. On the Schedule tab configure a schedule as desired. This is the same Schedule tab you see when configuring a log file.

Using Memory and Processor Performance Counters

You can use Performance to check out the performance of memory and the processor—and even the paging file. By monitoring these objects, you get a clear view of system and application usage and how memory and the processor are holding up under the demands placed on them. If you are feeling a bit overwhelmed by the number of counters and objects

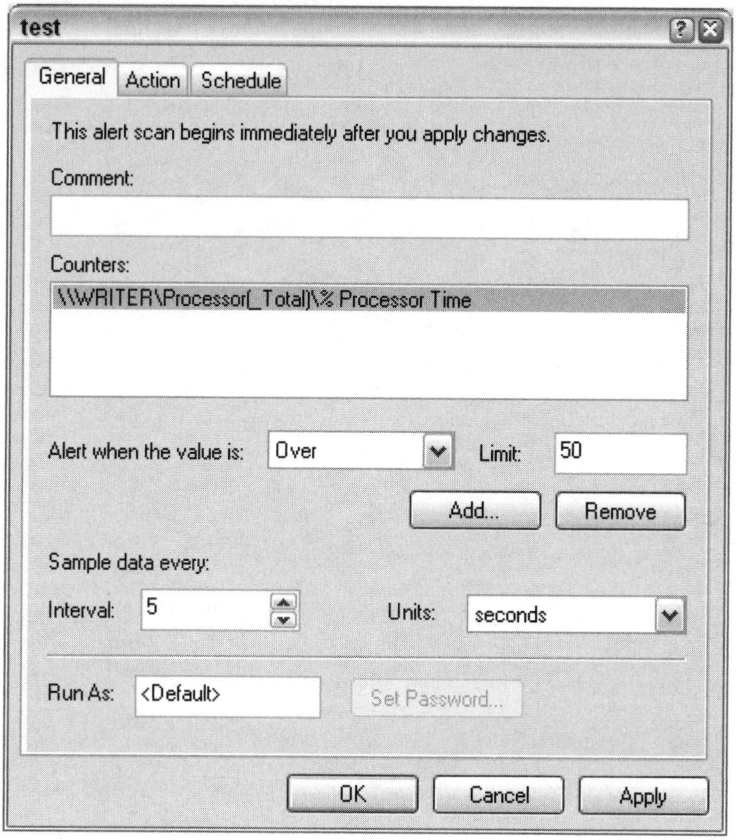

Figure 15-9: General tab for new alert settings.

you should monitor, here's a quick list of common counters and objects that can really help you.

For the processor object, use these common counters:

- **% Interrupt Time:** The amount of time the processor spends receiving and servicing hardware interrupts. This counter can help you see whether the processor can handle the system's hardware needs.
- **% Processor Time:** The percentages of time the processor spends to execute a non-idle threat. This counter tells you how much time the processor requires to meet system and application threads.
- **Interrupts/sec:** The average rate at which the processor receives and services interrupts.

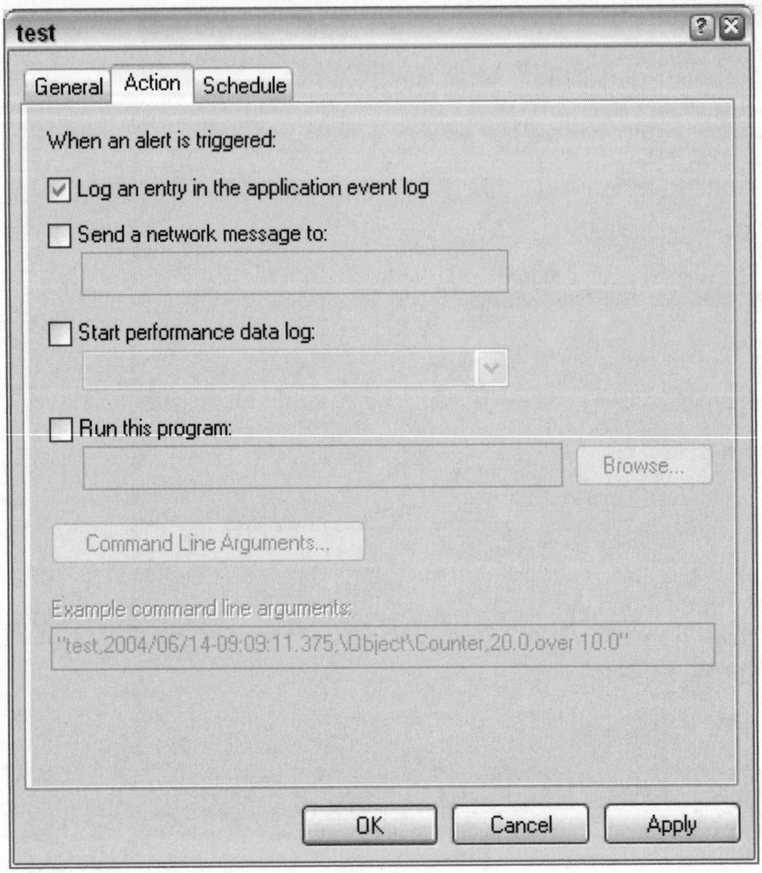

Figure 15-10: The Action tab for new alert settings.

- **% Idle Time:** The amount of time that the processor is idle during a sampling period. If there seems to be no idle time, this may indicate that the processor cannot keep up with system, application, and hardware demands.

For the memory object, keep these counters in mind:

- **Page Reads/sec:** The amount of pages read in a monitored second.
- **Page Writes/sec:** The amount of pages written in a monitored second.
- **Pages/sec:** The rate at which pages are written to or read from a disk.

For the paging file object, keep these counters in mind:

- **% Usage:** The amount of page file instances in use.
- **% Usage Peak:** The peak usage of the paging file, as a percentage. A high percentage indicates that more RAM may be needed on the system because the paging file is being used excessively.

Using the Event Viewer

One way you can keep track of errors and problems that occur in Windows XP is through the Event Viewer. This viewer console in Administrative Tools tells you all the events that have been recorded. It's a good place to check from time to time and see whether you find any constantly occurring problems that need addressing.

Open the Start menu and select Control Panel ➪ Administrative Tools ➪ Event Viewer. The console appears, showing you that an Application, Security, and System log are available to review. If you select one of the log files in the left console pane, you'll see the events that have occurred (see Figure 15-11).

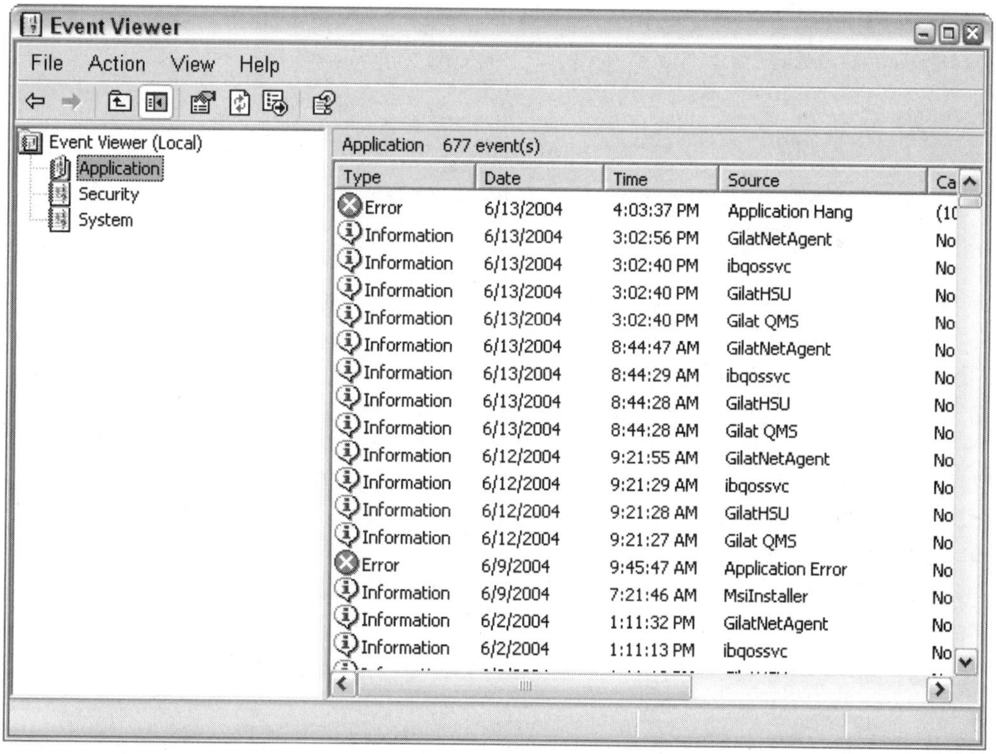

Figure 15-11: This event log shows you what has happened on your system.

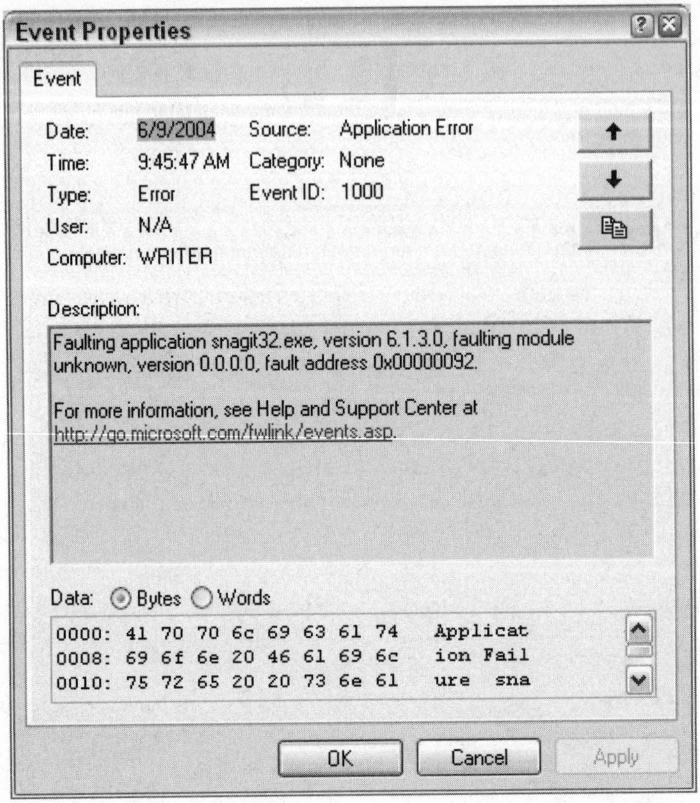

Figure 15-12: Double-click an item to open the Event Properties dialog box.

Notice that there are various types of entries. You may see information concerning comments on entries, but also error entries—which is what you should pay attention to. You'll also see audit entries and warning entries.

If you want to view an entry, double-click it. This action open the Event Properties dialog box, which gives you additional information about the entry (see Figure 15-12). The Event Viewer allows you only to view events that have been recorded. There is nothing you can do here to resolve problems that may be occurring, but the Event Viewer is a good source of information nonetheless.

Part V

Appendixes

IN THIS PART

Appendix A

Helpful Web Sites

If you are like me, you are always on the prowl for new ideas and tricks to get more speed out of Windows XP. One of the best places you can look for new tactics is, of course, the Internet. In this appendix, I show you some of my favorite Web sites devoted to speeding up and optimizing Windows XP. Check these sites out for more great ideas. However, keep in mind that I have not tested every tactic and piece of advice you may find here, so follow any instructions you read at your own risk, and make sure you back up your computer regularly in case something goes wrong.

PC Magazine

PC Magazine brings you all kinds of news and information from the world of technology. You can find numerous speed and optimization articles and utility downloads here. Visit the site at `www.pcmag.com` (see Figure A-1).

TweakXP.com

TweakXP.com offers numerous tips and tricks to optimize Windows XP, speed it up, change basic configurations, and much more. At this site you'll find easy-to-browse categories and a search feature so you can pinpoint what you are looking for. Visit the site at `www.tweakxp.com` (see Figure A-2).

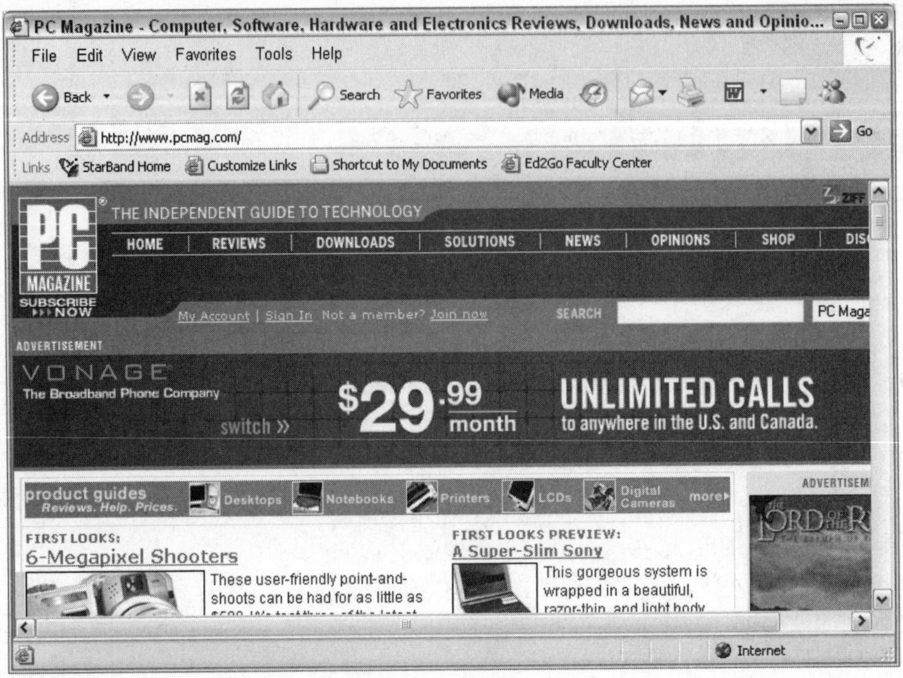

Figure A-1: The *PC Magazine* Web site.

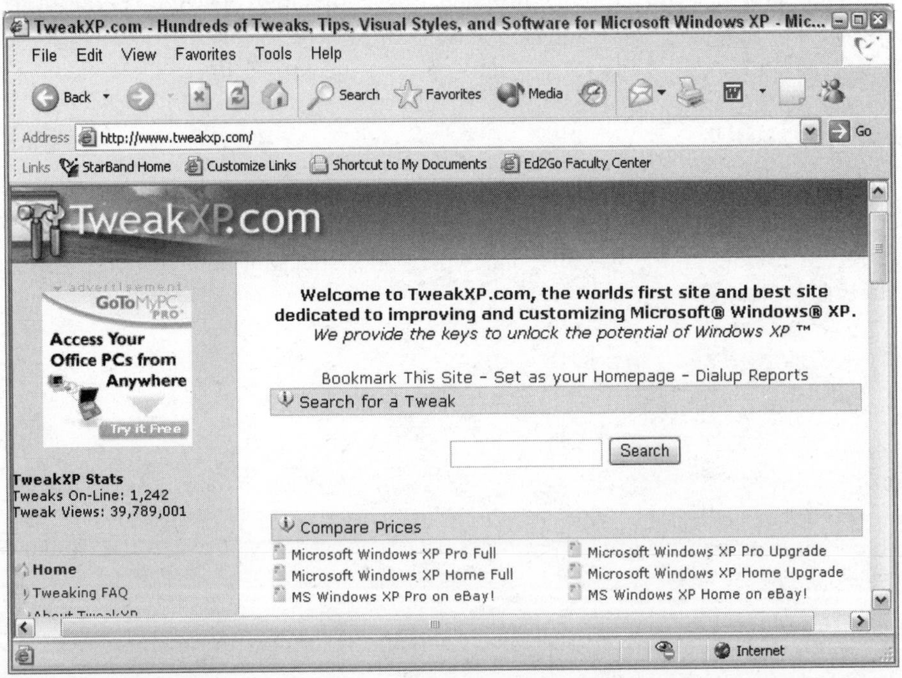

Figure A-2: TweakXP.com.

ExtremeTech

This is a good general site containing information about all kinds of technical issues. You can search for articles and discussions about a variety of topics, including speed and optimization solutions. You can also learn about important utilities and tools. Visit this site at `www.extremetech.com` (see Figure A-3).

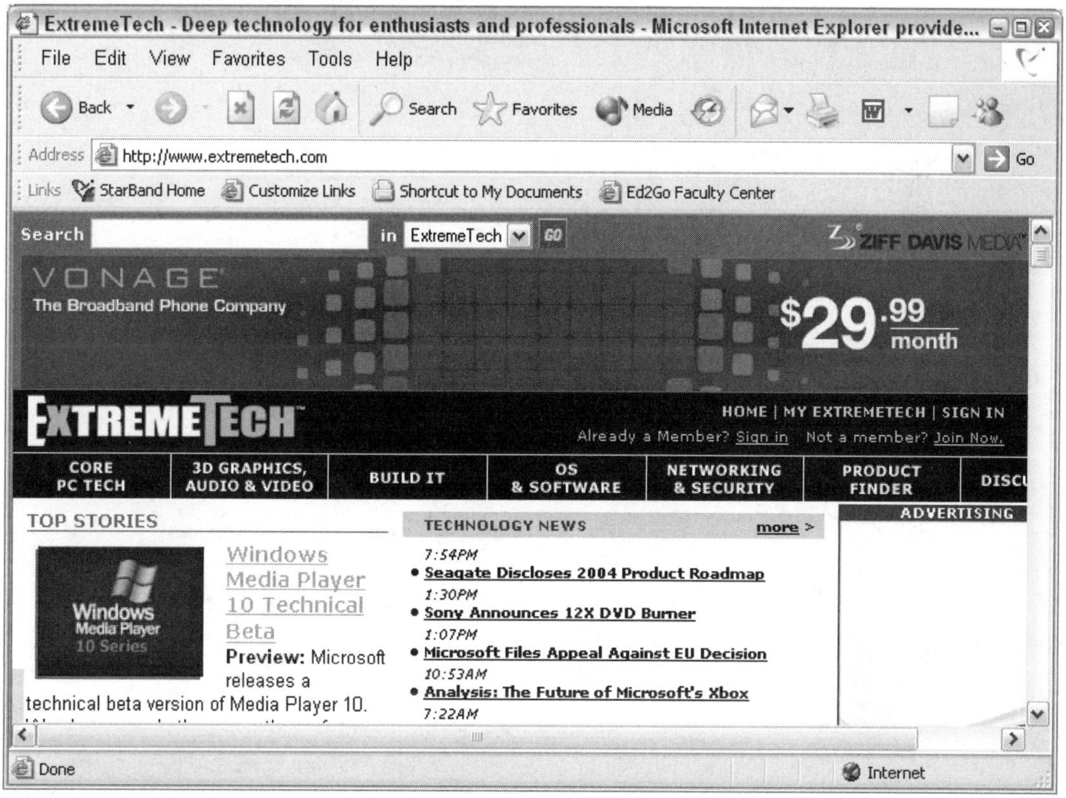

Figure A-3: ExtremeTech.

PuPpYpc.com

This site contains a good selection of tweaks, optimization tactics, and various tips for making Windows XP work more quickly. This is a good site to peruse and read articles about a variety of fixes you can make to Windows XP. Visit the site at `www.puppypc.com/windows` (see Figure A-4).

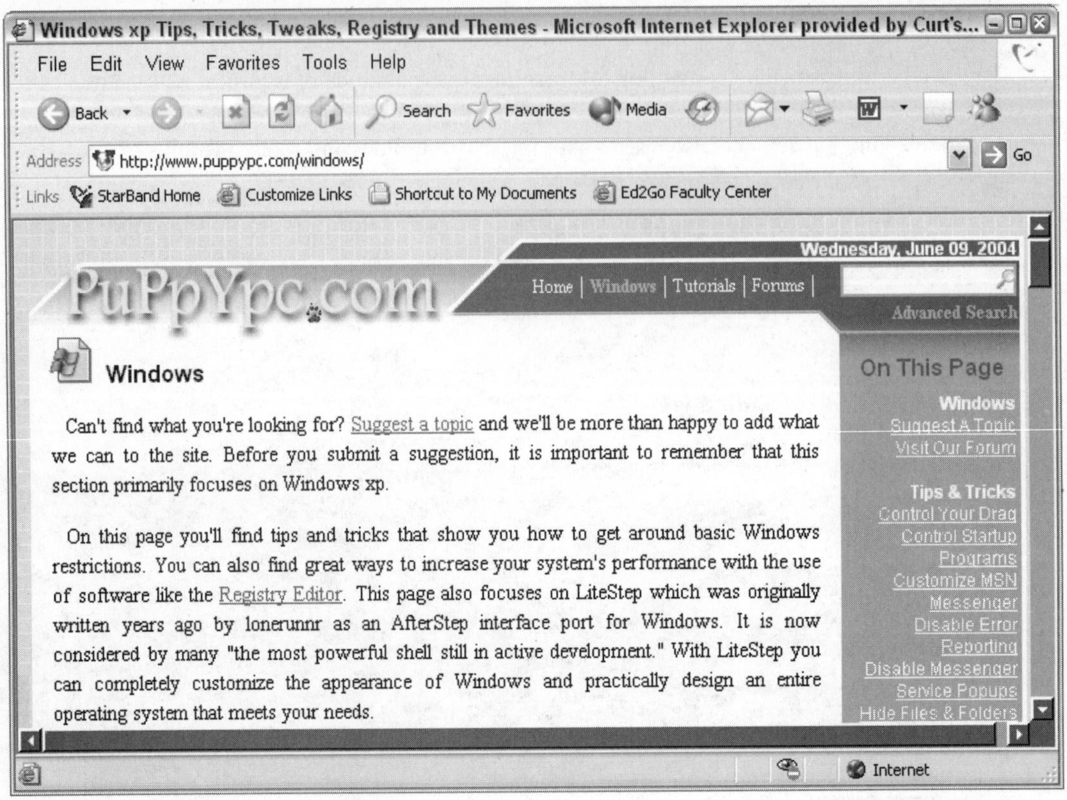
Windows xp Tips, Tricks, Tweaks, Registry and Themes - Microsoft Internet Explorer provided by Curt's...
File Edit View Favorites Tools Help
Back
Search
Favorites
Media
Address http://www.puppypc.com/windows/
Go
Links StarBand Home Customize Links Shortcut to My Documents Ed2Go Faculty Center
Wednesday, June 09, 2004
PuPpYpc.com
Home | Windows | Tutorials | Forums |
Advanced Search
Windows
Can't find what you're looking for? Suggest a topic and we'll be more than happy to add what we can to the site. Before you submit a suggestion, it is important to remember that this section primarily focuses on Windows xp.
On this page you'll find tips and tricks that show you how to get around basic Windows restrictions. You can also find great ways to increase your system's performance with the use of software like the Registry Editor. This page also focuses on LiteStep which was originally written years ago by lonerunnr as an AfterStep interface port for Windows. It is now considered by many "the most powerful shell still in active development." With LiteStep you can completely customize the appearance of Windows and practically design an entire operating system that meets your needs.
On This Page
Windows
Suggest A Topic
Visit Our Forum
Tips & Tricks
Control Your Drag
Control Startup Programs
Customize MSN Messenger
Disable Error Reporting
Disable Messenger Service Popups
Hide Files & Folders
Internet

Figure A-4: PuPpYpc.comc

PurePerformance.com

This site is focused on PC performance across a number of Windows platforms, and it can be a great site to research performance issues on your PC. Here you'll find plenty of articles and information that can help you squeeze extra power from Windows XP. Visit the site at `www.pureperformance.com` (see Figure A-5).

SpeedGuide.net

This site focuses on Internet performance issues, Windows performance issues, and other issues concerning speed for what it calls a "technically aware" audience. You'll find some great articles and solutions here. Visit the site at `www.speedguide.net` (see Figure A-6).

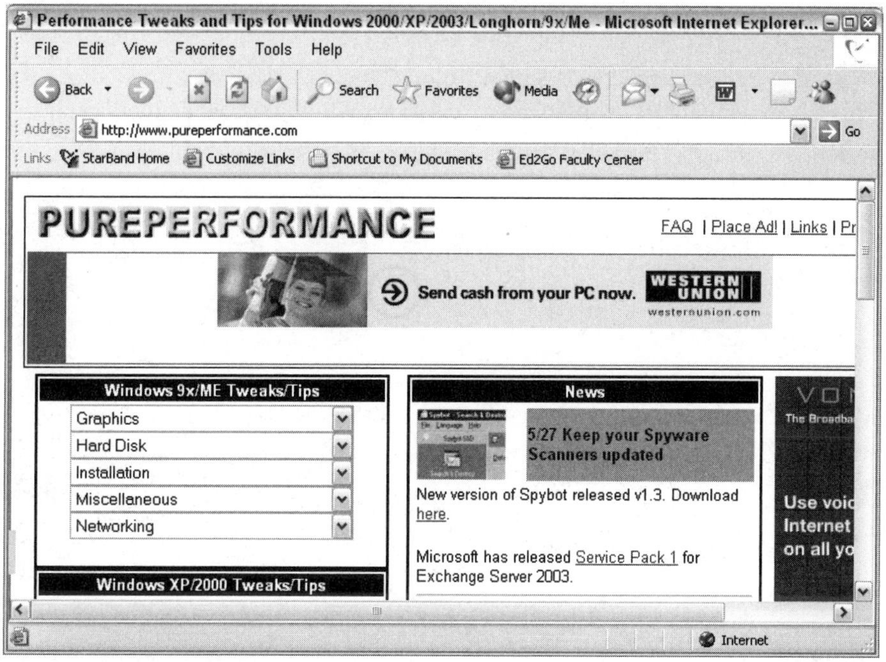

Figure A-5: PurePerformance.com.

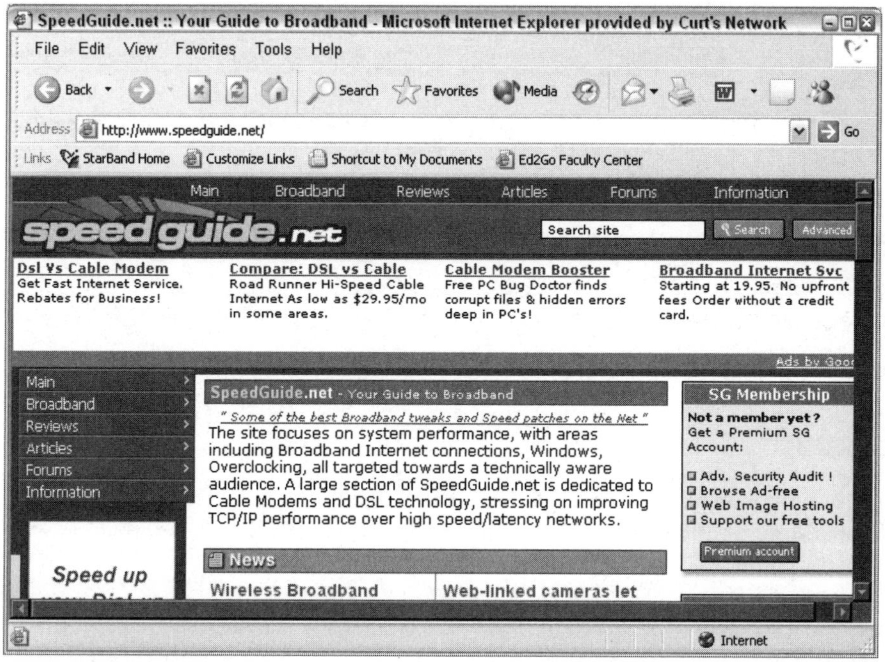

Figure A-6: SpeedGuide.net.

WinXPcentral.com

This is a good overall site that contains information about speed and optimization issues, along with other configuration matters and concerns for Windows XP and other operating systems, as well. Visit the site at www.winxpcentral.com (see Figure A-7).

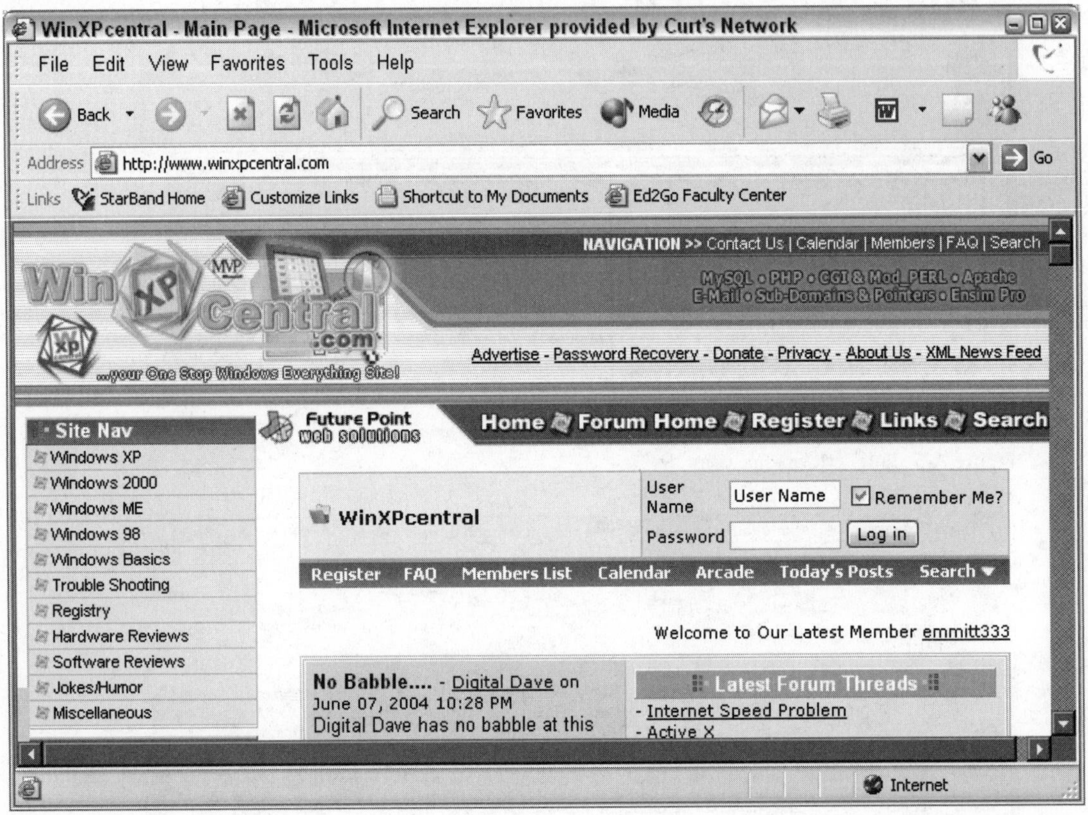

Figure A-7: WinXPcentral.com.

XPTuneup

This site has a number of tips for giving Windows XP a tune-up. You'll find a variety of speed features and configuration options. This site is easy to read and the information you want is easily found. Visit the site at www.xptuneup.com (see Figure A-8).

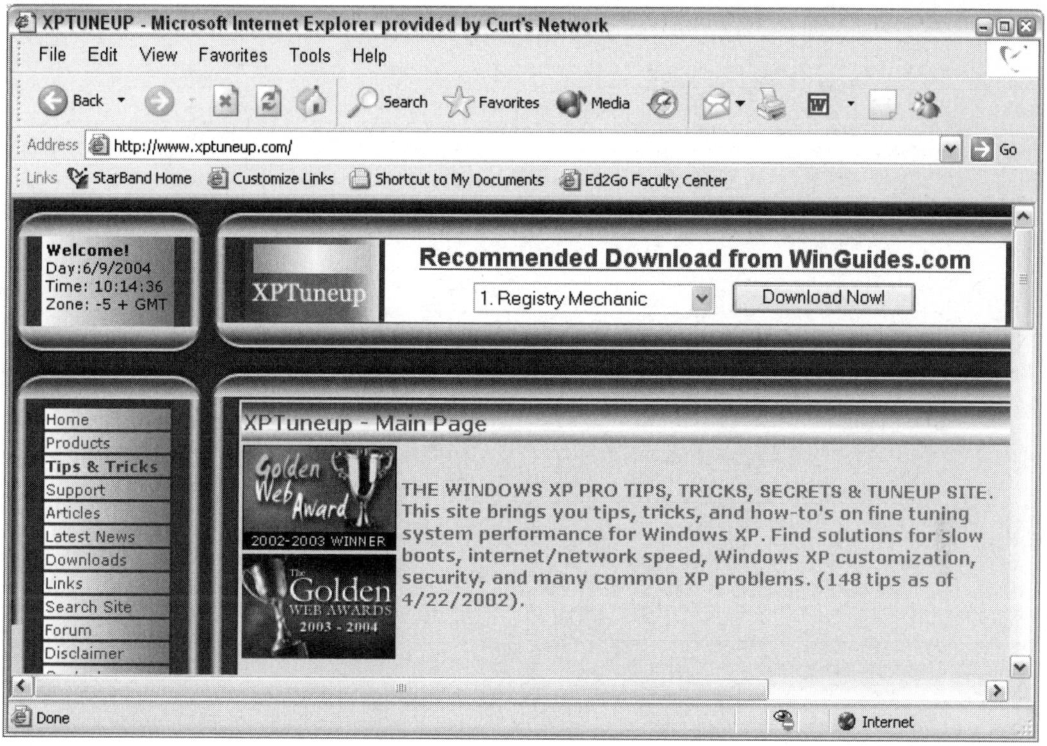

Figure A-8: XPTuneup.

Appendix B

Running a Clean Windows XP Installation

A radical but helpful way to optimize your system and get some speed back is to perform a clean installation of Windows XP. If Windows XP just isn't performing well for you—as it used to—and if you have tried most everything else in this book, you just may discover that a clean installation goes a long way toward getting your PC's life back on track.

Before you run a clean installation, make sure you have backed up all of your personal data and e-mail. Also make sure you have the latest drivers for all of your hardware devices (see Chapter 8). A clean installation requires you to reinstall all of your software programs, as well. So first make sure that a clean installation really is necessary. If you believe it is and you want to try and correct some speed problems (as well as other OS problems that may have occurred), the clean installation is rather easy.

The Windows XP installation CD is bootable. Start the installation by simply booting from the CD, if your computer supports CD booting. If your computer does not support booting from a CD, simply start the installation from the Windows desktop by accessing the Windows XP installation CD. In an upgrade or clean installation scenario, insert the CD while you are booted into your current operating system and follow the setup instructions. You can then start the installation by accessing your CD drive and running setup.exe.

At the Welcome to Microsoft Windows XP screen, you can launch the setup program or have it check your system for compatibility. Setup is rather straightforward; the following steps guide you through it:

1. Launch the CD or run setup.exe, as necessary, for your particular installation.

2. Setup begins and collects information about your computer. In the Welcome to Windows Setup screen, you can use the drop-down menu to select New Installation or Upgrade. Choose New Installation and click Next.

3. The Licensing Agreement dialog box appears. Read the agreement, click the I Accept This Agreement option, and click Next.
4. The Product Key dialog box appears. Enter the 25-character product key found on the yellow sticker on the back of your CD case, and click Next.
5. The Setup Options dialog box appears. If you selected the New Installation option in Step 2, at this point you can change the Accessibility Options and language, if desired, and you can also click the Advanced button.
6. In the Advanced Options dialog box you have the following options:
   - **Installation file copy:** Specify the location from which the setup files should be copied. This feature can be useful if you need to start setup from a CD but actually want the files copied from another location.
   - **Folder location:** Specify the folder name to which the files should be copied. C:\Windows is the default folder and typically what you should use.
   - **Copy all installation files from the Setup CD:** Copy all files to the computer's hard drive before beginning installation. This feature can be helpful if you need to install several computers but only have one CD. You can copy the files and continue with installation without the CD so that it can be used on another machine.
   - **I want to choose the install drive letter and partition during Setup:** Choose a drive letter and select a partition you want to use for the installation of Windows XP.

   Make any desired selections, click OK, and then click Next.
7. The Setup Files dialog box appears. You can choose to connect to the Internet and check for updated files that can be downloaded and used during installation. Your current operating system must be configured with an Internet connection for this option to work, but you should use the option if you have a connection. Choose either Yes or No and click Next.
8. At this point, the file copy process begins. Setup copies necessary files to your computer's hard drive and then automatically reboots your computer (make sure there is no floppy disk in the disk drive.

   Once the computer reboots, the MS-DOS portion of setup begins. The Setup Notification dialog box appears. Press Enter to continue.
9. In the Welcome to Setup dialog box, you can choose to install Windows XP Professional now by pressing Enter, repair an existing installation by

pressing R, or quit setup by pressing F3. Press Enter to continue with Setup.

10. Depending on your upgrade or clean install choices, you may see a partition window where you can choose the desired partition in which you want to install Windows XP Professional and format that partition as well. Follow the setups that appear to select a desired partition, create a partition from unpartitioned space, and to format that partition.

11. Once the partition is established and formatted with a file system, the file copy process begins. This may take some time and requires no intervention from you.

    After the file copy process is complete, the computer automatically reboots. At this point, you see the Windows XP setup screen and installation continues. The approximate amount of time that setup will require is displayed here, as well. It is not unusual for the screen to flicker several times during this phase of setup.

12. During the installation of Windows XP Professional, the Regional and Language Options dialog box appears. You can click the Customize button to choose a different language or region, or you can click the Details button to view information about your current regional configuration. Click Next to continue.

13. In the Personalize Your Software dialog box, enter your name and organization. Click Next.

14. In the Computer Name and Administrator password box, enter a name for the computer (or accept the default) and an administrator password. The password will be used in conjunction with the Windows XP Professional administrator account and should be kept private. Typically, for the best security, the local administrator password should be at least seven characters long and should contain both letters and numbers. Click Next.

15. In the Modem Dialing dialog box, choose your country and enter your area code and outside line number (if necessary). This dialog box does not appear if you do not have a modem attached to your computer. Click Next.

16. In the Date and Time Settings dialog box, use the drop-down menus to choose the correct time, date, and time zone. Click Next.

17. Setup continues and a Networking Settings dialog box appears if a network adapter card is installed on the computer. You can choose Typical Settings, which installs TCP/IP, Client for Microsoft Networks, and File and Printer Sharing for Microsoft Networks. If you want to select the services and IP address you will

configure, choose the Custom Settings option and click Next to complete the information.

18. The Choose Workgroup or Computer Domain dialog box appears. Choose a desired work or domain name and click Next. If you are creating a new workgroup, enter the desired name in the provided dialog box.

Setup continues and may require another 30 minutes or longer before the computer reboots. Once the computer reboots, Windows XP Professional boots for the first time. Once setup completes, a few questions appear, such as the configuration of an Internet connection, the user's name, registration, and so on. You can also activate Windows at this time.

Appendix C

Quick Catalog of Helpful Third-Party Utilities

I've mentioned a number of third-party utilities throughout this book, but I also wanted to include this appendix of helpful and fun utilities you can grab from the Internet. Some of these relate to speed solutions, while many of them simply make Windows XP more customized to meet your needs. Some of them are just for fun, as well. Unless otherwise noted, all of these utilities can be found and downloaded from the *PC Magazine* Web site at `www.pcmag.com`.

Note

You must purchase a subscription to *PC Magazine* (around $20 per year) to download premium offerings, but the cost is well worth the material you get in return.

FolderMon

This folder monitoring utility allows you to get up-to-the-minute data about changes that have occurred on file folders you monitor. The tool is particularly helpful with network folders because you are notified when something has been added or removed from the folder by another user. FolderMon (see Figure C-1) is easy to use and can save you time by keeping you informed about what goes on throughout your network.

Dupeless

I've talked a lot about managing folders and files on your hard disk and keeping the clutter cleaned up. Dupeless (see Figure C-2) seeks out duplicate files that are unneeded and gets rid of them. Fortunately, the utility allows you to control what duplicate files are deleted, so you don't have to worry about losing something you want to keep.

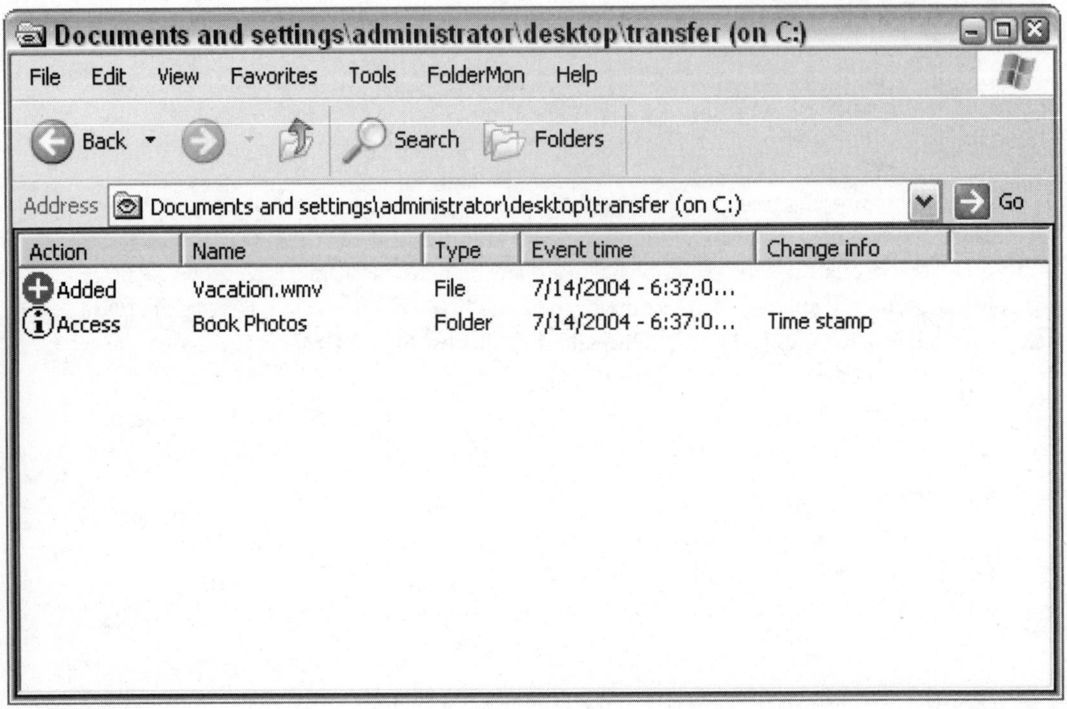

Figure C-1: FolderMon.

FindOrphans

This is another nice utility that looks for orphaned files on your computer and removes them. Orphaned files can take up precious space on your system and slow it down. Using this utility is a good way to get rid of them.

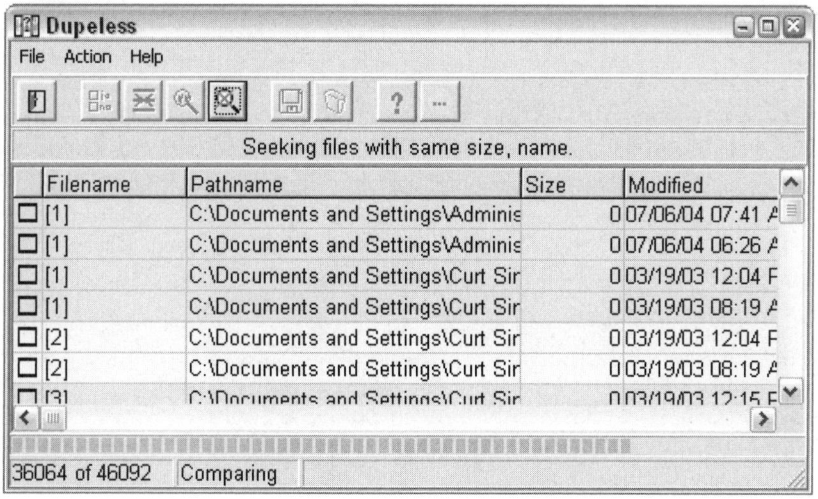

Figure C-2: Dupeless.

FileSnoop

If you want to find information quickly about the files on your system, FileSnoop can do that for you. Use this utility to gather all the available information about a particular file.

HDValet

This is another good utility that seeks out files on your hard disk that are unnecessarily wasting space. The tool allows you to scan files and clean up the ones you don't want, and it has a confirmation step that reduces the likelihood of your making a mistake.

Shred 2

After you delete a file, it's not really gone for good. You can ensure that files you delete are truly destroyed with Shred 2. This utility erases the file's contents so that it cannot be recovered from your hard drive. This is a good one to have if you work with sensitive data and you need to make certain that it cannot be recovered.

Slice32

If you need to transport a large file on a floppy disk that cannot contain the file in its entirety, Slice32 (see Figure C-3) can help you chop the file apart, save it, and then reassemble it again. This is a helpful utility if you are having problems moving a big file from one location to another.

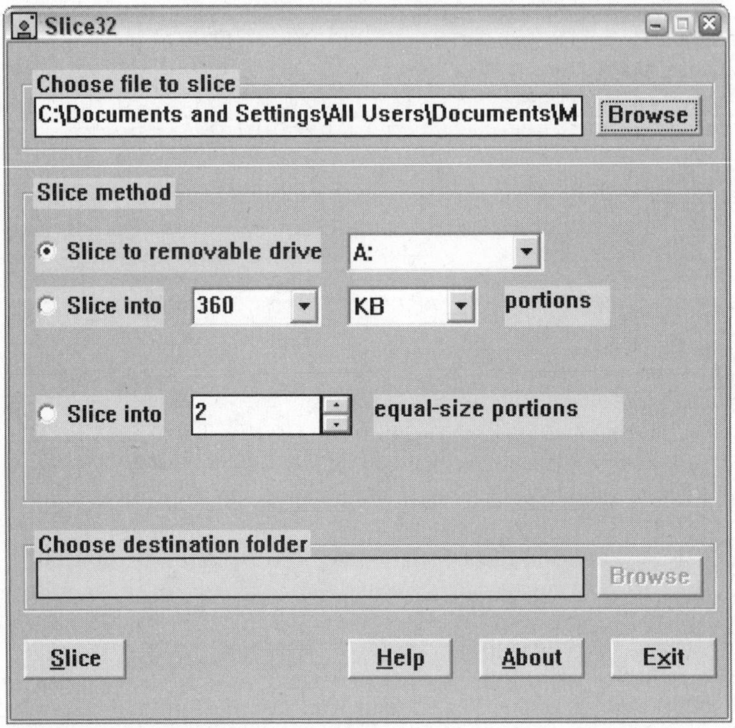

Figure C-3: Slice32.

ListZapper

This is a good utility to use if you need to keep information private from other users. ListZapper allows you to locate and manage lists that are kept by your computer of your usage actions. For example, when you access files, a Most Recently Used list is maintained, so someone else could potentially see what you've been doing. With ListZapper, you can easily manage and destroy those lists to keep your activities private.

ClockRack

This utility allows you to tell time around the world. Fun and easy to use, ClockRack (see Figure C-4) shows the time with a simple clock interface.

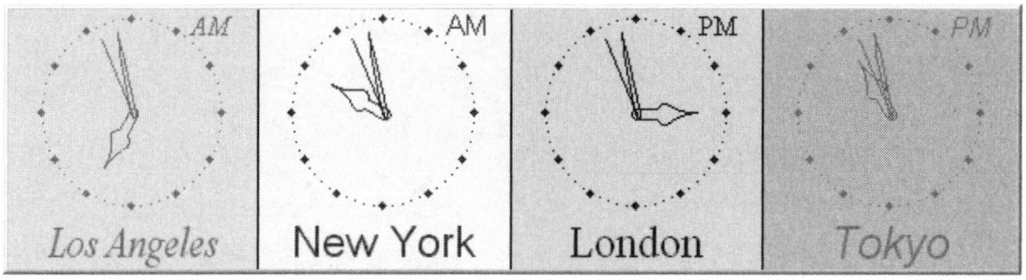

Figure C-4: ClockRack.

DaysEase

Use this utility to create a customized and nice-looking calendar for any month or year. The calendar is suitable for printing and hanging on the wall, if you like. If you need custom calendars, DaysEase can do the job.

TrayMin

This utility is helpful because it allows you to put essentially any icons you want in the Notification Area, even if the icons are not designed for it. TrayMin gives you great flexibility while using Windows XP.

ThemeCrafter

This utility allows you to customize Windows XP by creating your own visual theme, including wallpaper, screen savers, system icons, and more. ThemeCrafter (see Figure C-5) works directly with the operating system's THEMES.EXE program and is rather easy to use.

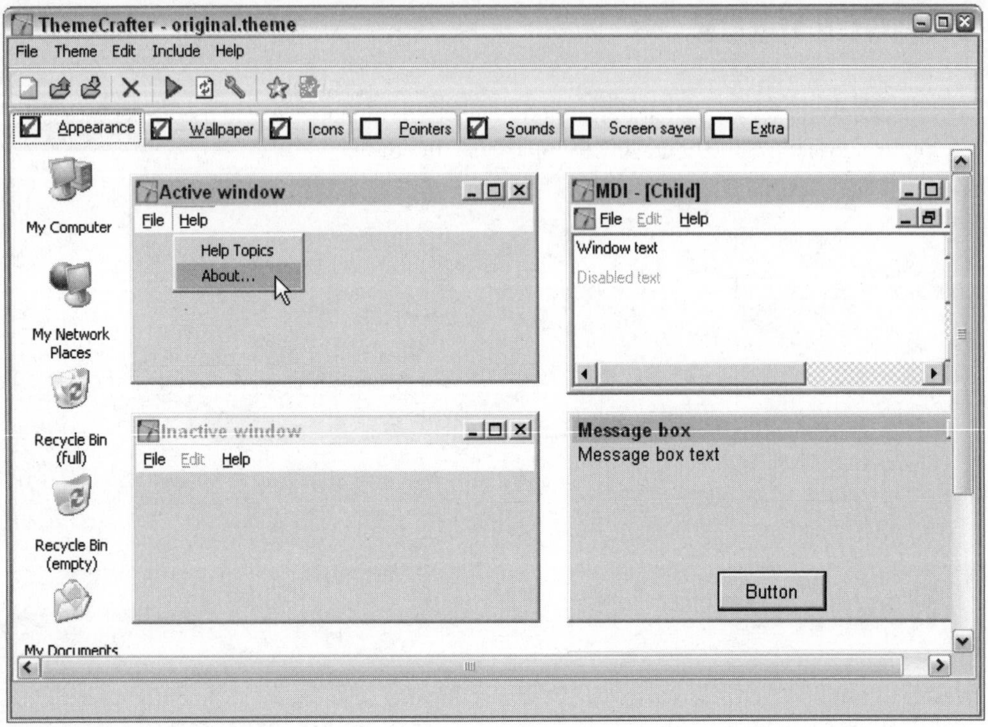

Figure C-5: ThemeCrafter.

Media Console

If you don't want to spend a lot of money on media management software, but you need something that makes digital media easier to use and manage, this utility might be for you. Media Console gives you a quick and easy way to view and manage all kinds of digital media on Windows XP. The configuration window (see Figure C-6) allows you to set up the program and determine what you want it to do. Try this one out!

IconJack 32

This fun utility allows you to grab basically anything on your PC and make it into an icon, including Windows folders, logos, photos, and essentially anything else. IconJack 32 is a fast and fun way to customize your PC.

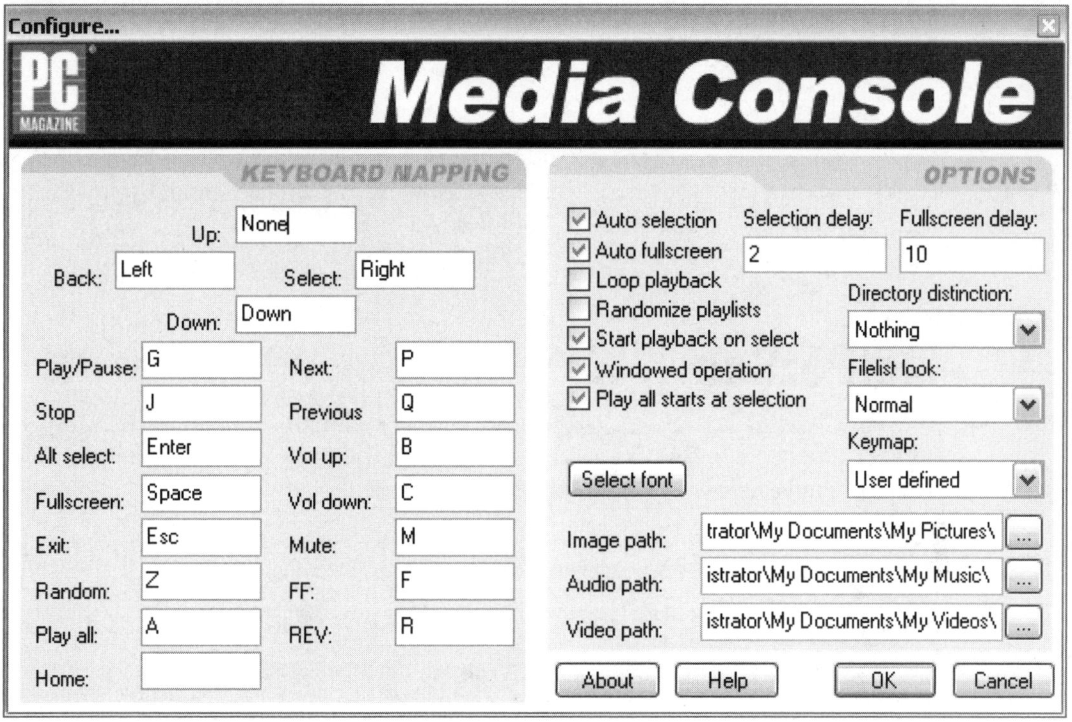

Figure C-6: Media Console.

RoboType 2

This utility allows you to create shortcut keys for chunks of text. RoboType 2 is helpful if you create documents that have the same kind of phrasing over and over. Avoid repetitive typing by creating the text and assigning a keystroke value to it.

FavesToGo

This utility allows you to take your Internet Explorer favorites with you wherever you go. FavesToGo grabs your favorites from Internet Explorer, or even bookmarks from Netscape, and puts them in a quick and easy-to-transport HTML file so you can make copies and keep your favorites with you at all times.

HandsDown

This utility creates a batch file from a list of Internet files that you want to download. You can then run the batch file and download all the items without having to babysit them. HandsDown is a helpful utility if you have a slow Internet connection and you want to download several items from different locations.

NetPerSec

This is a nice utility to have. Run NetPerSec (see Figure C-7) at any time to find out how fast your Internet connection is working at the moment.

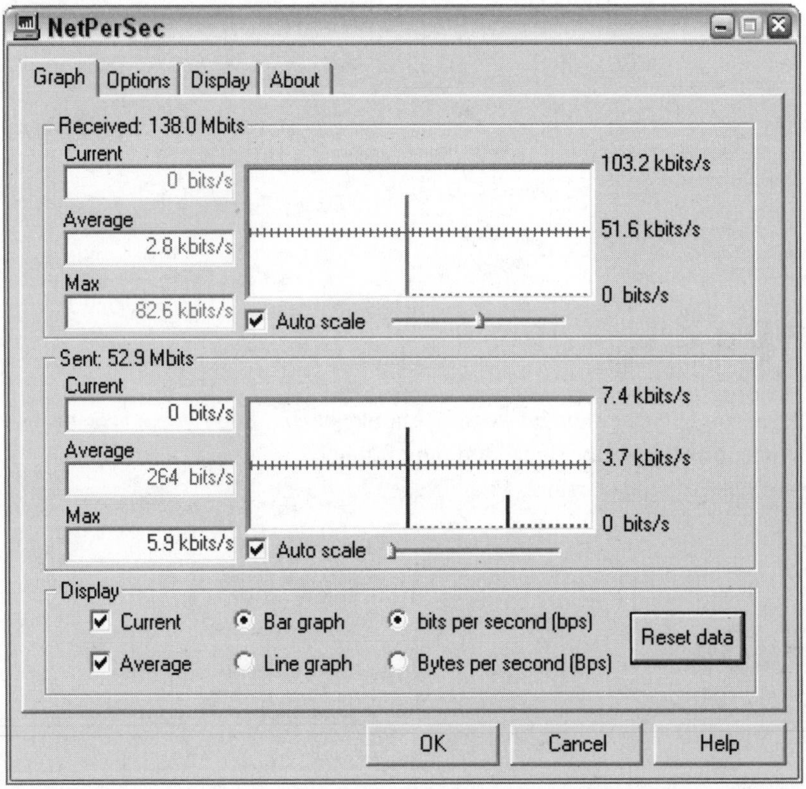

Figure C-7: NetPerSec.

Security Scout

This is basically an informational utility that gathers data from reliable sources over the Internet, such as CERT, about current Internet security issues and problems. You can view the data each day and make any necessary decisions to keep yourself protected. Security Scout is a great way to stay "in the know" concerning Internet security.

Web Highlighter

This utility enables you to highlight text and links on Web pages as you read them. It works with Internet Explorer 4.0 or higher. Once it is enabled, all you have to do is select the text you want to highlight and right-click it. Web Highlighter (see Figure C-8) is a great way to keep track of information on a Web site, particularly sites that have a lot of articles and text.

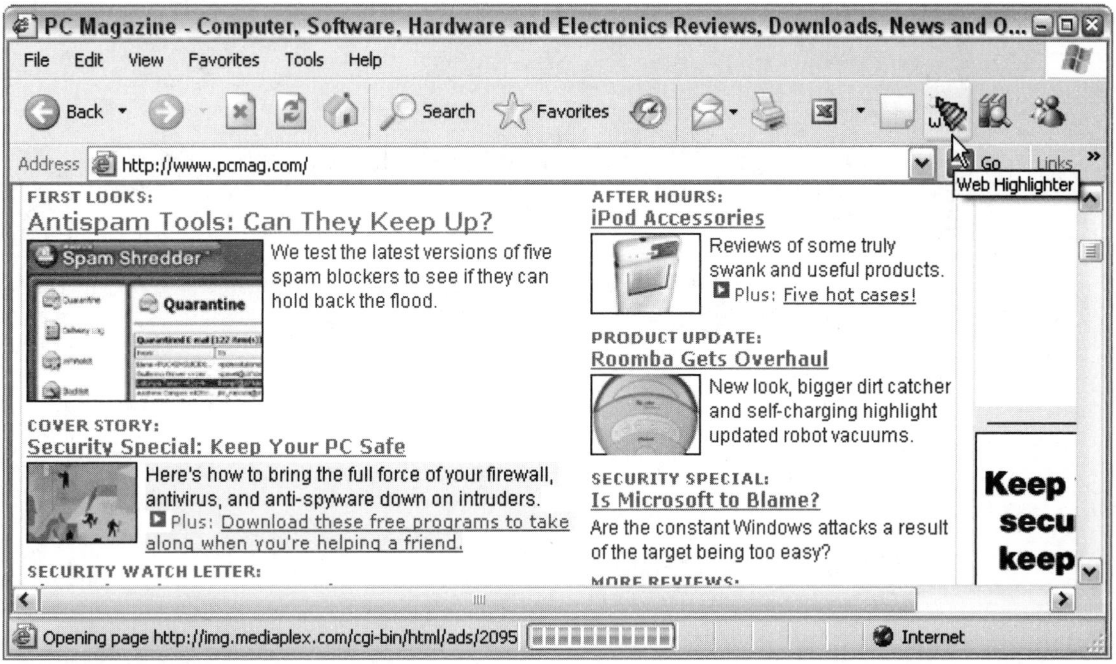
PC Magazine - Computer, Software, Hardware and Electronics Reviews, Downloads, News and O...
File Edit View Favorites Tools Help
Back
Search
Favorites
Address http://www.pcmag.com/
Go
Links
Web Highlighter
FIRST LOOKS:
Antispam Tools: Can They Keep Up?
Spam Shredder
Quarantine
We test the latest versions of five spam blockers to see if they can hold back the flood.
AFTER HOURS:
iPod Accessories
Reviews of some truly swank and useful products.
Plus: Five hot cases!
PRODUCT UPDATE:
Roomba Gets Overhaul
New look, bigger dirt catcher and self-charging highlight updated robot vacuums.
COVER STORY:
Security Special: Keep Your PC Safe
Here's how to bring the full force of your firewall, antivirus, and anti-spyware down on intruders.
Plus: Download these free programs to take along when you're helping a friend.
SECURITY SPECIAL:
Is Microsoft to Blame?
Are the constant Windows attacks a result of the target being too easy?
SECURITY WATCH LETTER:
Keep
secu
keep
Opening page http://img.mediaplex.com/cgi-bin/html/ads/2095
Internet

Figure C-8: Web Highlighter.

DiskPie 2

Windows XP does a good job of giving you a graphical interface to view disk configuration, but DiskPie 2 (see Figure C-9) gives you more: an Explorer view of your disks and the disk usage portions of folders in Windows XP.

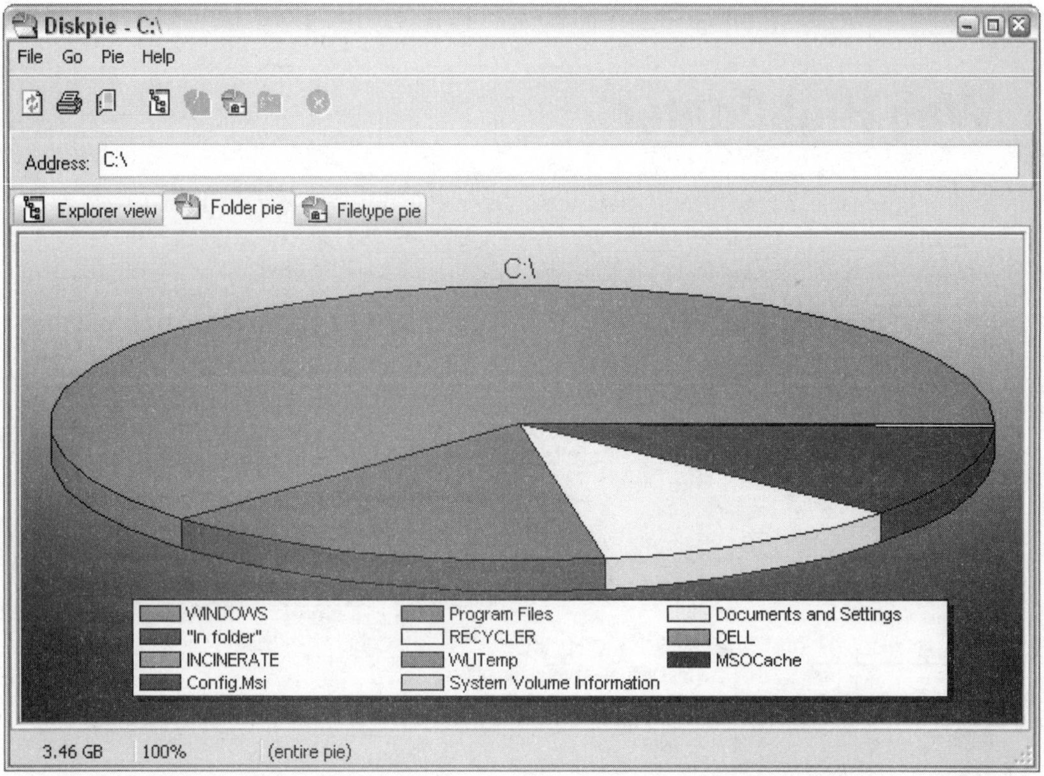

Figure C-9: DiskPie 2.

Registry Detective

This is a good tool for searching the Registry. You can search on any value quickly and find the Registry key, the value itself, and the data. Registry Detective (see Figure C-10) is flexible and easy to use.

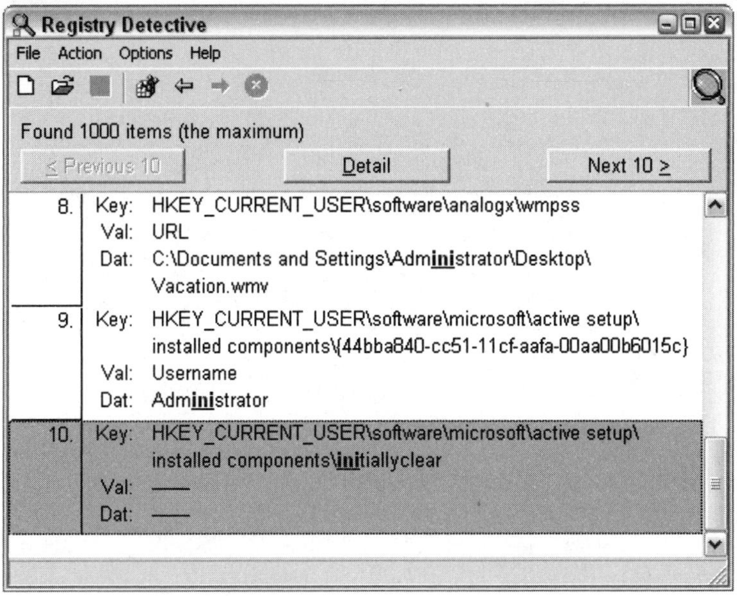

Figure C-10: Registry Detective.

RegistryRobot

This utility allows you to make a number of tweaks and changes through a folder-based interface. RegistryRobot (see Figure C-11) is great to have if you want to make some helpful changes but don't really like the idea of wading around the Registry yourself.

Startup Cop

This tool helps you manage startup programs. While you can manage them directly through the MSCONFIG interface (see Chapter 3), Startup Cop easier to use and much more graphical.

TaskPower

This program gives you an easy way to manage services and processes along with applications. It's a lot like Windows Task Manager but it provides greater flexibility and more

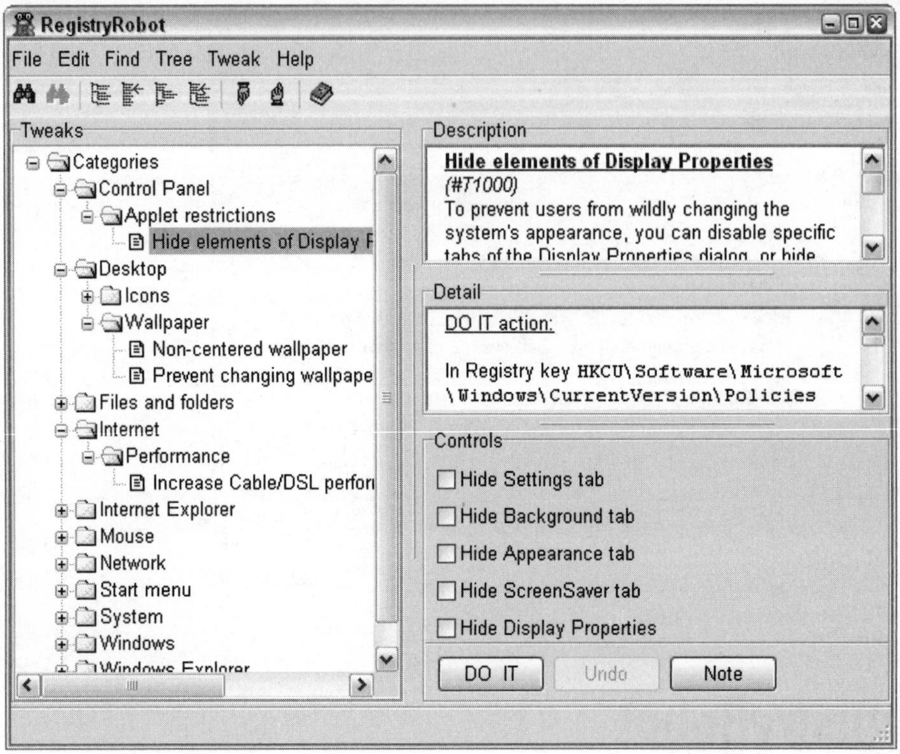

Figure C-11: RegistryRobot.

control options. You can even see what drivers are in use at the moment. If you want to keep control of your system, TaskPower (see Figure C-12) is good to have on hand.

CubeShow

This utility allows you to use your photos as a slideshow screen saver. It displays the images on a three-dimensional cube that moves around the screen. CubeShow works with many types of picture files, such as JPEG, BMP, and so on. Overall, it's a fun product to use.

FaveLock

This is a quick tool that allows you to lock your Favorites folder. Because Favorites can contain a large amount of personal information—such as the sites you visit, online banking

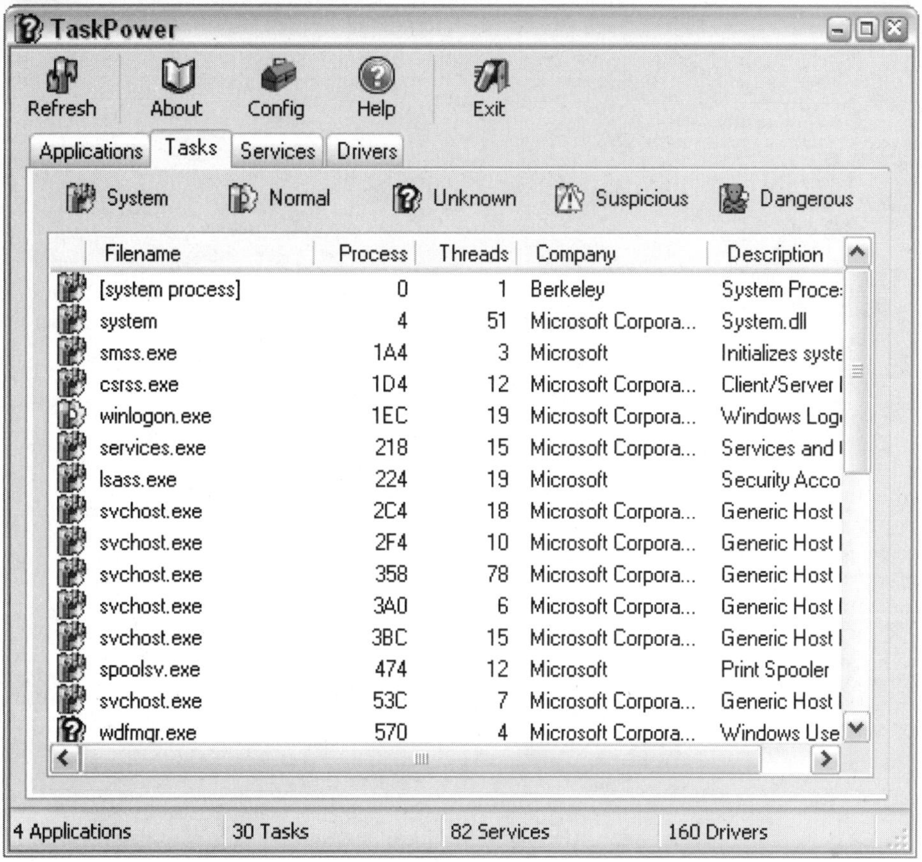

Figure C-12: TaskPower.

data, stocks, and so on—you can use FaveLock to lock the folder and keep everything safe from prying eyes.

Tip

Be sure to check out the free PowerToys for Windows XP, an assortment of fun and helpful programs you can download directly from Microsoft. Visit the site at `www.microsoft.com/windowsxp/downloads/powertoys/default.mspx`.

Appendix D

Keeping Your Computer Secure

In the past, security was a concern for corporations whose sensitive data needed to be protected from both the inside and outside. They carefully guarded Internet access and their servers held critical files in "lockdown." In those days, home and small-office users didn't have to worry much about security.

Unfortunately, times have changed. Each of us faces an onslaught of potential intrusions and problems from both within and without, and the issue of security has become a common one for all computer users. You'll know how important security is when a computer virus, Trojan horse, or hacker—or just someone from your office or home—tinkers around in your private files. Fortunately, in spite of security problems elsewhere, there are quite a few security features built into Windows XP that can make your computer, your data, and any personally identifiable information much more secure. While I explored some of these throughout this book, I want to pull all of the information together here.

Managing Users

As you think about security, one of the issues you must face concerns the people who use your computer. If you are the only user of your computer, you have little to worry about. However, the odds are good that several family members also use your computer. If your Windows XP computer is located on a small home or office network, you have to protect yourself from people who log on to the computer or access the system over the network. Windows XP gives you the tools you need to manage that access.

Managing Shared Folders

If your computer resides on a network, you can share data, printers, CD drives, and just about anything else with network users, which is the purpose of the network in the first place. However, you do not want users to be able to access everything on your computer—that's where the problems tend to crop up.

If you are connected to a network, you can share any folder by right-clicking the folder and selecting Sharing and Security. This opens the folder's Properties pages where you can choose to share the folder (see Figure D-1). Notice that when you share the folder, users are given read-only access. If you want users to be able to change your files, you can give them that permission as well by clicking the provided option.

PEP Properties
General
Sharing
Customize
Local sharing and security
To share this folder with other users of this computer only, drag it to the Shared Documents folder.
To make this folder and its subfolders private so that only you have access, select the following check box.
Make this folder private
Network sharing and security
To share this folder with both network users and other users of this computer, select the first check box below and type a share name.
Share this folder on the network
Share name:
PEP
Allow network users to change my files
Learn more about sharing and security.
OK
Cancel
Apply

Figure D-1: You can easily share a folder on the network.

If you are using Windows XP Home Edition, this is the only sharing option you have; however, if you are using Windows XP Professional, you can invoke additional sharing and security features. Windows XP tries to make folder sharing easy through the basic sharing interface you see. This is called Simple File Sharing. It makes the sharing process easier for users. However, if you want more power and control, you can turn off Simple File Sharing and use NTFS permissions, where you can tailor the rights and privileges of shared folders more strictly.

In the Control Panel, open Folder Options. Click the View tab and scroll to the bottom of the dialog box. Clear the "Use simple file sharing (Recommended)" check box (see Figure D-2) to turn off Simple File Sharing.

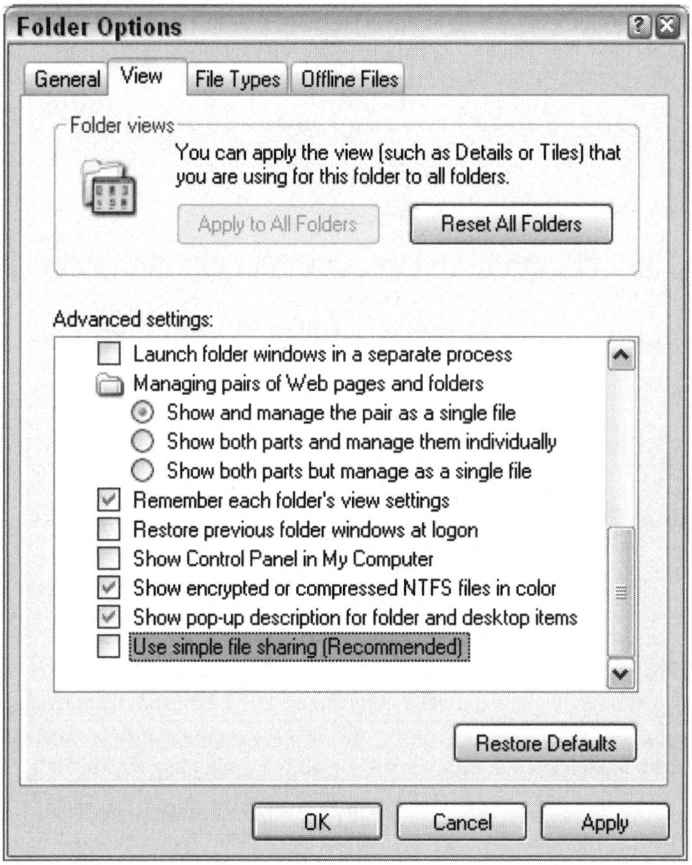

Figure D-2: Turn off Simple File Sharing.

Once you have turned off Simple File Sharing, the Sharing tab changes to a Windows 2000–style tab (see Figure D-3), which permits you to use the Permissions button to set permissions on the folder.

Once you click the Permissions button, you can assign specific permissions to specific users. This feature enables you to give some users read-only access, some users write access, some users full control. You can also block some users from accessing the folder altogether.

Figure D-3: The Sharing tab changes after you turn off Simple File Sharing.

Unlike Simple File Sharing, which is a catch-all process, NTFS permissions give you greater flexibility for sharing data over your network (see Figure D-4). Use the Add button to browse for the desired user, select the user, and then set the level of permission you want to apply. Keep in mind that NTFS permissions can get complicated, and you can invoke many other permission settings that are beyond the scope of this book. If you want to learn more about security and permissions, the Windows XP Help files are a good place to start. You can also find plenty of books about Windows XP security that will guide you along the way.

Using Encryption

Windows XP features an easy-to-use encryption method that allows only you to read a file or folder. This is a quick way to protect sensitive files and data. However, don't encrypt everything on your computer. Because encryption adds overhead, encrypt only files or folders that you deem rather sensitive. This way, even if someone from your network or the Internet manages to get into your computer, those files will still be protected by encryption.

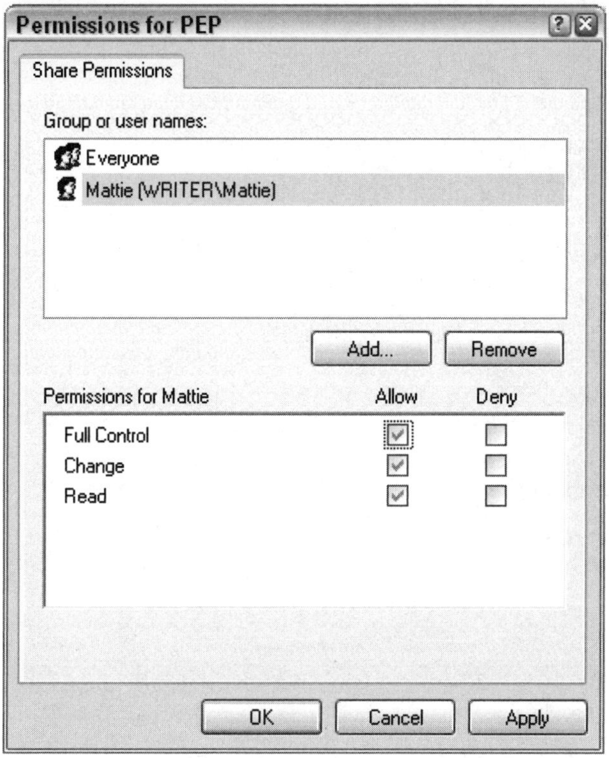

Figure D-4: You can set individual permissions for each user.

Once you encrypt a file or folder, you can open it and use it as you normally would, but no one else can gain access without the encryption key, which is tied to your account. To turn on encryption for a folder or file, follow these steps:

1. Right-click the desired folder or file and click Properties.
2. On the General tab, click the Advanced button.
3. In the Advanced Attributes dialog box (see Figure D-5), click the "Encrypt contents to secure data" option and click OK.

As you work with Windows XP, it is important to keep in mind that your encryption key is tied to your user account. In most cases, this will never cause you any problems, but should you ever create a backup file and encrypt it, and then perform a clean installation of Windows XP, you will no longer be able to open the backup file without retaking permission of it, which can be tricky. The point is to keep your encrypted files in mind, especially if you ever do anything radical with your user account or perform a clean installation.

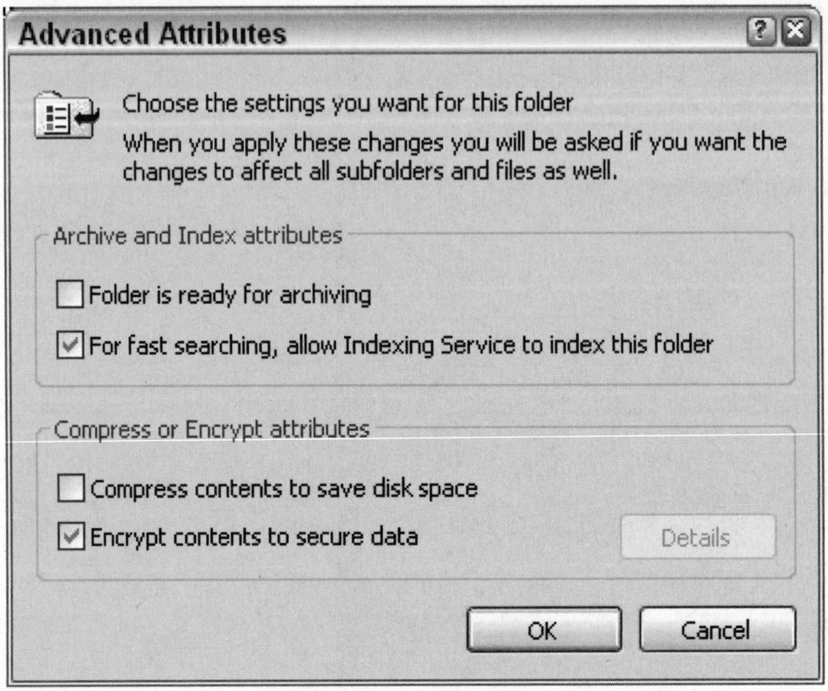

Figure D-5: You can easily encrypt the contents of a folder or file.

Tip

You can turn encryption off on any file or folder at any time by simply returning to the Advanced Attributes dialog box and clearing the "Encrypt contents to secure data" check box.

Managing Accounts

One of the best ways you can protect yourself and the data on your computer is through the effective management of accounts on your computer. If you are the only person who uses your computer, this isn't a big issue. The only thing you should do is make sure you use a password so that someone else cannot easily gain access. However, if several people use your computer, you need to take steps to secure the computer and those accounts and make certain that your computer is not easily accessible.

Only one person should have an administrator account on your computer. When you first install Windows XP, a default administrator account is created, which may be the account you currently log on with. You can create more accounts with administrator privileges using the Users applet in the Control Panel; however, it is generally not a good idea to do so. The more accounts you grant administrator privileges, the more likely you are to experience security problems. Only you should have the kind of power on your system that the administrator account provides.

Another issue concerns passwords. To make life easier on home users, Windows XP provides the option for blank passwords. With this feature, the user only has to click his or her username on the Welcome screen to log on. Naturally, anyone can click the different user accounts and log on, so blank passwords provide you absolutely no protection. If you want to make the computer secure, each user account should have an effective password assigned to it.

Effective Passwords

If a password is easy to guess, it doesn't do any good. As you think about enforcing passwords, make sure those passwords are effective. Here are some tips to keep in mind:

- **Minimum length:** Effective passwords are generally between five and eight characters in length. Avoid passwords under four characters.
- **Combinations:** Effective passwords should contain letters and numbers. "Pass457" is a much more effective password than "Password."
- **No identifiable information:** Do not use passwords that contain your name, names of family members, phone numbers, names of pets, names of favorite activities, or anything else that can be associated with you.
- **No real words:** Although these are more difficult, passwords that avoid words at all are better. "Gtvd789" is an effective password because the lettering combination doesn't mean anything and no one is likely to guess it outright.
- **Different case:** Passwords are case-sensitive, so mixing case strengthens passwords. For example "GtVD789" is more effective than "Gtvd789." Of course, the user must type the correct case, but the tactic provides additional security.

To make sure you have good account configuration and passwords, you can check out the account settings with the Users applet in the Control Panel. If you are a Windows XP Professional user, you can also use the Computer Management console and invoke additional features, which I explore in a moment. Make sure you are logged on with the administrator account and open User Accounts in the Control Panel. This lets you see a description of each account on the computer, the type of account, and whether or not the account is password-protected (see Figure D-6).

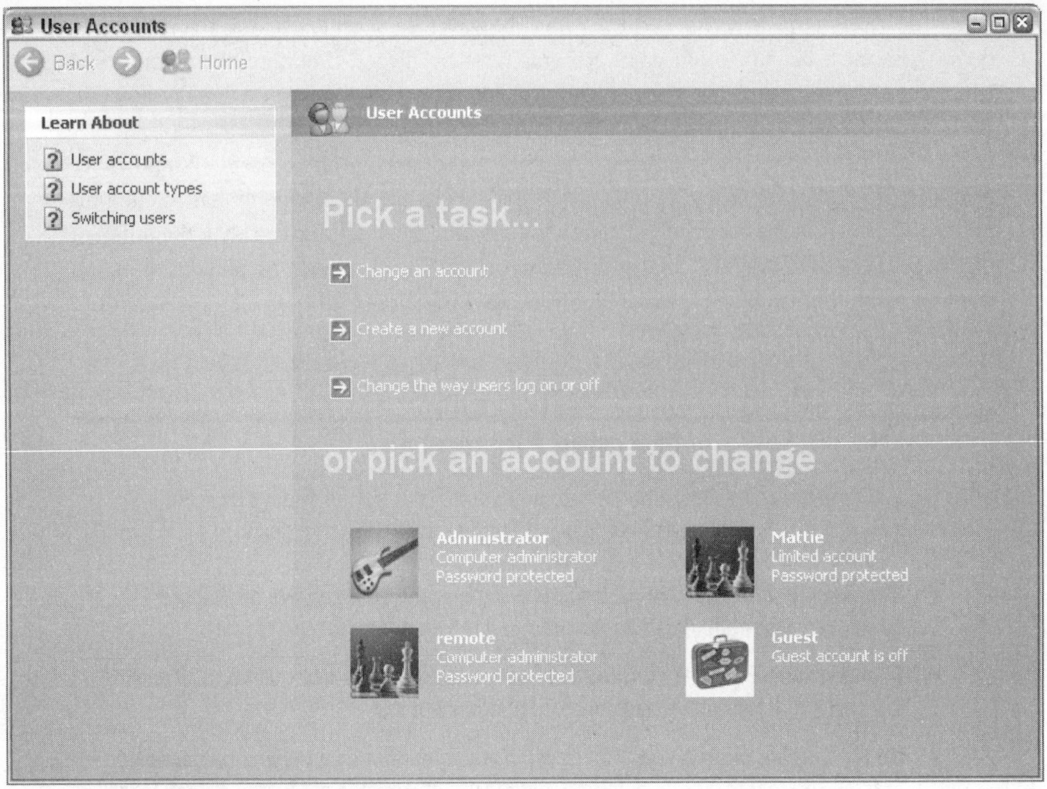

Figure D-6: Examining user accounts.

Select the desired user account and click the "Change an account" link to change it. The interface is easy to use and understand. Just make sure you have only one administrator account and that all accounts are password-protected with effective passwords.

Windows XP Account Types

If you haven't spent any time creating accounts in Windows XP, you need to know that there are two types of accounts: Administrator and Limited. Administrator accounts can basically do anything, except access private files of other users. However, the administrator can add and delete accounts, make systemwide changes, add or remove programs and hardware, and do essentially anything else. The Limited account can make changes within the account, such as changing the wallpaper, editing documents, viewing and creating files, and so forth. The Limited user may not be able to install programs, and the user cannot make any systemwide changes. In essence, the Limited account allows someone to use the computer but not make any changes that affect anyone else or the operation of the computer itself.

Performing Advanced User Account Management

The User Accounts applet in the Control Panel may work well, but there are additional account management features you may wish to invoke. You can access these if you are using Windows XP Professional and you are logged on with the administrator account. The available account features give you some additional security. For example, you can force users to create their own passwords at the next logon, or stop them from changing passwords. Think about your security needs and decide if these additional security enhancements are necessary.

1. Log on with an Administrator account.
2. Open the Control Panel and select Administrative Tools. Double-click the Computer Management icon.
3. In the Computer Management console, expand Local Users and Groups and select the Users container (see Figure D-7).

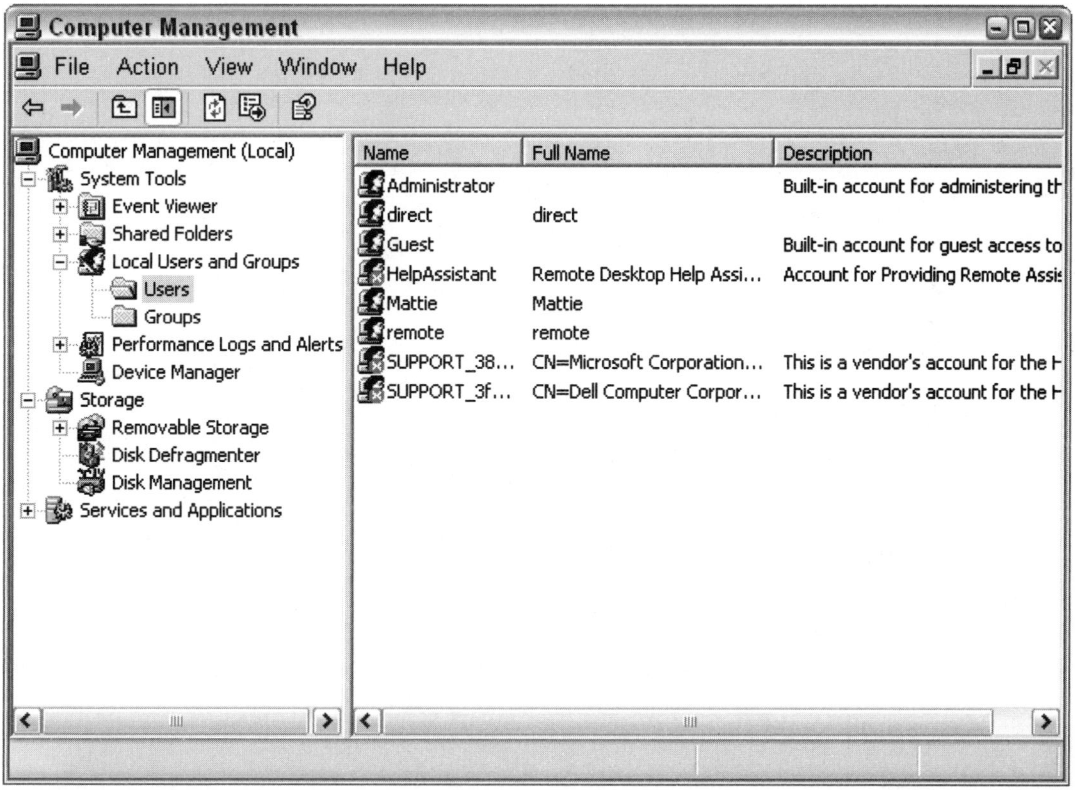

Figure D-7: The Computer Management console.

4. In the right pane, double-click the desired user icon.
5. Notice that on the General
   tab, you can make some restrictions concerning the use of passwords and changing passwords (see Figure D-8). Make any desired changes and click OK.
6. Close the Computer Management console.

Figure D-8: Setting user account properties.

Using Group Policy

Another way to manage accounts and general security is to use Group Policy—a powerful tool in Windows XP that enables you to control what users can and cannot do on the computer. You can invoke settings that affect user logon security, general security settings,

Internet Explorer settings, and many more. I won't wade through all of the Group Policy options and features, but I do want to show you the user account security settings that you might find useful. Keep in mind that you can invoke these settings so that they impact all users on the local machine. You cannot individually apply these settings to specific users. Depending on your security needs, you may not need to use any of them, and if you don't need them, don't enable them. However, if your computer resides in an insecure location, these additional settings can help you out:

Note

Group Policy Editor is not part of Windows XP Home Edition.

1. Log on with an Administrator account.
2. Select Start ➪ Run, type **gpedit.msc**, and click OK. This opens the Group Policy console.
3. Expand Computer Configuration ➪ Windows Settings ➪ Security Settings ➪ Account Policies (see Figure D-9). Notice that you have a container for Account Policies and Account Lockout Policy.
4. If you double-click a container, you can see which policies are available. For example, if you double-click Account Lockout Policy you see that there is an option for a Minimum Password Length policy. Double-click the policy and a dialog box appears, allowing you to determine the minimum length (see Figure D-10).
5. Other Group Policy settings follow the same pattern. Locate the desired policy and double-click it to enable or configure it. When you're done, simply close the Group Policy console.

Stopping Internet Threats

The greatest security threats are those coming directly from the Internet. The Internet can pose a number of potentially serious problems, from viruses to hackers, and so on. Fortunately, you can take steps either to eliminate or greatly decrease the likelihood of experiencing security problems from the Internet. Carefully consider and implement the following tactics.

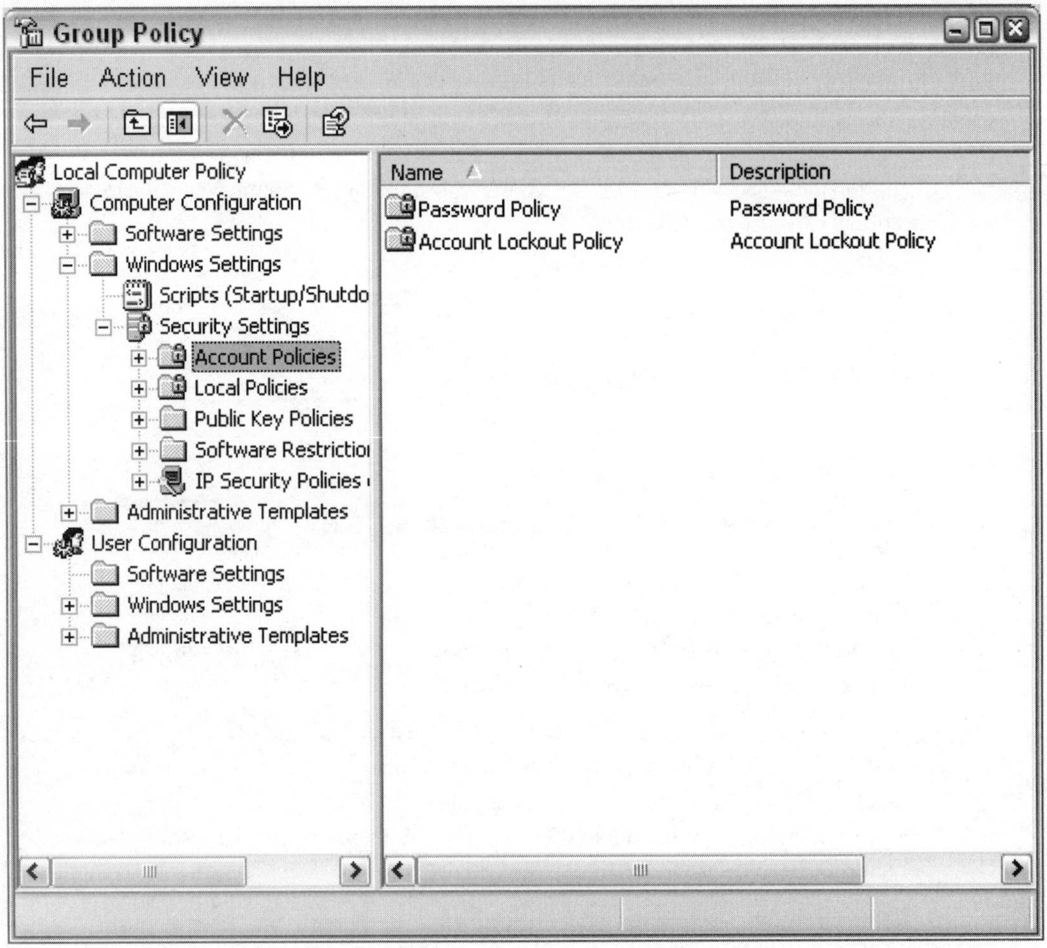

Figure D-9: Using the Group Policy console.

Using Antivirus Software

Always use antivirus software and keep that software up to date. The protection it provides at minimal expensive is worth every penny. Without antivirus software, you have no protection from viruses of any kind, and it will always be too late once you get a virus. Visit Symantec Corporation (`www.symantec.com`) or McAfee (`www.mcafee.com`) to get started. If you prefer to save money, Grisoft (`www.grisoft.com`) offers a free version of its antivirus software, called AVG Anti-Virus Free Edition, for single home computer use only.

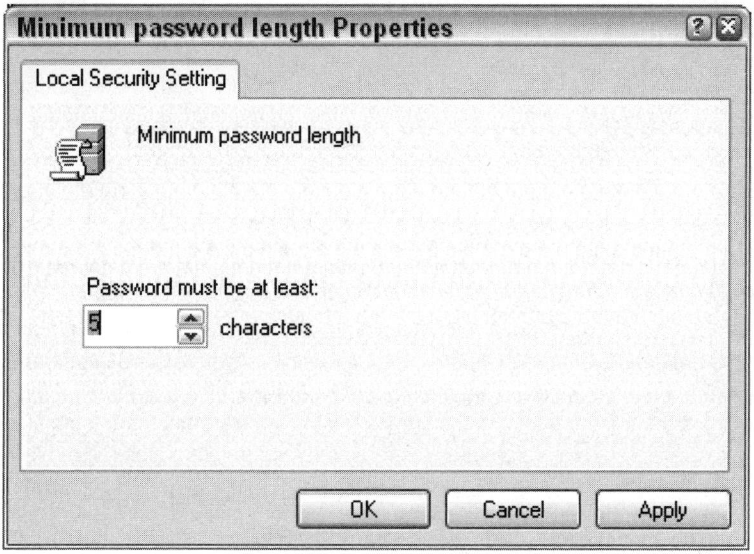

Figure D-10: Set the value for the minimum password length.

Configuring Internet Explorer Security

Internet Explorer provides security settings that can help prevent attacks from the Internet. Configure Internet Explorer security in a manner that provides you the best protection but does not hamper your surfing needs. (I explore these features, along with cookie management, in Chapter 12.)

Using a Firewall

A firewall is software, or a hardware device, that acts as a security boundary for your computer. The firewall's job is to ensure that traffic entering your computer from the Internet is allowable and nonthreatening. You can purchase a hardware firewall or firewall software, or you can use Windows XP's firewall, which is installed and free, but you should always use one.

While Windows XP's firewall works well and won't cost you anything, it doesn't give you the flexibility that other firewalls may provide. No matter your choice, the firewall greatly reduces the chance of someone hacking into your computer from the Internet. If you want to use a third-party firewall, I recommend Norton Personal Firewall (`www.symantec.com`), McAfee Personal Firewall Plus (`www.mcafee.com`), or Zone Labs

ZoneAlarm (www.zonealarm.com). If you want to configure and use the Windows XP firewall, I'll show you how in this section.

The Windows XP firewall works on an exclusion basis. Essentially, it allows anything that you request from the Internet, such as a Web page or file download. However, it doesn't allow anything to enter the computer that you have not directly requested, such as attacks from a hacker. Overall, the firewall works well and provides you with a strong measure of security.

The Windows XP firewall has been revamped in Service Pack 2, so if you are not using Service Pack 2, you should use Windows Update to get it. If you are using Service Pack 2, you know that there is a new Security Center in the Notification Area, where you can see information about the firewall, automatic updates, and whether or not antivirus software is installed. You can also directly access Internet Options, System, and Windows Firewall settings by clicking the provided icons (see Figure D-11). Click the Windows Firewall icon to access the firewall properties.

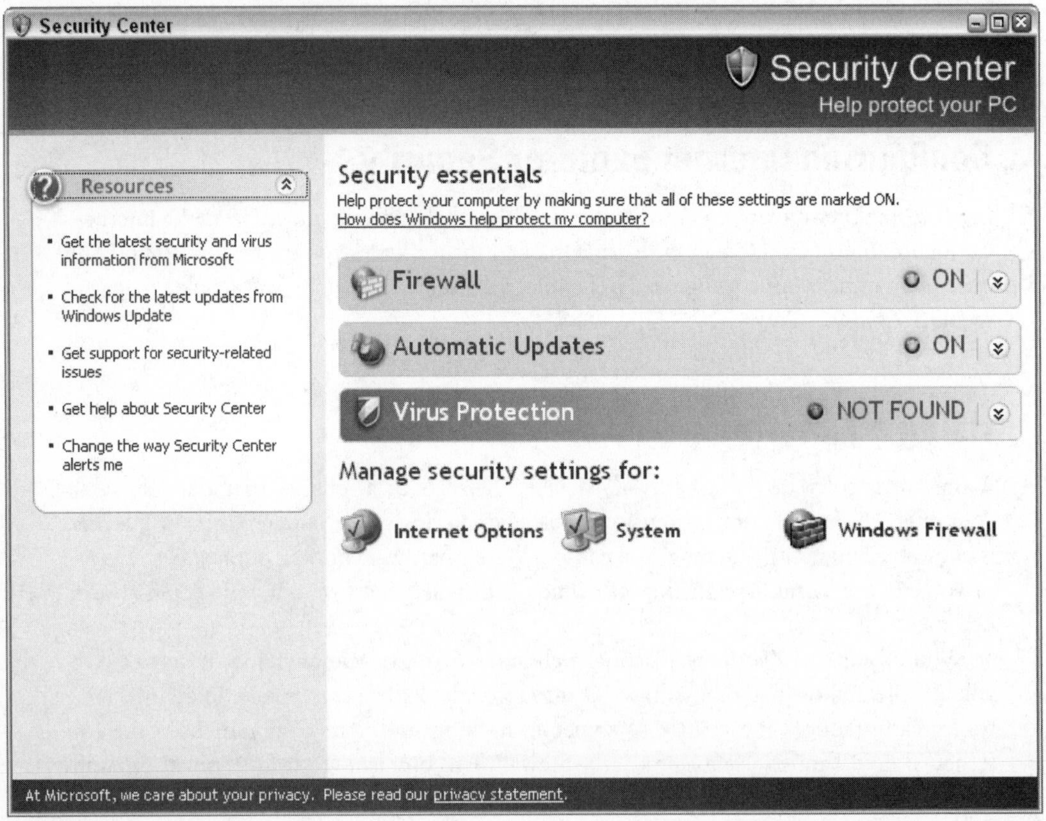

Figure D-11: The Security Center in Windows XP.

Windows Firewall properties provide you with three tabs. On the General tab (see Figure D-12) you can turn the firewall on or off. You can also prevent any exceptions from being configured. Because you may want to create some exceptions, leave this check box unselected for the time being.

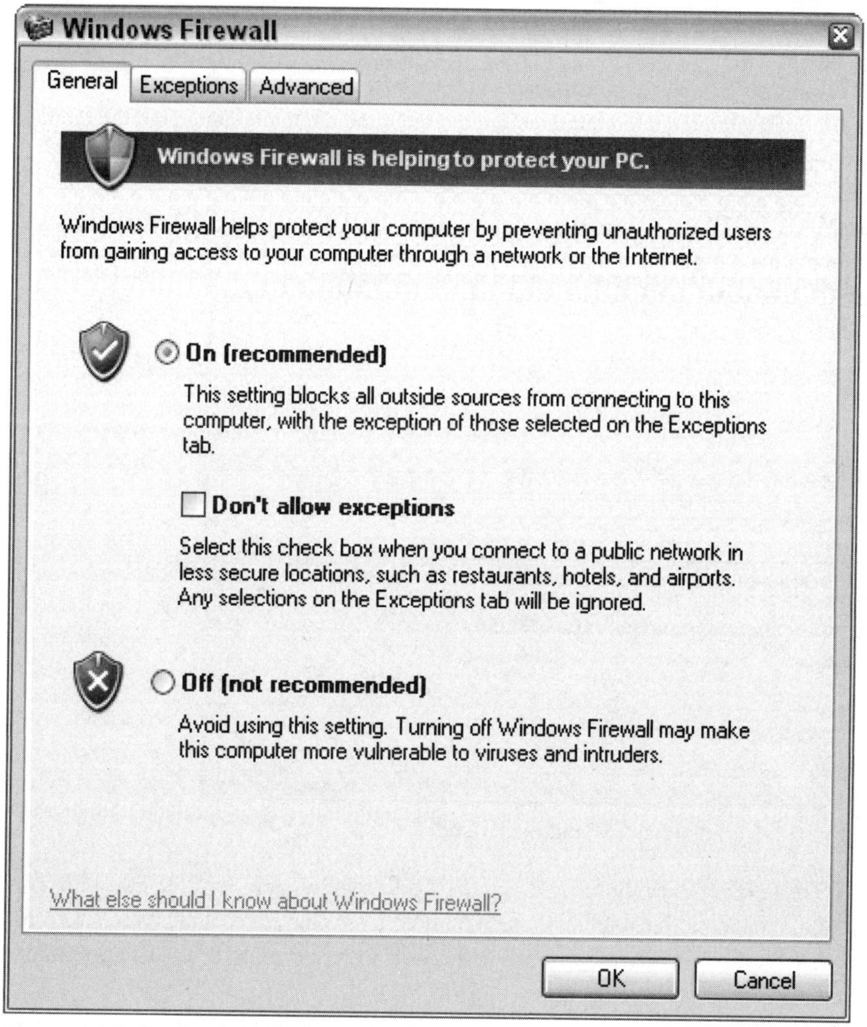
Windows Firewall
General
Exceptions
Advanced
Windows Firewall is helping to protect your PC.
Windows Firewall helps protect your computer by preventing unauthorized users from gaining access to your computer through a network or the Internet.
On (recommended)
This setting blocks all outside sources from connecting to this computer, with the exception of those selected on the Exceptions tab.
Don't allow exceptions
Select this check box when you connect to a public network in less secure locations, such as restaurants, hotels, and airports. Any selections on the Exceptions tab will be ignored.
Off (not recommended)
Avoid using this setting. Turning off Windows Firewall may make this computer more vulnerable to viruses and intruders.
What else should I know about Windows Firewall?
OK
Cancel

Figure D-12: The General tab of Windows Firewall.

On the Exceptions tab you can allow exceptions to the firewall. For example, Remote Desktop functions by directly contacting the remote computer. The firewall on the remote computer will automatically block this activity. So if you want your computer to be contacted by a remote computer, you need to create an exception for this to occur. In this case, all you need to do is enable the provided check box (see Figure D-13).

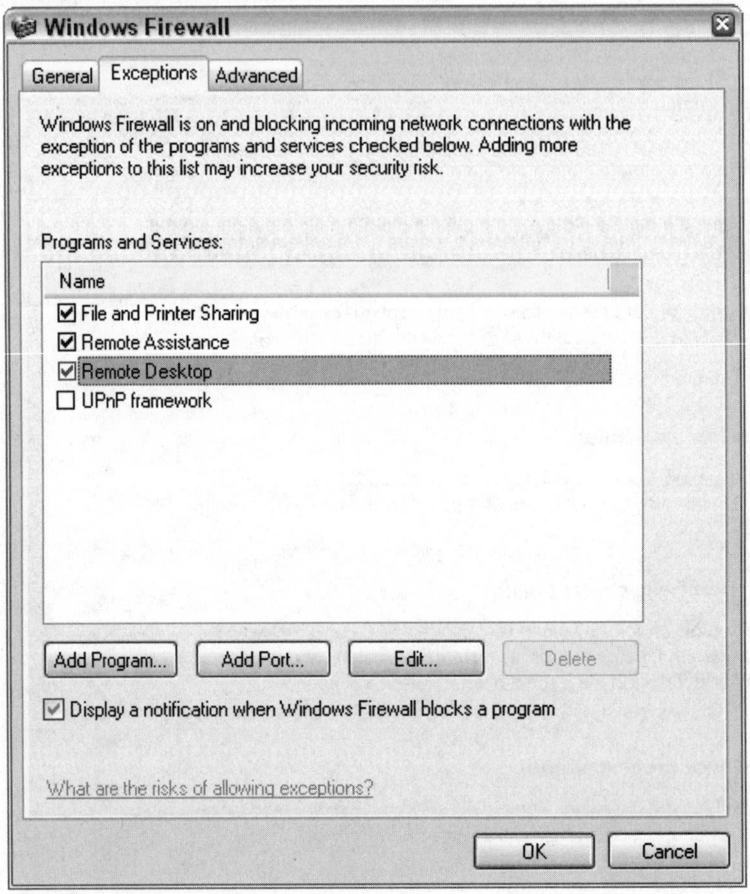

Figure D-13: The Exceptions tab of Windows Firewall.

You can create other exceptions by using the Add Program, Add Port, or Edit buttons. Generally, you should not enable anything here unless you have a specific reason for doing so. If a program you are using requires firewall exceptions, refer to that program's documentation for specific instructions.

The Advanced tab (see Figure D-14) provides you with several different settings you may find helpful:

- **Network Connection Settings:** You can enable the firewall for your Internet connection as well as your location area connection. Click the Settings button to determine the services that you want to enable for the different connections.

Windows Firewall
General
Exceptions
Advanced
Network Connection Settings
Windows Firewall is enabled for the connections selected below. To change settings for an individual connection, select it, and then click Settings.
Dial Up
Local Area Connection
Settings...
Security Logging
You can create a log file for troubleshooting purposes.
Settings...
ICMP
With Internet Control Message Protocol (ICMP), the computers on a network can share error and status information.
Settings...
Default Settings
To restore all Windows Firewall settings to a default state, click Restore Defaults.
Restore Defaults
OK
Cancel

Figure D-14: The Advanced tab of Windows Firewall.

- **Security Logging:** You can have the firewall record a security log, which you can then view. This enables you to see the denied requests that may have come to your computer. Click the Settings button to enable it.
- **ICMP:** Computers on a network can use Internet Control Message Protocol to share error and status data. If you like to ping other computers, ping is an ICMP tool. These tools are all blocked by default but if you want to enable some ICMP features, click the Settings button and choose the type you want to allow.
- **Default Settings:** If you have made some changes and need to go back to the default settings, just click the Restore Defaults button.

Index

R

V

W

X

Z